CONTENTS

176
Woodworking
Projects

◆ ◆ ◆ ◆ ◆

By the Staff of
Workbench Magazine

Sterling Publishing Co., Inc.
New York

10 9 8 7 6 5 4 3 2 1

Library of Congress Cataloging-in-Publication Data Available

Published in 2003 by Sterling Publishing Co., Inc.
387 Park Avenue South, New York, NY 10016

©1987 by Modern Handicraft, Inc.
Originally published by Modern Handicraft, Inc. in 1985 under the title *The Workbench Treasury of Weekend Wood Projects.*
Also published in part in 1984 in *The Workbench Treasury of Infants' and Childrens' Furniture* and *The Workbench Treasury of Decks, Patios, Gazebos, and More* by Modern Handicraft, Inc., and also in *Workbench* magazine, published by Modern Handicraft, Inc.

Distributed in Canada by Sterling Publishing
c/o Canadian Manda Group, One Atlantic Avenue, Suite 105
Toronto, Ontario, Canada M6K 3E7
Distributed in Great Britain by Chrysalis Books
64 Brewery Road, London, N7 9NT England
Distributed in Australia by Capricorn Link (Australia) Pty. Ltd.
P.O. Box 704, Windsor, NSW 2756 Australia

Sterling ISBN 1-4027-0884-X

Introduction

Here, for your enjoyment, is a broad selection of woodworking projects that range from simple household items and gifts to furniture for children and the home to more elaborate plans for decks and patios that can significantly add to the value and enjoyment of your home. All of the projects, which have appeared in *Workbench* magazine, can be made with basic hand tools. However, those home craftsmen who have one or more power tools can often do the job faster, easier, and in some instances, with more precision.

By building a deck or patio designed by do-it-yourself homeowners, you can save hundreds of dollars. You'll get step-by-step descriptions including problems that might arise and how they can be solved. And all you need to know is basic carpentry. After you take a few moments for advance planning and selection of materials—because whatever you create will become a permanent part of the landscape—you can begin a project that can be completed in a weekend or two.

Building furniture and toys for children can be a highly rewarding experience for the craftsman. Not only will the projects be appreciated and long remembered, the hobby-crafter will enjoy the hours of satisfying the urge to be creative. All of the plans for children's furniture adhere to *Workbench* magazine's rigid criteria for utmost safety and usefulness.

Many hobbyists are called upon from time to time to make some small items for a gift or to answer a household need. Care has been taken to include extremely simple designs for the eager beginner, rough-hewn plans for the rugged individualist, and projects with delicate artistry to challenge the experienced woodworker.

Please be sure to read instructions in their entirety and study the plans before beginning any of these projects to be sure you have all the materials and tools required. Choose those which best fit your budget, needs, and expertise. And don't be afraid to dare to be a little original or creative if the situation arises.

In order to provide you with as many projects as possible within these pages, plans have been simplified or reduced in size, explanations kept short, or eliminated where construction details are obvious. Please note that in some cases squared drawings are provided on grids with no dimensions given. This enables you to determine your own dimensions for the project from miniature to billboard size to fit your own application.

To enlarge to actual from a squared drawing, first determine the scale you need. In other words, determine that one size of individual square in the original drawing equals one inch, or two inches, or whatever scale you set. Then draw a full-size grid of these actual-size squares on paper or on the actual stock to be used. Finally, draw in the details of the design in the same relative positions in the squares of the full-size drawing. Squared drawings also make it easier to adapt plans to the actual dimensions of stock you will be using.

METRIC EQUIVALENCY CHART

MM—MILLIMETRES   CM—CENTIMETRES

INCHES TO MILLIMETRES AND CENTIMETRES

INCHES	MM	CM	INCHES	CM	INCHES	CM
⅛	3	0.3	9	22.9	30	76.2
¼	6	0.6	10	25.4	31	78.7
⅜	10	1.0	11	27.9	32	81.3
½	13	1.3	12	30.5	33	83.8
⅝	16	1.6	13	33.0	34	86.4
¾	19	1.9	14	35.6	35	88.9
⅞	22	2.2	15	38.1	36	91.4
1	25	2.5	16	40.6	37	94.0
1¼	32	3.2	17	43.2	38	96.5
1½	38	3.8	18	45.7	39	99.1
1¾	44	4.4	19	48.3	40	101.6
2	51	5.1	20	50.8	41	104.1
2½	64	6.4	21	53.3	42	106.7
3	76	7.6	22	55.9	43	109.2
3½	89	8.9	23	58.4	44	111.8
4	102	10.2	24	61.0	45	114.3
4½	114	11.4	25	63.5	46	116.8
5	127	12.7	26	66.0	47	119.4
6	152	15.2	27	68.6	48	121.9
7	178	17.8	28	71.1	49	124.5
8	203	20.3	29	73.7	50	127.0

YARDS TO METRES

YARDS	METRES	YARDS	METRES	YARDS	METRES	YARDS	METRES	YARDS	METRES
⅛	0.11	2⅛	1.94	4⅛	3.77	6⅛	5.60	8⅛	7.43
¼	0.23	2¼	2.06	4¼	3.89	6¼	5.72	8¼	7.54
⅜	0.34	2⅜	2.17	4⅜	4.00	6⅜	5.83	8⅜	7.66
½	0.46	2½	2.29	4½	4.11	6½	5.94	8½	7.77
⅝	0.57	2⅝	2.40	4⅝	4.23	6⅝	6.06	8⅝	7.89
¾	0.69	2¾	2.51	4¾	4.34	6¾	6.17	8¾	8.00
⅞	0.80	2⅞	2.63	4⅞	4.46	6⅞	6.29	8⅞	8.12
1	0.91	3	2.74	5	4.57	7	6.40	9	8.23
1⅛	1.03	3⅛	2.86	5⅛	4.69	7⅛	6.52	9⅛	8.34
1¼	1.14	3¼	2.97	5¼	4.80	7¼	6.63	9¼	8.46
1⅜	1.26	3⅜	3.09	5⅜	4.91	7⅜	6.74	9⅜	8.57
1½	1.37	3½	3.20	5½	5.03	7½	6.86	9½	8.69
1⅝	1.49	3⅝	3.31	5⅝	5.14	7⅝	6.97	9⅝	8.80
1¾	1.60	3¾	3.43	5¾	5.26	7¾	7.09	9¾	8.92
1⅞	1.71	3⅞	3.54	5⅞	5.37	7⅞	7.20	9⅞	9.03
2	1.83	4	3.66	6	5.49	8	7.32	10	9.14

DECKS, PATIOS & OUTDOOR FURNITURE

King-size Deck

One of the most economical ways to expand the living space of a single family home is to add a deck. If it can be located off the kitchen or family room, much of the congestion that occurs in these rooms when friends and relatives visit can be relieved.

The amount of time a deck can be used depends on the climate where you live. But it can be used comfortably more often than the concrete patio that now is hidden under this model deck.

Many homes have a concrete slab at the rear of the house and with some landscaping it becomes a patio. The rear of the house in the photograph faces east and portions of the deck/patio area receive the summer sun until about 2 P.M. The concrete pad would soak up the sun's energy during this time and then in the evening the concrete would radiate the heat back. This would be great in the winter, but in the summer, even though the area was shaded when used, the concrete pad made it unbearably hot for many hours.

Now the patio-covering deck remains much cooler, since the wood does not absorb and retain heat like concrete and may even be used more often in the winter. It does not seem to get as cold as concrete.

While building a deck may be a relatively inexpensive way to expand space, if it will be larger than the standard advertised 10 × 12 ft., and if any extras are added, it still might cost several thousand dollars. So lots of study and planning should go into deck design.

This king-size deck measures approximately 19 × 25 ft. This seems rather large, but to host parties, which as many as fifty people may attend, requires a roomy deck. With a large deck, most of them are kept out of the house. Thus, the first step in planning is to decide the size deck you need.

The next step is to determine the type of material to use. Here pressure-treated lumber was used for all parts of the deck that had ground contact or that would be within six inches of the ground. For the rest, construction-grade lumber was used, in the interest of economy.

The first step in construction was to be removal of an old privacy fence. The fence posts were found to be set in concrete nearly 4 ft. deep. They were cedar posts and in good condition, so rather than remove them and set new posts they were used as deck supports.

After the fence sections were removed from the posts, plants and shrubs were transplanted and the ground around the concrete slab filled to ensure good drainage away from the house. The concrete slab, of course, remained in place. The joint between it and the house foundation was grouted and sealed with a liberal application of roofing tar.

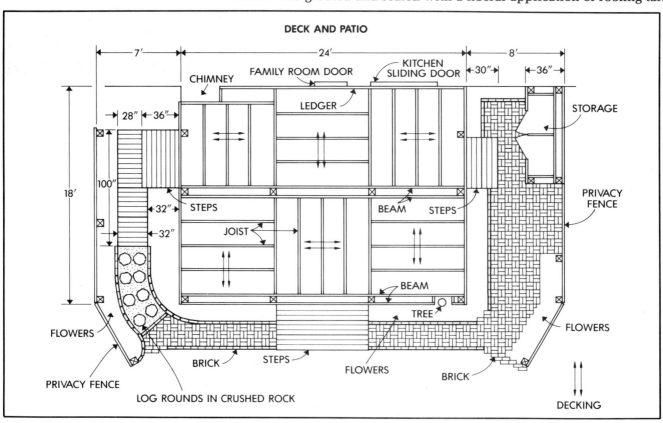

DECK AND PATIO

The whole area under the deck later was covered with heavy polyethylene sheeting so water would not collect. Weeds and grass also were prevented from growing.

Two posts had to be located in the patio slab. Six-inch diameter holes were cut for the posts. First, using a carbide masonry bit, a circle of holes about 2 in. apart was drilled around the circumference of the intended hole. The concrete was removed from the circle with an air chisel. A 4-in. hole then was bored about 3 ft. deep in the ground and pressure-treated posts were set in fresh concrete.

Framing for the deck was constructed as shown in the drawings. Typically, a deck is built with posts supporting beams on which rest joists. The decking then is nailed to the joists. Because of the space limitations under the level of the decking (less than 16 in. at the foundation) the typical system was modified here. Rather than the joists

Some shrubs were cut out, others moved.

Project began with installation of posts.

Ledger was installed first, fastened to studs.

Posts were cemented in holes in slab.

Beams and joists in place ready for deck.

Jig ensures even spacing between boards.

being installed on the beams and ledger, they were suspended between the beams with joist hangers.

When doing the initial layout of the beams, it is important to get everything level. The ledger first is attached to the house. Next the face plates projecting out from the house on either side of the deck are temporarily installed. The ends of these then are checked to be sure they are level. Once sure all is in order, the face plates and beams are bolted to the posts using galvanized carriage bolts. As shown in the photographs, joists here were installed in alternating patterns to provide the correct nailing support for the decking, which has an alternating design. With all the supporting structure in place, it was stained and sealed because it would be inaccessible later.

Installing the decking can be the most time-consuming part of the job. There are a large number of individual boards that must be fitted and nailed. Here 2 × 4s spaced ¼ in. apart were used. Pieces of ¼-in. perforated hardboard were employed as spacers. A short length of dowel was placed in a hole to keep the spacers from falling through the cracks. A straight length of 2 × 4 is rare, so most must be pushed, pulled and even levered into position and nailed while held there.

Once nailed in place they will stay. The decking was stained on the bottom side before it was installed.

Each of the three sets of steps is different and was intended to be that way. The intent of the landscaping around the deck, of which the steps are a part, was to minimize the symmetrical look. Because of their proximity to the ground, the steps were made of pressure-treated lumber.

Railings and benches can be designed in an infinite number of ways. The benches described here were open style, but you can get extra storage space by enclosing them with exterior-grade plywood and hinging the seats. Also be sure the spacing of the side rails or balusters around the perimeter meets the requirements of your local building code and will prevent small children from crawling through and falling to the ground.

Quite often decks are built high enough above the ground that a storage closet can be built under them. That certainly was not the case here. Because storage space was needed, a storage closet was added, camouflaged so it would appear to be part of the newly built privacy fence.

Pressure-treated 4 × 4s were used for the posts, as for the fence, set in concrete. A lower framework of 2 × 6s and an upper framework of 2 × 4s was spiked in place and the tool storage closet lined with exterior plywood.

The walkway around the deck is mostly of used paving brick. If you live in an area where it freezes, be sure to use pavers (paving brick). Ordinary brick will break up after just a few seasons of freezing and thawing. One section of walkway was made of log rounds and crushed stone lined with brick.

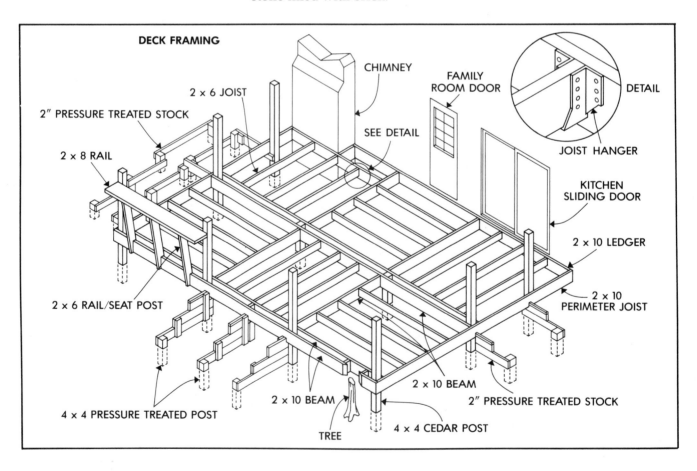

DECK FRAMING

CHIMNEY

FAMILY ROOM DOOR

DETAIL

2 × 6 JOIST

2" PRESSURE TREATED STOCK

SEE DETAIL

JOIST HANGER

2 × 8 RAIL

KITCHEN SLIDING DOOR

2 × 10 LEDGER

2 × 6 RAIL/SEAT POST

2 × 10 PERIMETER JOIST

4 × 4 PRESSURE TREATED POST

2 × 10 BEAM

2 × 10 BEAM

2" PRESSURE TREATED STOCK

TREE

4 × 4 CEDAR POST

Same post design is used to support railing, with or without seats.

Paving bricks are set in sand base.

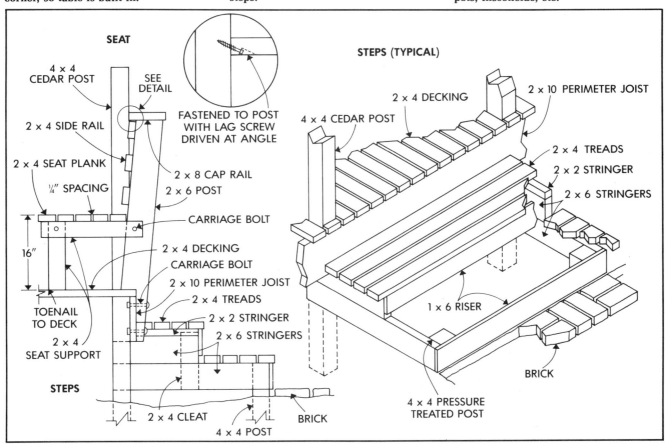

Because of tree, bench cannot extend to corner, so table is built in.

Pressure treated posts, stringers support steps.

Storage closet is built into fence, stores garden tools. Shelves in one end hold pots, insecticide, etc.

SEAT

4 x 4 CEDAR POST

2 x 4 SIDE RAIL

2 x 4 SEAT PLANK

¼" SPACING

16"

TOENAIL TO DECK

2 x 4 SEAT SUPPORT

STEPS

SEE DETAIL

FASTENED TO POST WITH LAG SCREW DRIVEN AT ANGLE

2 x 8 CAP RAIL

2 x 6 POST

CARRIAGE BOLT

2 x 4 DECKING CARRIAGE BOLT

2 x 10 PERIMETER JOIST

2 x 4 TREADS

2 x 2 STRINGER

2 x 6 STRINGERS

2 x 4 CLEAT

4 x 4 POST

BRICK

STEPS (TYPICAL)

2 x 4 DECKING

4 x 4 CEDAR POST

2 x 10 PERIMETER JOIST

2 x 4 TREADS

2 x 2 STRINGER

2 x 6 STRINGERS

1 x 6 RISER

BRICK

4 x 4 PRESSURE TREATED POST

Modular Deck System

Sometimes the scope of a dream deck is so broad and all-encompassing that one can't afford the total expense all at once. Or perhaps the limited amount of free time available to construct it prevents its completion before snow flies. Whatever the reason, here's how a complete sun deck, solar shade, potting bench, outdoor workbench, etc. "system" can be built—one module at a time.

In this situation there is a sliding glass door on the back side of the house with a three-ft.-high step down to the ground. The plan calls for adding a 14 × 18-ft. balcony deck outside this door, just large enough to hold a few flower pots, the barbecue, perhaps a bird feeder or two. Ample room is provided to accommodate some chairs and a table, perhaps built-in benches.

Using the sliding glass door as the starting point, all measurements begin there and the outline of the deck is staked off. Next come stakes to locate the footings for support posts and these important measurements are duly marked.

The actual construction of the deck is fairly standard. The holes for the footings are dug about 8 in. in diameter and below the frost line, then poured full of concrete. U-shaped bars are pushed down into the fresh mix; the bars are ⅛ × 1-in. steel flats, 3 ft. long, bent to shape by hand. The spacing at the surface of the concrete is sized to fit a 4 × 4.

For concrete forms, use 3-lb. coffee cans. Both ends are removed and the cans are cut in half with a friction saw blade. The can halves are fitted down over the bars into the fresh concrete, then are filled with a thick mix of concrete. This creates a surface about 3 in. above the ground to assure quick drainage away from the bottoms of the posts. To season it, the concrete is covered with newspapers that are kept wet for a week.

When it is time to install the support posts, if some of the U-shapes have closed to less than the size of a 4 × 4, or have moved out of line with others, cut vertical notches in posts so they will fit between the U-shaped bars. Cutting a notch deeper on one side may be required in some cases to move a post one way or the other.

With the outside line of posts in position—not yet cut—it is time to determine their heights. This can be done by going back to the sliding glass door and starting ⅛ in. below the sill. The top 2 × 4—fastened to the foundation with anchors and lag screws—has to be 14½ in. plus ⅛ in. below the door sill.

A straight 2 × 8 is placed on the ledger, leveled and clamped to the corner, outboard post. Decks usually are sloped ⅛ in. to the running foot, which means 1¾ in. for the 14 ft. So, the position of the leveled 2 × 8 is marked, then moved down 1 in. and spiked to the post. The end posts are left full height for a possible future roof or sunshade.

A chalk line and string level now are used to locate a 2 × 8 beam at the other corner post. The chalk line also locates the ends of the other 2 × 8 beams, and shows where the posts should be cut to fit under them. Most of the posts between the end ones and the house are simply cut off and the beams set on them. Toenail in from each side to keep the 2 × 8s in place. Where the posts are offset, they are notched and cut flush with the tops of the 2 × 8s.

If the sliding glass door is in a "hanging closet," which is a projection of a room set on joists that extend past the foundation, it will be necessary to notch a couple of the 2 × 8 beams to fit under it, and set on the ledger.

Once the 2 × 8 beams are in place, the rest of the construction is fairly simple. The 2 × 6 joists are spaced on 24-in. centers parallel to the house, and toenailed to the beams. As can be seen in the photos, some of the 2 × 6s used here were short, so were overlapped on a beam and spiked together at the overlap.

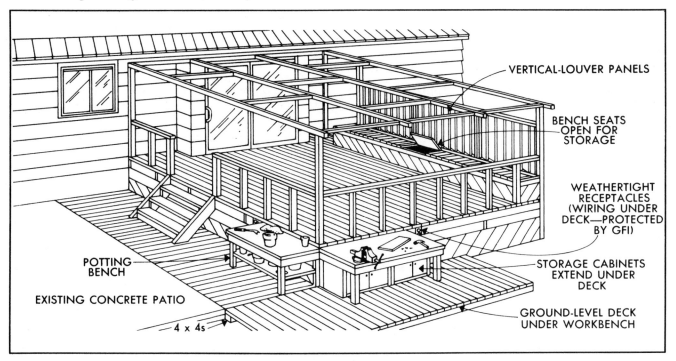

POTTING BENCH

EXISTING CONCRETE PATIO

4 x 4s

VERTICAL-LOUVER PANELS

BENCH SEATS OPEN FOR STORAGE

WEATHERTIGHT RECEPTACLES (WIRING UNDER DECK—PROTECTED BY GFI)

STORAGE CABINETS EXTEND UNDER DECK

GROUND-LEVEL DECK UNDER WORKBENCH

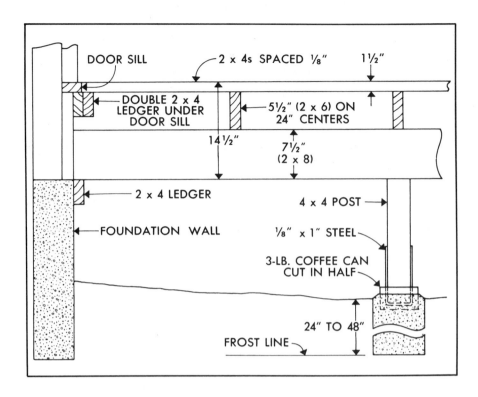

Short lengths of 2 × 6 are cut and fitted between the ends of the joists, both to box them in for appearance and to keep the joists from twisting or warping.

The flooring of 2 × 4s laid flat starts with the straightest 2 × 4 in the pile, which is nailed solidly to the joists at one end of the deck framing. Then the rest of the 2 × 4s are spaced by using 16-penny nails as spacers.

Some lower grades of redwood occasionally are green and unseasoned. If this is the case, curved and twisted pieces must be pried over, then wedged back or twisted down as the work proceeds. In a couple of weeks, however, the wood will season and the boards then will stay in place and be as solid as the floor of a well-built house.

With the deck surface now completed, a three-step stairway now is added at the appropriate place to reach ground level. Because safe, sturdy, well-designed, yet easily built stairways are important to various deck projects, they are covered in detail in the next section.

After the stairway is added, a long bench/seat can be framed in. The framing for the bench/seat is made wide enough to support the louvered wind diverter, sunshade and privacy screen built above it to form a "wall" on the west side.

This wall can prove to be a great boon by providing cooling shade from the afternoon sun, as a diverter to steer prevailing winds away from that side of the house and smoke from the barbecue outward on a breezy day.

Storage is important, as a deck accumulates its own furnishings like a house. Lift-up bench seats are a logical place for storage. This requires only hinging the seats; 2-in. stock as used for the seats shown is heavy enough so no hold-down catches are required.

If the deck is high enough above ground, as this one is, "lockers" in the deck itself can provide additional storage. A locker is simply a box made of exterior-grade plywood spiked to the joists or beams. The lid is a piece of plywood somewhat larger than the box to ensure it is weathertight. A section of the deck boards is cut free and nailed to the lid.

Heavy galvanized steel hinges are used, bent or positioned so the hinge pin is flush with the top of the deck boards. This permits the lid to pivot back for complete access to the locker.

Logical additions to the "system" might include a potting bench on the ground-level deck that can be made by spiking 2 × 4s to 2 × 2s set into the ground. An extension on this deck could be built around the corner and a workbench for outside maintenance might be constructed on it with storage under the workbench allowed to extend under the deck. It would be possible to store even 15-ft. lengths of lumber for the project in this spacious area, for example.

An "egg-crate" roof covered with plastic panels could be the capping climax. This truly would make the deck an "outdoor living room."

After concrete is poured flush with ground, half of coffee can is used to "form" concrete to ensure drainage.

"Beams" are 2 x 8s spaced about 4 ft. with 2 x 6 joists on top of them spaced about 2 ft. for solid framing.

Where 4 x 4 posts are out of line, beams are recessed into them or, as here, are set on projecting beams.

At two ends of deck the 2 x 6 joists are boxed in.

At this point decking of 2 x 4s nailed flat is well under way.

It takes several pounds of galvanized nails to fasten 2 x 4s to deck.

This view clearly shows how 4 x 4 posts are well clear of ground, framing is uniform and as rigid as house floor.

Where joists or beams are not long enough, they are overlapped a couple of feet, then spiked together.

Three step stairway to ground level deck is added.

Louvered screen on west side of deck is designed to divert prevailing northwest wind away from house.

Bench is built along west side, under louvered screen. Storage is provided under hinged seats of bench.

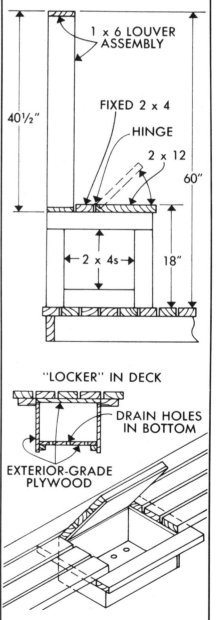

1 x 6 LOUVER ASSEMBLY

FIXED 2 x 4

HINGE

2 x 12

40½"

60"

2 x 4s

18"

"LOCKER" IN DECK

DRAIN HOLES IN BOTTOM

EXTERIOR-GRADE PLYWOOD

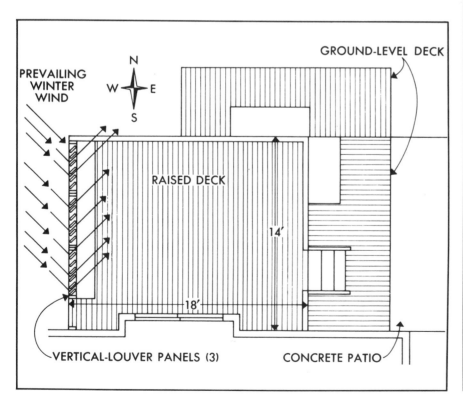

PREVAILING WINTER WIND

N
W — E
S

GROUND-LEVEL DECK

RAISED DECK

14'

18'

VERTICAL-LOUVER PANELS (3)

CONCRETE PATIO

Stairway Layout and Construction

Simple three-tread stairway is cleat type, built of wood to match deck. Two risers are open, two closed.

Designing and building stairways is not really the difficult job it might seem to be, although some ingenuity is required, plus careful workmanship and strong materials.

You need only some basic dimensions plus a 2-ft. carpenter's square for the layout, and ordinary woodworking tools for the actual construction.

The first two dimensions required are the total rise and total run, Fig. 1 (next page). You'll need these dimensions whether the stairway is a simple two- or three-step approach to a porch or deck, or a full reach from one floor to another, with one or more landings between.

The total rise is the vertical distance between two floors, the total run is the horizontal distance from the face of the top riser to the face of the bottom riser.

Some basic definitions: "tread" is the horizontal surface on which you step (also termed "unit run"). "Riser" is the vertical support between treads (also called "unit rise"). On service stairs, as from a basement, the riser can be open. "Stringer" is the notched member on which the treads and risers are fastened, Fig. 2 (page 19). A "built-up" stringer is a straight piece of lumber on which triangular-shape blocks are nailed to create the notches.

Main stairways should be at least 36 in. wide, and wider is better. The stair should be wide enough to allow the comfortable passing of two people and easy movement of furniture.

Headroom is another important dimension, Figs. 1 and 3 (page 19). This is the distance from the outside corner of the tread and riser to the ceiling directly above. The FHA specifies 6 ft. 8 in., but a more practical height is 7 ft. 4 in. to 7 ft. 7 in. This allows an average person to swing his arms above his head without touching the overhead.

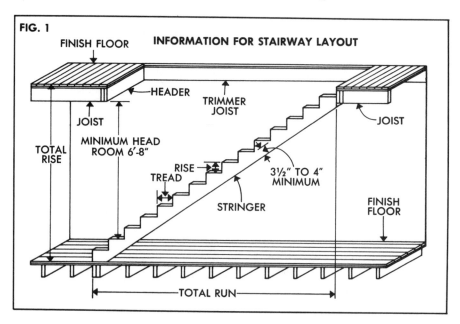

FIG. 1

INFORMATION FOR STAIRWAY LAYOUT

When a stairwell is 10 ft. or longer, a post usually is fitted at one corner to support the header and trimmer. When a platform is used, the post can be alongside the platform.

You start the layout of a stairway by taking the total rise and dividing it by 7 in., which is the "ideal" height for a riser. A "rule of thumb" says the width of tread and height of riser should add up to about 18 in. So, a 7-in. riser means a 10- or 11-in. tread.

Taking a hypothetical situation, with an 8-ft. ceiling, 2 × 8 joists and 1-in. decking, we start with 104¼ in. (96 plus 7½ plus ¾ in.). Dividing 104 by 7 (disregarding the fraction) we get 14⁵⁵⁄₆₄—15 in round numbers.

The next step is to determine the total run, which is figured by multiplying the width of the treads by the number of risers. Staying with our 15 risers, 11-in. treads require a length of 165 in., 10-in. treads will need 150 in. and 9-in. treads 135 in. It's obvious that a relatively small change in tread width makes a considerable difference in the total run.

When there is not sufficient free space in one direction for the required total run, one or more landings may be the answer.

When you figure for a platform, the total run does change direction, but there still must be floor space for the full length.

The total run also is influenced by the method used to attach the stringers at the upper end, Fig 4 (next page). In Detail 1 there is a complete tread in the top, which means you have an equal number of treads and risers. Detail 2 has only a part of a tread at the top. The number of complete treads then is one less than the number of risers (14 in our example). The total run will be 14 times the tread width (9, 10 or 11 in.) plus the width of the partial tread at the top. In Detail 3 there is no tread at the top; the finished floor is the tread. The number of treads then is one less than the number of risers.

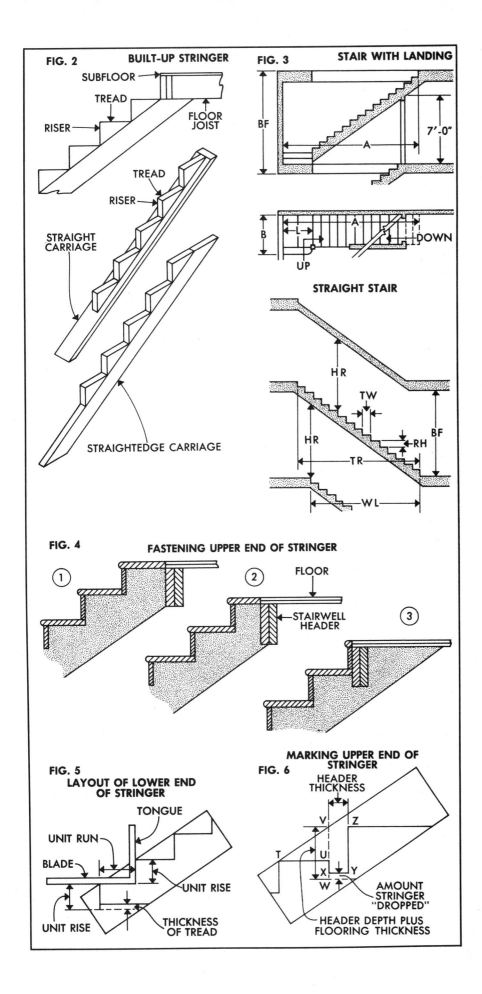

FIG. 2 BUILT-UP STRINGER

SUBFLOOR
TREAD
RISER
FLOOR JOIST
TREAD
RISER
STRAIGHT CARRIAGE
STRAIGHTEDGE CARRIAGE

FIG. 3 STAIR WITH LANDING

BF
A
7'-0"
B
L
A
DOWN
UP

STRAIGHT STAIR

HR
TW
HR
RH
BF
TR
WL

FIG. 4 FASTENING UPPER END OF STRINGER

① ② FLOOR
STAIRWELL HEADER
③

FIG. 5 LAYOUT OF LOWER END OF STRINGER

TONGUE
UNIT RUN
BLADE
UNIT RISE
UNIT RISE
THICKNESS OF TREAD

FIG. 6 MARKING UPPER END OF STRINGER

HEADER THICKNESS
V Z
T U
X Y
W
AMOUNT STRINGER "DROPPED"
HEADER DEPTH PLUS FLOORING THICKNESS

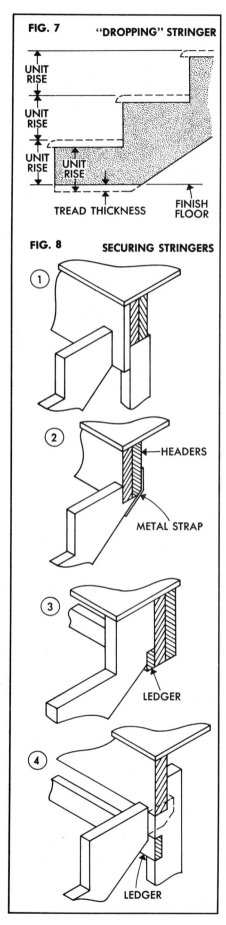

FIG. 7   "DROPPING" STRINGER

UNIT RISE

UNIT RISE

UNIT RISE

UNIT RISE

TREAD THICKNESS

FINISH FLOOR

FIG. 8   SECURING STRINGERS

①

②   ← HEADERS

    METAL STRAP

③   LEDGER

④   LEDGER

There are four ways to determine the approximate length of the stringers: the first is the Pythagorean theorem, where the square of the length of the hypotenuse (stringer) of a right triangle equals the sum of the squares of the lengths of the other two sides. For some of us a few years out of school, this is not realistic.

A second method is to lay out the stairway full size on a driveway or other large surface—not always practical. Third, you can make a scale drawing of the layout—not too accurate when you are dealing with fractions of an inch.

The final way is with the aid of a 2-ft. square. Measure diagonally—for our hypothetical stairway—from 8½ in. on one leg (for the 8 ft. 8 in. total rise) to 13¾ in. (for the 13 ft. 9 in. total run) on the other leg. It measures about 16¼ in. This means the stringer should be about 16¼ ft. long. Add 3 or 4 ft. to allow for waste and fitting.

Start the stringer layout at the bottom, using a 2-ft. square with blocks clamped to mark tread and riser, Fig. 5 (page 19). Start back far enough from the end of the 2 × 12 to make sure there is room to mark the first riser.

Mark the first unit run and rise on the stringer along the edges of the square. Now, reverse the square and mark the first riser. Finish marking off the correct number of treads and risers.

Go back to the first riser and shorten it by the thickness of the first tread. This is called "dropping the riser," and is done to ensure that all steps are the same height.

To make a stringer fit snugly under the stairwell header, Fig. 6—9 using the method in Detail 3, Fig. 4 (page 19)—the depth of the notch is shortened by the amount the stringer was dropped, Fig. 7. Carefully cut the first stringer, check it for fit, then cut the other stringer.

In most cases just two stringers are used. But if the stairway is more than 30 in. wide, or the treads less than 1⅛ in. thick, a third stringer should be centered under the steps for more support.

Freestanding stairways have the stringers attached at the top in a variety of ways, Fig. 8. When the stairway is between walls, the stringers can be spiked to the studs their full length. No matter how a stairway is attached, the main idea is to create a structurally sound, safe assembly. An improperly supported stairway will feel shaky and probably develop squeaks.

For the main stairway, finish nails are used to attach the treads and risers to the stringers. Check the first tread and riser for level and plumb, and also level cross between the stringers to make sure the steps will be level. Make adjustments now, not after the steps are assembled.

Handrails should be installed on at least one side of a stairway. The rail should be 30 in. above the treads at the outside edge, and 34 in. above the floors of landings.

Cleat-type stairways, Fig. 9 (next page), as used for reaching porches and raised decks, are relatively inexpensive to build, need no risers and usually are built of weather-resistant or pressure-treated softwood. They are designed and built the same as interior stairways, using the total rise and total run. Divide the rise by 7, then respace to get equal spacing in the total rise.

For the first tread, measure vertically from the bottom of the stringer to mark the riser height—minus the thickness of the tread. Set an adjustable T-bevel to the angle formed by the front edge of the stringer and the ground, then move the T-bevel up and mark the first tread. Repeat this for each riser height.

Nail 1 × 2 (or heavier) cleats with their upper edges on these marks. Install the stringers, then cut the treads to fit. You also can cut the treads to length and assemble the stairway before you install it. The assembly may get a bit heavy, considering you probably are using 2-in. stock for treads, risers and stringers.

If the stringers will contact the ground, they should be placed on concrete blocks or bricks to keep them clear of moisture.

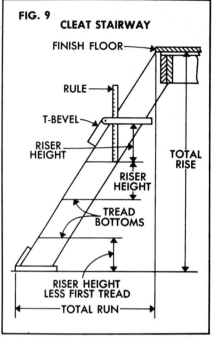

FIG. 9 CLEAT STAIRWAY

FINISH FLOOR
RULE
T-BEVEL
RISER HEIGHT
RISER HEIGHT
TREAD BOTTOMS
TOTAL RISE
RISER HEIGHT LESS FIRST TREAD
TOTAL RUN

Compact Deck

Compact enough to fit in almost any yard, this 10 × 12-ft. redwood deck still is large enough for family cookouts or a play area for youngsters, and it's ideal for sunbathing, or relaxing on lazy summer days, or enjoying cool evenings.

Cost is kept down by utilizing less expensive construction-grade redwood that contains knots and creates a rustic appearance. Redwood has a high resistance to insect damage and decay.

The first step is to determine the location of the deck that best fits your situation. Generally, this should be adjacent to the house so it can be reached through a kitchen or family room door. A freestanding arrangement, however, makes sense if your family's favorite spot in the yard is under a particular tree or somewhere else away from the house.

Nails and other hardware for the deck should be aluminum, or hot-dipped galvanized. Common steel nails will cause black stain streaks. Also, be sure to drill clearance holes for nails when working near the ends of boards to prevent the wood from splitting.

If attached to the house, as in this example, position the deck so the top surface is either just about 1 in. below the door level or 4 to 7 in.

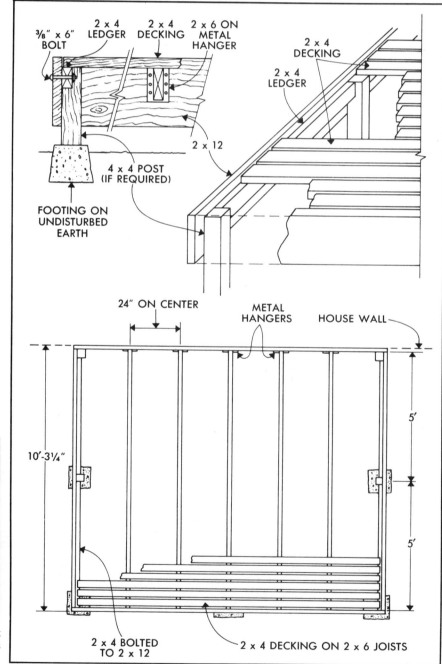

Joists for the deck are heart redwood 2 x 6s. Attach them to the skirt boards with metal joist hangers on 2 ft. centers.

below it. In other words, you want an easy step out or down, not a shallow stumble or a back-jarring drop.

Mark the top of the skirt board along the house at the level you want the deck to be. Attach the skirt board, a 12 ft. 2 × 12, to the wall with the simplest anchoring method permitted by the local building code. This can be lag screws directly into studs or expansion bolts into a concrete foundation.

From the skirt board, project a right angle a distance of 10 ft. 3¼ in. from each end. Locate wooden stakes at these spots. Measure between the stakes, then on the diagonals, which should be equal, to ensure that the deck framework will be square.

Five concrete footings are used to support this deck: one at each outside corner, one at the center of the outside skirt board.

Precast concrete footings about 1 ft. square at the bottom and tapering to the top with a wood-nailing block embedded, can be purchased at some lumberyards and building supply dealers. Or you may choose to pour or fabricate your own. Extend the 10-ft. side skirt boards out from the house and level them by using blocks or other devices, then measure from the lower edges to the ground. This distance will indicate how deep you will have to set the footing blocks into the ground.

With the footings in place, toenail the skirt board to the nailing block after first nailing the skirt boards at the corners with 16-penny galvanized nails. Two 4 × 4 posts are used against the house.

If posts are needed, set the footings in place first, then measure from the top of each footing to the top of the leveled skirt boards. Subtract 1⅝ in. from this distance, then cut the posts to that length. Toenail the posts to the nailing blocks in the footings, attach the skirt boards to the posts with ⅜ × 6-in. lag screws, then nail the skirt boards together at the corners.

Attach five 2 × 6 joists to the skirt boards on 24-in. centers, using metal joist hangers. The joists are placed below the tops of the skirt boards so that 2 × 4 deck boards will be flush with the tops of the skirt boards. Bolt 2 × 4 ledger boards along each of the 10-ft. skirt boards, also below the tops to allow for the thickness of the decking. If posts are used, cut the ledger boards to fit between them. The ledger boards support the free ends of the deck boards that are placed across the joists. This deck is designed to accept thirty-two 2 × 4s spaced apart the width of a 16-penny nail. Place larger knots in the decking directly over joints where possible. Check for this by laying the boards loosely over the joists and arranging them for best position.

Deck boards need not be full length of deck, but should be joined over joists. Predrill nail holes at these locations also.

To avoid splitting deck boards when nailing near ends, as shown here, drill through deck boards into joists.

Proper spacing between deck boards provided by placing 16d nail loosely between them. One nail at each joist.

Airfoil Patio Roof

It's a mathematical equation in three dimensions, it's a challenge to a carpenter (professional or do-it-yourself amateur), a very fine roof for your patio and certainly a conversation piece.

It's quite likely the whole neighborhood will want to know how you bent all those boards to make them follow the curves of the roof.

You can be modest and tell everyone it was simply a matter of utilizing your natural skill, talent and ability, or you can tell the truth and say that every strip of wood in the roof is straight.

They probably will be more inclined to believe the former than that the boards in the roof really are straight. But they are; not one stick of lumber is curved or bent. Unless it was that way before you nailed it in place.

The first order of business is to decide whether to build a patio or deck first, or to build it after the roof is finished. Building either surface might be easier before the support posts are in the way, but working in the shade of the roof might be a help also.

In either case, first locate the positions of the four posts that support the roof. You will want to build the deck, or pour the patio (or lay it in stone, brick, etc.) so that it leaves space for the holes in which the roof supports are anchored.

The drawing shows the 4 × 4 support posts set 2 ft. in the ground. In a mild climate, such as California, this might be deep enough. In colder areas the post should be set below the frost line, and that could be 3 or 4 ft. in northern locations.

Also, while 4 × 4s are sturdy enough for most areas, if your locality is subject to occasional strong winds, you might better consider 4 × 6 or 6 × 6 columns.

In an area where gentle winds (winter or summer) are the rule, you will want to align the roof so the two high points are in line with the wind. This will ensure a nice breeze on a hot summer day, which will both cool you and blow away the smoke from a barbecue.

If winds are strong, it would be better to align the roof so the low points were in line with the prevailing wind. Or, locate the axis of the low points about halfway between the prevailing wind and right angles to the wind.

The point is that the shape of the roof is an "airfoil" and wind pressure under the high sides could create a lifting effect that might tear the roof loose from the posts. Which means you must make sure there are strong connections at each post. Long ⅜- or ½-in. bolts through the 2 × 6 framing and the posts would be a good idea.

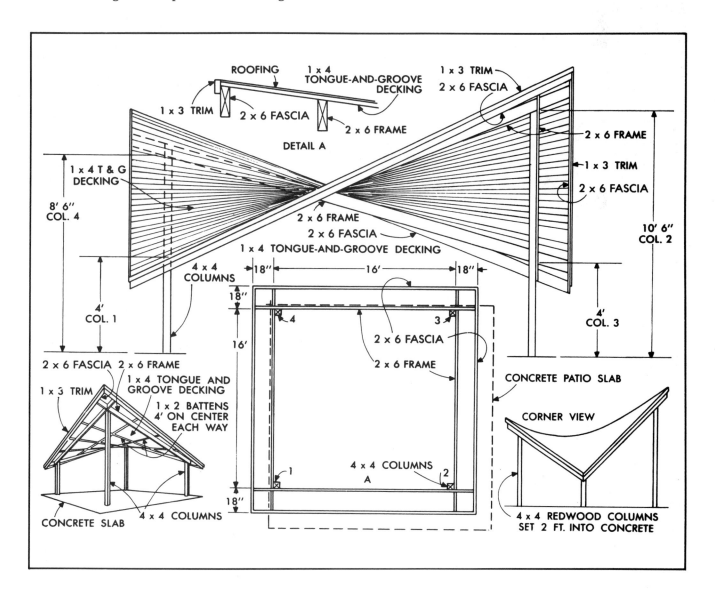

If your posts do not project exactly as dimensioned, make sure they are a bit higher so they can be trimmed to the heights shown. Plumb the posts with a level and use braces to hold them plumb until the concrete sets. Additionally, the ground where the posts are located should be relatively flat. That is, the tops of the short pairs of posts should be at the same level, regardless of the slope of the ground.

You can check this with a small string level fitted on a line drawn taut between the posts, or one of the leveling devices that utilizes a garden hose and water could be employed.

Next, spike (or bolt) the 2 × 6 framing to the posts. It will be necessary to half-lap the 2 × 6s at the corners where they meet at the posts. The 2 × 6 fascia goes on next, then the 1 × 2 battens are run from one side of the frame to the other, spaced 4 ft. on centers. It may be a bit tricky to join the 1 × 2s where they cross, but they can simply be toenailed, or temporarily tack nailed until the decking is in place. The 1 × 2s then can be nailed to the underside of the decking and to each other at the intersections.

Roof decking is 1 × 4 tongue-and-groove lumber made for the purpose. The tongue-and-groove assembly is much more rigid than would be plain edge planks.

After the decking is nailed to the framing and battens, apply roll roofing. In colder climates it might be a good idea to first install some plain roofing paper. This would help seal the roof.

The color of the roofing paper can be selected to match that on the roof of the house. It is not recommended that shingles be used because the unusual slopes of the roof would make any such application certain to lean and/or blow off in the wind.

After the roofing is applied, a trim of 1 × 3 stock can be nailed to the edge of the fascia to conceal the edges of the roll roofing.

The completed structure can be stained or painted, and a contrasting color on the fascia and trim will emphasize the unusual shape of the roof.

Children's Picnic Table

When my three small grandsons indicated they would like a picnic table "just like the big one," I combed through several years worth of various magazines looking for plans but found none. The table shown is my own design, based on some 1-in. lumber I had on hand. Two 1 × 12s 44 in. long determined the size of the top. Although 2 × 4s generally are used for full-size picnic tables, I decided that 2 × 2 lumber would be strong enough for this scaled-down version. I cut the legs with a 25-degree angle at each end so they were 22½ in. long.

Braces for the top and the seats are cut from the 1-in. (¾ in. net) lumber, with the lower corners cut at 45 degrees to eliminate sharp corners. To make the assembly more rigid, I dadoed the legs to accept the seat and top braces. Position the braces, clamp them in place, then mark the locations of the dadoes. They can be cut by making several passes on a table or radial-arm saw, or even with a portable saw, with the depth of cut at ½ in.

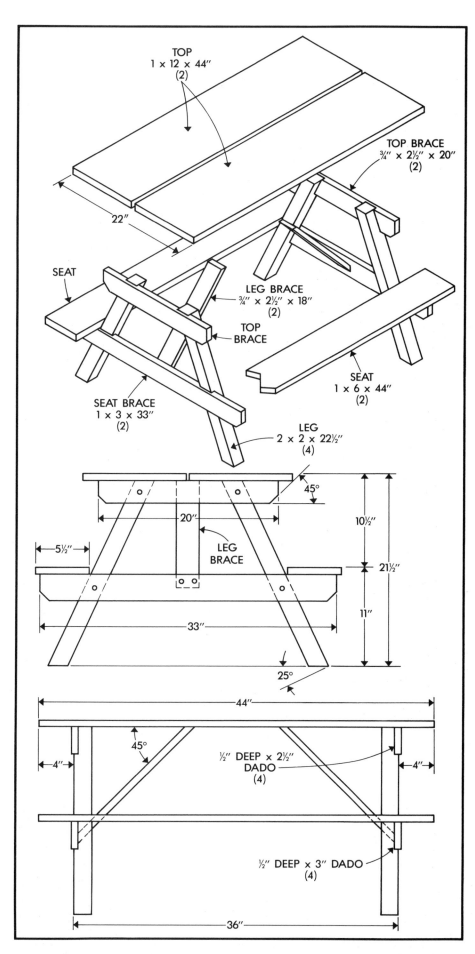

TOP
1 × 12 × 44″
(2)

TOP BRACE
¾″ × 2½″ × 20″
(2)

22″

SEAT

LEG BRACE
¾″ × 2½″ × 18″
(2)

TOP BRACE

SEAT
1 × 6 × 44″
(2)

SEAT BRACE
1 × 3 × 33″
(2)

LEG
2 × 2 × 22½″
(4)

45°

20″

LEG BRACE

5½″

10½″

21½″

11″

33″

25°

44″

45°

4″

½″ DEEP × 2½″ DADO
(4)

4″

½″ DEEP × 3″ DADO
(4)

36″

MATERIALS LIST
(All 1″ stock except legs)
Top, 1 × 12 × 44″ (2)
Top brace, ¾″ × 2½″ × 20″ (2)
Seat, 1 × 6 × 44″ (2)
Seat brace, ¾″ × 3″ × 33″ (2)
Leg brace, ¾″ × 2½″ × 18″ (2)
Leg, 2 × 2 × 22½″ (4)

I used glue and one countersunk no. 8 × 1¼-in. flathead wood screw at each joint. With the legs and braces assembled, it was easy to place the two 1 × 12s on the assemblies and attach them with two countersunk flathead screws driven through each board. A 1 × 12 ripped in half lengthwise created the two seats, and they were fastened to the braces with two countersunk flathead wood screws driven into each brace. The final step was to invert the table and attach the two diagonal braces between the legs and top with a couple of countersunk flathead wood screws driven through each end.

A natural finish was applied, but the boys wondered why some of the wood looked new and some old. The reason was because I'd had the 1-in. material on hand for awhile and the 2 × 2s for the legs were new. So, I painted the table with some gray deck paint left over from painting wooden steps. The boys now enjoy the table not only for eating outside, but also for inside activities such as coloring and building models.

Sunshades and Windscreens

There are two sides to solar heating; in the winter you want it in the house; in the summer you want to keep it out. That's where sunshades come in. They not only keep out the hot sun, they also can create a spot where cooling breezes can be enjoyed on a hot summer day.

Sunshades can take a number of forms, from a simple wooden frame with an "egg crate" top, or a roof of translucent plastic, or an elaborate structure utilizing wooden beams to break up the sun's direct rays, or even a lattice work, as used on porches in the past to provide shade and a place for vines to climb to add their coolness and wind protection to porch, patio or deck.

A shade trellis of simple post-and-beam construction can be attached to a house, fence, garage, carport or built as a freestanding structure on 4 × 4 posts. The trellis overhead or roof can be flat, which is easiest to build, or sloped, gabled or even made in a pyramid shape. Here's an opportunity to try one's own hand at designing.

Depending on its use and the climate, a shade trellis can vary considerably in design. In hot, dry areas, the trellis should be open and can be assembled from laths, "egg crate" blocking, or straight or angled "louvers." These assemblies cast interesting shadow patterns, filter harsh sunlight and form a windbreak or even a privacy shield that still allows vertical circulation of the air for cooling.

In an area subject to frequent summer rain squalls, consider covering the overhead with shingles, shakes, reed or sapling fencing, bamboo, canvas or translucent plastic. Such a roof covering makes the area usable year-round for such things as barbecuing. Making some sections of the roof removable so that screens can be installed, or simply left out, allows better control of wind, sunlight and ventilation, depending on the time of year.

Lumber used for a sunshade, windscreen trellis or patio cover should be a weather- and insect-resistant type, such as redwood. Lumber in contact with the ground should be the pressure-treated type that also is rot and insect resistant. For all assemblies, use aluminum or hot-dipped galvanized nails to avoid rust streaks. Lag bolts and other fasteners also should be galvanized for the same reason.

To construct a simple 8 × 12-ft. patio shelter adjacent to the house, for example, Fig. 1, start by anchoring a 2 × 4 ledger to the side of the house. Position the ledger on the house wall far enough below any roof overhang to permit installing 2 × 6 "rafters."

Prepare for anchoring the 4 × 4 posts that will support the 4 × 6 beams on which the outer ends of the 2 × 6 rafters will be supported. If the shelter is to be built over a concrete patio, secure the bottoms of the posts with rust-resistant metal fasteners. "Post bases" are shaped from galvanized sheet metal, and designed for this purpose, Fig. 3. A masonry bit will have to be used to bore holes in the concrete so the post base can be fastened to the patio with lag screws and screw anchors.

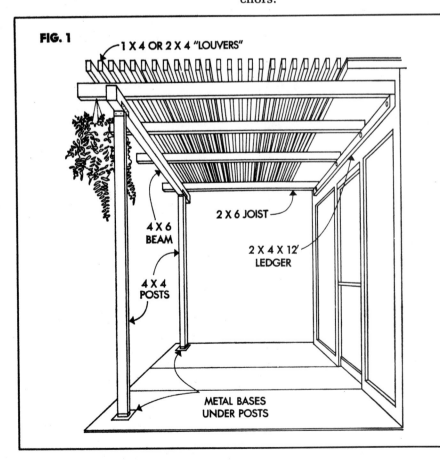

FIG. 1

1 X 4 OR 2 X 4 "LOUVERS"

2 X 6 JOIST

4 X 6 BEAM

2 X 4 X 12' LEDGER

4 X 4 POSTS

METAL BASES UNDER POSTS

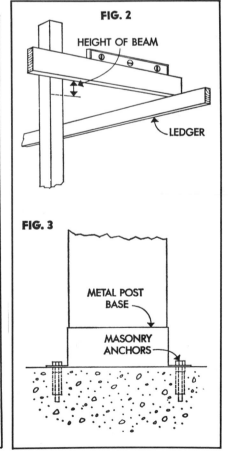

FIG. 2

HEIGHT OF BEAM

LEDGER

FIG. 3

METAL POST BASE

MASONRY ANCHORS

If the shelter is built over a wooden deck, the same post bases can be fastened with 16-penny nails, or lag screws.

Where a patio surface is brick, stone or concrete patio blocks, remove enough at each post location to permit setting a precast anchoring block, available from building supply dealers who sell sand, gravel, cement and concrete blocks.

There are two main types of anchoring blocks. One has a wooden nail block cast into it, and the bottom of the support post is simply toenailed to fit, Fig. 4. The other type block has a metal pin at its center. In this case, you bore a hole in the bottom of each post to fit over the pin. The pin-type block is used for structures that will have enough mass to hold the posts down on the pins.

In areas where there is a lot of wind, and especially if the structure is fairly small and light, the nail block anchor is best. As an alternative, dig a hole a couple of feet deep (in very cold areas dig it down below the frost line) and about 1 ft. square. Pour concrete in the hole, then push a U-shape steel flat bar down into the concrete, spacing the ends of the U-shape to fit against the 4 × 4 post.

Tack-nail strips of wood to the posts to hold them vertical, Fig. 5, then cut off the posts at the correct height to support the 4 × 4 or 4 × 6 beam that will in turn support the ceiling joists or rafters.

Proper height of each post is determined by resting one end of a rafter on the ledger that is attached to the house, and clamping the other end of the rafter on the post, using a level, Fig. 2.

Note that this position is the location of the rafter, which means you have to subtract the height of the beam, then cut off the post, Fig. 2. Carefully repeat this procedure for the other two or more posts that will support the beam.

Since the posts are not yet fastened, they can be removed to permit sawing them to length in a more convenient manner than doing the job up on a ladder and sawing horizontally. Once the posts are trimmed to length, replace them, readjust them to vertical and replace the support boards to hold them.

Attach the bottoms of the posts to the anchor blocks. It is not recommended that posts be set directly on concrete as the bottoms will rot away in just a few years. Pressure-treated lumber, cedar or redwood will, of course, last longer. No matter what kind of wood, make provision for fast drainage of moisture from the posts to minimize the chances of rotting.

Carpenter ants and other insects attack wet, rotting wood much more quickly than dry wood.

When all the posts have been fitted in place, and plumbed vertical, use metal post caps to attach the beam, Fig. 6.

Space 2 × 6 joists on 4-ft. centers, with the ends resting on the ledger and the beam. Secure the joists to ledger and beam with galvanized 8-penny nails, toenailing them from each side into ledger and beam.

Next, "louvers" of 1 × 4 or 2 × 4 stock are spaced about 3 in. apart and toenailed to the joists, Fig. 7 (next page). You might want to space the 2 × 4s farther apart, say 4 or 5 in., to reduce the weight and the "closed-in" appearance of the heavier lumber.

For overheads on shelters where trunslucent plastic is used, the louvers are eliminated, and the joists are spaced farther apart. There also must be cross joists to support the ends of the panels and provide a nailing surface.

FIG. 4

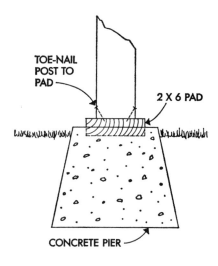

TOE-NAIL POST TO PAD

2 X 6 PAD

CONCRETE PIER

FIG. 5

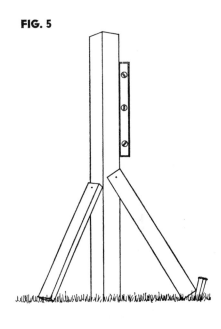

FIG. 6

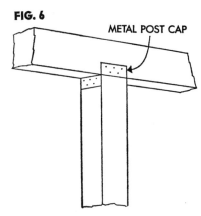

METAL POST CAP

FIG. 7

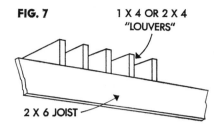

1 X 4 OR 2 X 4 "LOUVERS"

2 X 6 JOIST

Benches, whether built as part of the structure, or as freestanding pieces of furniture, can reflect the structure of the roof. That is, 2 × 4s, 2 × 2s or 3 × 3s can be used for the seats. It's not recommended that 1 × 4s be used, as the stock is a bit too thin to provide a comfortable seating surface.

When building a windscreen around an existing patio, by keeping the structure on the outside of the patio surface, the size of the patio is not reduced. Rather, the screen expands the size of the patio, both visually and practically.

Scrap-wood Patio

This rough-hewn patio was made from scraps of 4 × 4 fencing material. The least expensive grade of redwood 4 × 4 stock, railroad ties, or pressure-treated lumber scraps might be substituted.

The patio can be any shape you wish; square, rectangular, round or free-form. One way of making a circle or free-form is shown, with a pipe driven into the ground for a center, and a spade or other cutting tool on the other end of a length of cord. One or two other pipes in between will create the free-form shape.

Strip the sod off to the depth required (3-½ in. for 4 × 4) to bring the boards flush or slightly above ground level. Tamp them down firmly, using a scrap piece of wood. Fill in the ground, or cut it out, as you place the random lengths of wood from the center outward.

Use a portable circular saw to cut the boards to length and angle on the outside ends. Make the first cut the one that will show, then make the second cut from the bottom of the 4 × 4 trying to match the first cut. Very few portable electric saws will cut all the way through a 4 × 4.

When all boards are in place, sweep dry sand over the patio. Repeat this until no more sand will drop between the boards, then sweep away the excess.

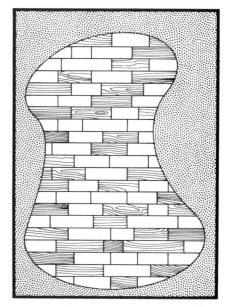

Boards are trimmed at one end to roughly conform to shape of patio. Scrap board is used to mark for portable saw.

Boards in patio are of random lengths, but no two joints are in line. Looks better, is more solid.

Length of 4 x 4 fence post makes handy tamper to help get boards level, bang them snugly together on ends.

One way of marking out patio is with cord tied to stake, and to cutting tool used to outline the area.

You can smooth, fill and/or dig out the soil as you install the various pieces of wood used for making patio.

Porch Swing

Modern homes often do not have a place to hang a porch swing, and even if there is a location for it, on occasion it's nice to move it out to a shady spot in the yard. This A-frame will support a "standard" porch swing and is assembled from four "landscape timbers" that are readily available at garden centers, lumberyards and home centers. The timbers are pressure treated and fairly uniform in quality and shape. Because three of the timbers will be ripped in half lengthwise, select those that have no cracks running lengthwise.

(*Editor's Note: The porch swing shown was purchased from a home center, but it would be easy to build and we have included plans for making one similar to it.*)

Purchase the hardware listed in the Materials List, and make sure it is rust-resistant (galvanized, aluminum or stainless steel). Start the project by ripping three of the timbers in half lengthwise for the A-frame. Because pressure-treated lumber is tough to cut, it may be easier to cut halfway through in one pass, then invert the timber and finish ripping from the other side.

Cut four legs 6½ ft. long from the half timbers. This will create four pieces 18 in. long that are used for braces. Cut another half timber into two 48-in. lengths, then cut two pieces 34 in. long from the remaining half timber. The beam from which the swing will hang is a full-size

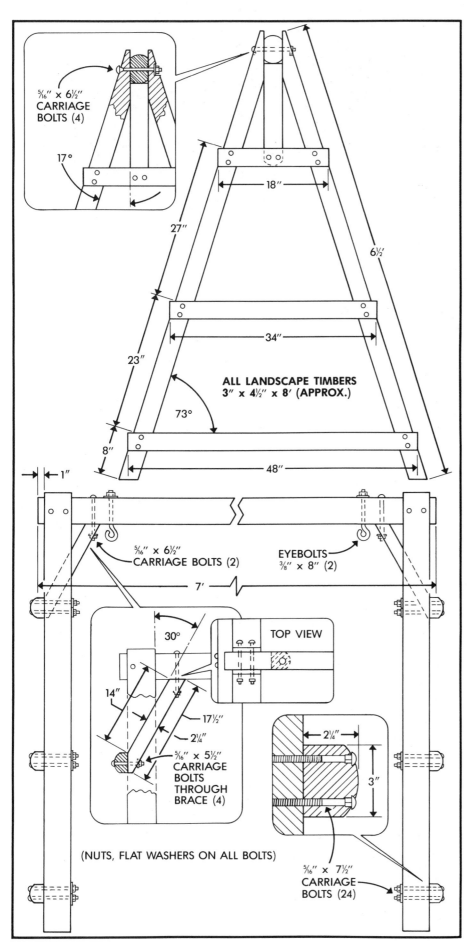

MATERIALS LIST

A-frame

Landscape timbers (approx.
  3″ × 4½″ × 8′) (4)
Hardware (all galvanized):
  Carriage bolts, 5/16″ × 4″ (4)
  Carriage bolts, 5/16″ × 6½″ (8)
  Carriage bolts, 5/16″ × 5½″ (24)
  Eyebolts, 3/8″ × 8″ (2)
  Flat washers, 5/16″ ID (36)
  Flat washers, 3/8″ ID (2)
  Nuts, 5/16″ (36)
  Nuts, 3/8″ (2)

Swing

Lumber, redwood suggested:
  Slats, 1 × 2 × 5′ (12)
  Slat, 1 × 2 × 57″ (1)
  Front rail, 1 × 3 × 5′ (1)
  Bottom support, 1 × 2 × 15″
    (4)
  Back support, 1 × 2 × 17½″
    (4)
  Arm, 1 × 2 × 17½″ (2)
  Arm upright, 1 × 2 × 10¼″ (2)

Hardware:

  FHWS, #10 × 1½″ (60)
  FHWS, #12 × 2″ (2)
  Eyebolts, 5/16 × 4″ (4)
  Carriage bolts, 5/16 × 2″ (4)
  Flat washers, 5/16″ ID (12)
  Nuts, 5/16″ (8)
  Chain, screweyes (2) to fit
    chain

35

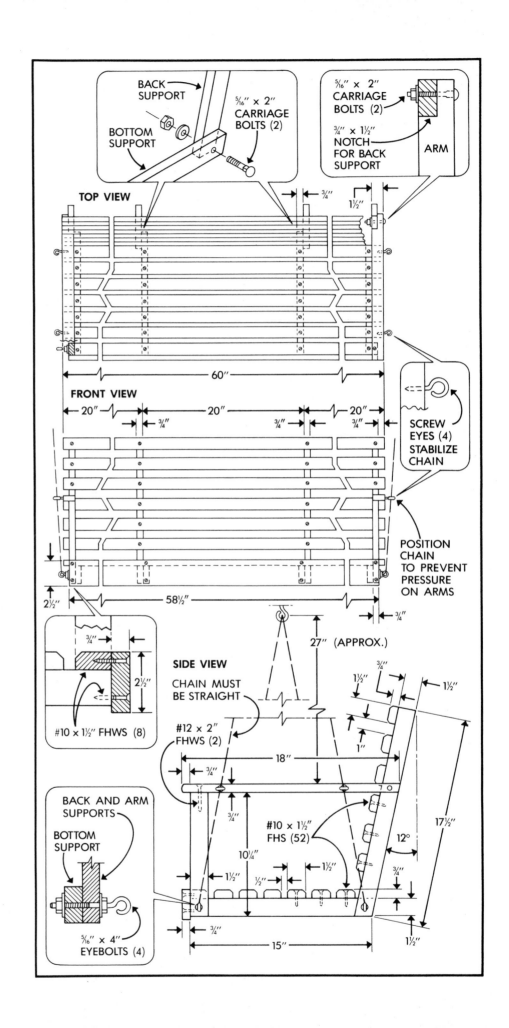

BACK SUPPORT

BOTTOM SUPPORT

⁵⁄₁₆″ × 2″ CARRIAGE BOLTS (2)

⁵⁄₁₆″ × 2″ CARRIAGE BOLTS (2)

¾″ × 1½″ NOTCH FOR BACK SUPPORT

ARM

TOP VIEW

¾″

1½″

60″

FRONT VIEW

20″

20″

20″

¾″

¾″

¾″

SCREW EYES (4) STABILIZE CHAIN

POSITION CHAIN TO PREVENT PRESSURE ON ARMS

2½″

58½″

¾″

¾″

2½″

#10 × 1½″ FHWS (8)

27″ (APPROX.)

SIDE VIEW

CHAIN MUST BE STRAIGHT

#12 × 2″ FHWS (2)

18″

¾″

¾″

1½″

¾″

1½″

1″

#10 × 1½″ FHS (52)

12°

17½″

BACK AND ARM SUPPORTS

BOTTOM SUPPORT

10¼″

1½″

½″

1½″

¾″

¾″

⁵⁄₁₆″ × 4″ EYEBOLTS (4)

¾″

15″

1½″

timber, and is cut 2 ft. longer than the swing. That is, if the swing is 4 ft. long, cut the beam 6 ft.; if the swing is 5 ft., cut the beam 7 ft. Because there is no need for the scraps left over from cutting the beam to length, cut it from the best part of the timber.

Begin construction by placing two legs on edge with their ends touching at the top, and separated at the bottom about 48 in. Position a 48-in.-long brace across the legs with the upper edge 8 in. above the lower ends of the legs. Drill two holes in each end of the brace and through each leg and bolt the brace to the legs with 5⁄16 × 5½-in. carriage bolts. Use flat washers under the nuts. Be sure the upper ends of the legs are in firm contact, then mark the width of the top beam on the frame. Your marks should be approximately 1½ in. on each side of the center line, which is where the upper corners of the legs contact each other. Also mark the lower ends of the legs parallel with the ground. Temporarily remove the two carriage bolts and cut the upper and lower ends of the legs. Repeat the operation on the other pair of legs.

Rejoin the legs with the 48-in. braces, leaving the bolts loose. Have someone hold the top beam vertically between the ends of one A-frame placed flat on the ground (and about 1 in. projecting past the legs), then drill two 5⁄16-in. holes through the legs and beam. Join the legs and beam with a 5⁄16 × 6½-in. carriage bolt with flat washer and nut. Repeat the operation to join the other pair of legs to the beam.

Tighten the nuts on the bolts in the 48-in. brace. Locate the 34-in. brace on each pair of legs, drill through it and the legs, then bolt the brace to the legs. Do the same for the 18-in. brace on each pair of legs. The two remaining 18-in. braces have their ends cut to 30 and 60 degrees as indicated, then they are positioned as shown and holes drilled through the braces, the 18-in. braces and the top beam. Attach the braces with 4-in. bolts through the 18-in. horizontal braces and 6½-in. bolts up through the top beam.

The swing is constructed primarily of 1 × 2 stock except for the front rail which is a 1 × 3. Be sure to select a wood species that will weather well, such as redwood. The dimensions provided will make a swing 5 ft. wide, but the dimensions can be adjusted to suit your needs.

Cut to size the several pieces, then bolt the bottom supports to the back supports with a loose fit. Drill countersunk pilot holes in the slats and screw them to the supports using flathead wood screws. Using a waterproof glue in addition to the screws will provide a longer-lasting joint.

When all the slats are in place, attach the arm uprights and the arms, screwing the arm to the upright and bolting it to the back support. The seat and back will rotate on the loose-fitting bolts that hold them together and will "fold" into position. The angle of the back with the seat can be adjusted by lengthening or shortening the arm.

Tighten the bolts and temporarily attach the chain to the bottom. Determine where it passes by the arm and mark the location of the screweyes. Attach the screweyes (they must be large enough so the chain will pass through them).

Apply a sealer to the swing to protect it from the weather, or paint it an appropriate color, if you prefer. Sealer, if used, should be applied each year for continued protection.

Locate and drill the holes in the top beam for the two eyebolts. The chain should not hang straight down but should be angled slightly so it will not exert undue pressure on the arms. In other words, the distance between eyebolts in the top beam should be greater than the distance between the chain supports (eyebolts) on the ends of the swing.

Install the bolts with flat washers between the nuts and the beam. Use two nuts on each eyebolt, the second nut locking the first so it will not turn. You also may want to slightly upset the threads on the ends of the bolts to further ensure that the nuts will not loosen.

Go over the A-frame and firmly tighten every nut. Do this every month or so, as the nuts may loosen when the swing is used. Hang the swing, adjusting the lengths of the chains so the swing is at a comfortable height for sitting.

Child's Two-seat Lawn Swing

This project is not difficult to make, and will provide many happy hours for your children or grandchildren.

Check the Materials List to determine the lumber and thin-wall electrical conduit needed. While assembling the swing is not difficult, it is important that all matching pieces be cut and drilled to match. For example, the ends of all four pieces for the A-frames should be cut at the same angle, and all holes for bolts or nails spaced the same.

The same is true for matching lengths of thin-wall conduit. Unless all hole spacings and lengths of matching pieces are the same, the swing will not sit level and will not swing smoothly. Your best bet is to cut and drill all matching pieces together. A drill press or drill stand will be a big help to drill through several pieces at once, and at right angles to the various surfaces.

Cut and assemble the A-frames from 2 × 4 lumber, cutting the angles on the ends to 30 degrees at the tops, 60 degrees at the bottoms. The difference in angles can be confusing, so one way to lay them out is to position the lower ends 78 in. apart as in the drawing, with the upper ends spaced 1½ in. apart. Mark the bottom ends parallel to the surface against which they rest, the top ends vertical to that surface: 30 plus 60 equals 90 degrees.

Join the four legs of the A-frames to a 44-in. length of 2 × 6 that is notched in two places 1½ in. wide × 2¾ in. deep. The two 18-in. lengths of 2 × 6 fit in these notches. Alternately, for greater strength, notch the two shorter 2 × 6s to fit the longer one.

2 × 6 × 18″
18″
30°
(APPROX., CUT TO FIT)
(2) 2 × 4 × 45″
78″
30°
30°
36″
1 × 4 × 36″
60°
78″
48″
2 × 4s

12d NAILS, ENDS UPSET
2¼″
1/8″ × 2″ × 14½″ STEEL STRAP
BUSHINGS
3/8″ × 2″ BOLT
3/8″
1″
CONDUIT ¾″

(APPROX.)
SLIGHTLY ROUND ALL EDGES
HOLES 17″ ON CENTER
2″ ¼″ DIA.
1″
12°
14″
18″
¼″ DIA. ¾″ × 2″ STOCK
SEAT BACK (2)
14″
24″
SEAT (2)
17″ 2″
FOOT REST
SLATS ¾″ × 2″ × 24″ (20)

SPACER 2 × 4 × 23¼″ (1)
44″
26¼″ 2¾″
12″
2 × 6 × 44″
2 × 6 × 35″ (CUT TO FIT) (2)
66″
56″
¾″ CONDUIT
24″
44″

18″
1″
3/8″ DIA.
1″
¾″ THINWALL CONDUIT × 56″
¼″ DIA.
¾″ THINWALL CONDUIT × 20″
FLATTEN ENDS OF SHORT PIECES OF CONDUIT
¼″ DIA.
18″
1″
6¾″
5¾″
12″
1″
16½″
18″

14″
2¼″
3/4″
2½″
¾″
17½″
¼″ DIA.
ARM ¾″ × 2½″ × 17½″ (4)

MATERIALS LIST

A-frame, 2 × 4 × 78″ (4)
Horizontal braces, 1 × 4 × 36″ (2)
Diagonal braces, 2 × 4 × 35″ (cut to fit)
Horizontal spacer, 2 × 4 × 23¼″ (1)
Seat back braces, ¾″ × 2″ × 14″ (4)
Seat braces, ¾″ × 2″ × 14″ (4)
Seat slats, ¾″ × 2″ × 24″ (20)
Seat arms, ¾″ × 2¼″ × 17½″ (4)
Thin-wall conduit, ¾″ × 56″ (4)
Thin-wall conduit, ¾″ × 20″ (4)
Steel straps, 1/8″ × 2″ × 14½″ (4)
Necessary nuts, bolts, washers

Bolt or nail the longer 2 × 6 to the legs of the A-frames, then bolt or nail the two 1 × 4 × 36-in. crosspieces to the A-frames 30 in. from their tops. Two angle braces that run from these crosspieces to the top 2 × 6 are lengths of 2 × 4. Ends of these braces are cut by marking them in place. Make sure the A-frames are at right angles to the top 2 × 6 when you mark these 2 × 4 braces. Nail or bolt them in place, and the assembly should be like the one shown in the photograph. The 2 × 4 spacer between the short 2 × 6s was in the original design, but not installed.

The steel straps bent around the ends of the short 2 × 6s are made next. I used ⅛ × 2-in. flat steel, each piece 14½ in. long, so the ends projected 1 in. below the 2 × 6s. After you bend them to a U-shape, slip a piece of 2-in. (1½ in. net) stock between the legs and drill for the ⅜-in. bolts that hold the lengths of conduit that support the swing and allow it to pivot. Make sure all the holes are located in the same position in the four U-shape brackets you bend. They all should be centered on the strap and 1 in. from the ends.

Next, assemble the swing itself that consists of the foot rest, the seats and the backs. All material is 2 in. wide, ripped from 1-in. (¾ in. net) lumber. Cut the various pieces to length, noting that some require an angle on one end, while the other end is rounded. These are the four pieces for the seat and backs.

All slats for the seats, backs and foot rest are 24 in. long, and there are 20 of them. Assemble the four L-shapes angled 12 degrees for the seats and backs and join them with slats. Space the slats equidistant and flush with the outside surfaces of the L-shapes so the conduit supports can move freely.

Supports are ¾-in. thin-wall electrical conduit. Drill a ⅜-in. hole 1 in. from one end of each long conduit, and ¼-in. holes 1, 13 and 18¾ in. from the other (bottom) end. Flatten both ends of the four short pieces of conduit about 3 in. and drill ¼-in. holes 1 in. from each of the eight ends. Round the sharp corners of the flattened section with a grinder or file. All projecting bolts should be sawed flush with the nuts, and any rough ends filed smooth; you want no sharp projections that could cause injury.

Assemble the conduit to the seats and foot rest, and the conduit to the A-frame with ⅜-in. bolts. I used wooden spacers on each side of the upper ends of the conduit. They can be short slices of 1-in. dowel center drilled ⅜ in. to fit over the ⅜-in. bolt. Alternately, use a number of flat metal washers.

Check the swing for smooth action and make any corrections necessary. If you have accurately located all the holes, there should be no problem.

The final step in construction is to make the four arms for the swing as detailed in the drawing. They are edge drilled for ¼-in. bolts that pass through the long conduit supports and for the bolts that pass through the back brace of the seat backs.

Because all bolts that pass through the conduit must allow the conduit to pivot on the bolts, do not tighten the nuts too firmly. Upset the ends of the bolts so the nuts will not turn off the ends.

Paint all parts of the swing with a quality exterior paint. When the paint is thoroughly dry, give each pivot point a shot from an aerosol can of lubrication and the swing is ready for action.

Depending on how rambunctiously your children (or their friends) operate the swing, you may want to drive stakes in the ground and spike or bolt the low ends of the A-frames to the stakes.

Old-fashioned Hanging Swing

There is no nicer way to spend a summer evening than swinging in an old-fashioned porch swing. And what better time to start this project than spring?

The swing pictured here was made from 1-in. oak flooring but any 1-in. hardwood stock can be used. Begin construction by cutting 1-in. stock to width, ripping down the center edgewise, then planing the wood to a ⅜-in. thickness. Alternately, you could purchase ⅜- or ½- in. lumber.

First make the back piece for the swing by cutting seventeen 3 × 8- in. boards for slats. Shape the slat at an 8-in.-diameter radius with a band saw or saber saw as indicated.

Cut top and bottom pieces for the back piece to the dimensions

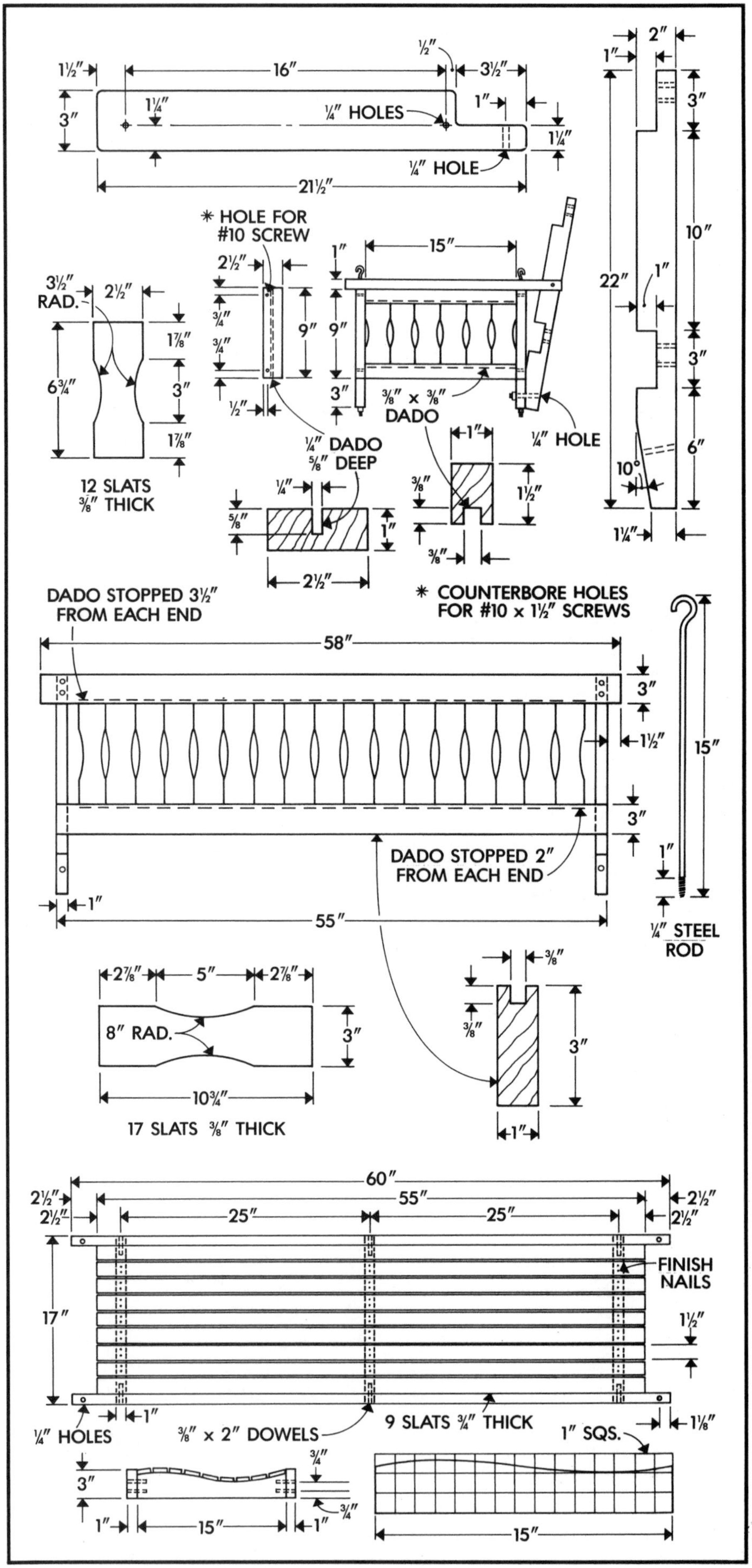

1½″
16″
½″
3½″
3″
1¼″
¼″ HOLES
1″
1¼″
¼″ HOLE
21½″
2″
1″
3″
10″
22″
1″
3″
6″
10°
1¼″
* HOLE FOR
#10 SCREW
2½″
3½″
RAD.
2½″
1⅞″
6¾″
3″
1⅞″
¾″
¾″
9″
½″
1″
15″
9″
3″
⅜″ x ⅜″
DADO
¼″ HOLE
12 SLATS
⅜″ THICK
¼″ DADO
⅝″ DEEP
¼″
⅝″
1″
2½″
1″
⅜″
1½″
⅜″
* COUNTERBORE HOLES
FOR #10 x 1½″ SCREWS
DADO STOPPED 3½″
FROM EACH END
58″
3″
1½″
15″
3″
DADO STOPPED 2″
FROM EACH END
1″
1″
55″
¼″ STEEL
ROD
2⅞″
5″
2⅞″
8″ RAD.
3″
10¾″
17 SLATS ⅜″ THICK
⅜″
⅜″
3″
1″
60″
2½″
55″
2½″
2½″
25″
25″
2½″
FINISH
NAILS
17″
1½″
1″
¼″ HOLES
⅜″ x 2″ DOWELS
9 SLATS ¾″ THICK
1″ SQS.
1⅛″
3″
¾″
¾″
1″
15″
1″
15″

given. The top and bottom rails have ⅜ × ⅜-in. dadoes stopped near both ends to accept the slats. Dadoes are cut with a table saw, then chiseled square at the ends.

Sand all pieces of the back, then assemble the slats and rails, glue and clamp and set aside to dry. Make sure the assembly is kept square.

Cut the two back supports next, then glue and screw to the back piece with 1½-in. flathead wood screws.

Make the seat by cutting the front and rear rails and seat supports to the dimensions shown. Enlarge the squared drawing to make a pattern for the three seat supports. The rails and supports are joined with ⅜ × 2-in. dowels. The holes are drilled first, then dowel centers are used to mark the holes in the supports.

There are nine slats in the seat assembly, each slat is 1½ in. wide and 55 in. long. The slats are glued and nailed to the support frame and are spaced ⅛ in. apart. Nails are set below the surface.

To make the side assemblies, cut twelve 3 × 6¾-in. slats and shape in the same manner as the back slats were done. Cut the top and bottom rails, then glue and clamp.

End pieces for the sides are cut to the dimensions shown, then glued and screwed in place with 1½-in. flathead wood screws.

Arm pieces are cut to 3 × 21½ in. with a 1¾-in. notch to fit around the back piece. Glue and nail the arm pieces to the side members.

Long eyebolts are made from 16-in. lengths of ¼ in.-steel rod. First, heat the steel with a torch, then bend around a piece of ¾-in. round stock. Thread the rods a length of 1 in. on the opposite end. The long bolts are inserted down through the sides with nuts and washers tightened securely. The back is put in place and fastened to the seat and arms with ¼ × 2½-in. bolts, washers and nuts.

Fill all nail holes and finish to suit. A polyurethane varnish is recommended due to its ability to withstand the elements. Chain for the swing can be bought at home centers or hardware stores.

Patio Chair

Stock 2 × 2s and 2 × 4s are used. Hand select lumber to get pieces that are straight and clear.

Use waterproof glue on all joints. Assemble with nails and dowels or screws (drawing on next page).

Locate the center of each leg and mark for half-lap joint. Even if slots are a bit off, just make sure the pair of X-shapes is identical. Seat is assembled from 2 × 2s, nailed or doweled between sidebars, front and back pieces. X-shape legs are topped with arms. Join the leg/arm assemblies with crosspieces. Two 11-in. lengths of 2 × 2 position seat at correct height. Back crosspiece is ⅞ in. lower than front so seat angles down to back. Glue and screw seat between legs on crosspieces. Assemble back side pieces, top and bottom members only. Fit assembly down against seat and between leg/arm assemblies. Drill through upright members of back into edges of arms, to create blind holes in arms 1 in. deep. Remove back. Install crosspieces. Fit the back in place and drive dowels through the sides into holes made in arms.

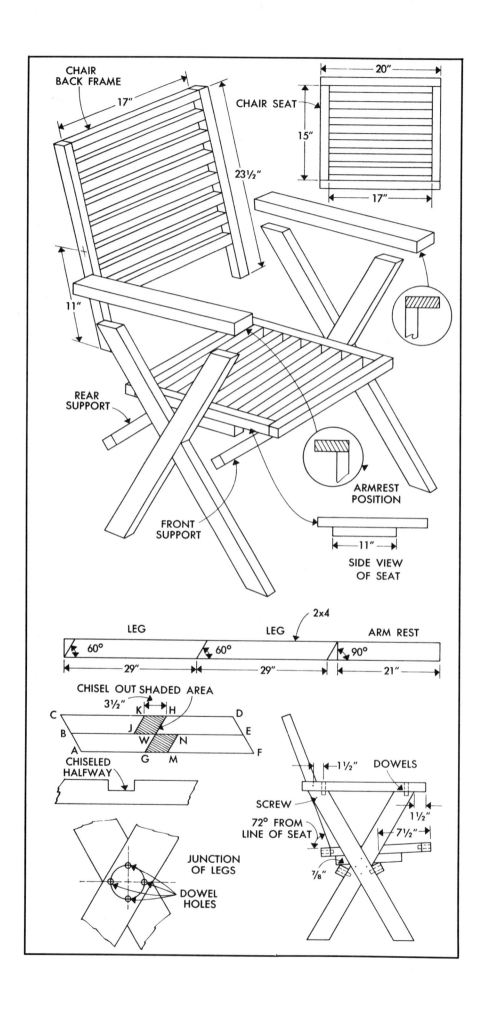

CHAIR BACK FRAME

17"

23½"

11"

CHAIR SEAT

20"

15"

17"

REAR SUPPORT

FRONT SUPPORT

ARMREST POSITION

SIDE VIEW OF SEAT

11"

LEG   LEG   ARM REST

2x4

60°   60°   90°

29"   29"   21"

CHISEL OUT SHADED AREA

3½"

C   K   H   D
B   J   E
          W   N
A   G   M   F

CHISELED HALFWAY

JUNCTION OF LEGS

DOWEL HOLES

1½"   DOWELS

SCREW

72° FROM LINE OF SEAT

1½"

7½"

⅞"

44

Folding Lounge Chair with Roto-Hinges™

Roto-Hinge™ blind pivot joint fasteners are relatively new, having been invented in 1982. The fasteners, or hinges, are manufactured by Abra, Inc. and can be used wherever a pivoting joint is needed in furniture or toy construction or any item made of wood. They are made of hardwood bushings and zinc-plated steel rivets and washers. You just drill two holes in the pieces to be joined, add glue and insert the hinge. It is invisible, strong and resists rust. Roto-Hinges are available in four diameters: ⅜, ½, ¾ and 1 in.

To try out these hinges, here are plans to make a folding rocking lounge chair, available from Abra, Inc., which has granted permission for us to reprint these plans so you can have this interesting chair for your deck or porch (drawings on pages 47-50).

Begin the project by cutting the individual pieces. Hardwood should be used, such as oak or maple. Sand and finish each piece before assembly. If the chair will be exposed to the weather, a couple of coats of

The Roto-Hinge is made of two bushings joined with plated steel pin, washers. Hole depth for ¾ in. hinge is ⁹⁄₁₆ in.

polyurethane or spar varnish would be appropriate, unless you decide to paint it.

Make the side assemblies by joining the legs to the leg connectors with Roto-Hinges. The correct sequence for assembly is: (for right side) insert two hinges into the long leg, fit both leg connectors onto these hinges. Insert two more hinges into the leg connectors, then fit the short leg. Repeat the procedure for the left assembly.

To install a Roto-Hinge, first put a few drops of glue into the hole. Coat the inside of the hole so there is not a bubble in the bottom. Too much glue in the bottom of the hole may cause the wood to crack when the fastener is inserted. Next, with the head of the rivet facing up, tap the hinge into position with a mallet. Repeat this procedure for the member to be joined. That is all there is to it; no clamping is needed.

After the side assemblies are complete, connect the crosspieces and arm rests with glue and screws. All screw holes are counterbored using buttons to cover the screws in the crosspieces and plugs in the

Holes are drilled in pieces to be joined, glue added and spread out, hinge tapped into position, second piece joined to hinge.

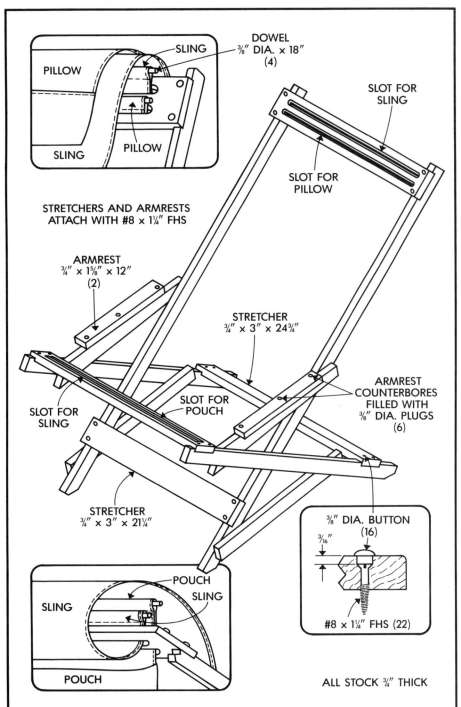

PILLOW

SLING

PILLOW

SLING

DOWEL
⅜″ DIA. x 18″
(4)

SLOT FOR
SLING

SLOT FOR
PILLOW

STRETCHERS AND ARMRESTS
ATTACH WITH #8 x 1¼″ FHS

ARMREST
¾″ x 1⅝″ x 12″
(2)

STRETCHER
¾″ x 3″ x 24¾″

ARMREST
COUNTERBORES
FILLED WITH
⅜″ DIA. PLUGS
(6)

SLOT FOR
SLING

SLOT FOR
POUCH

STRETCHER
¾″ x 3″ x 21¼″

⅜″ DIA. BUTTON
(16)

³⁄₁₆″

#8 x 1¼″ FHS (22)

POUCH

SLING

SLING

POUCH

ALL STOCK ¾″ THICK

MATERIALS LIST

Hardwood:
  ¾″ × 1⅝″ (20 lineal ft.)
  ¾″ × 3″ (11 lineal ft.)
Dowels: ⅜″ × 36″ (2)
Buttons: ⅜″ dia. (16)
Plugs: ⅜″ dia. (6)
Roto-Hinges: ¾″ dia. (8)
Wood Screws: No. 8 × 1¼″ (22)
Awning fabric: 2 yards.
*Batting, synthetic (for pillow), 2
  sq. ft.*
*Nylon thread, #69 industrial
  grade (1 spool)*

arm rests. Pay attention when joining the crosspieces as it is possible to assemble the rocker "inside out."

Awning material was used for the sling, pillow and pouch, but duck or heavyweight denim also would work. Sew the material as shown in the drawing. Depending on the weight of fabric used, you may need to have it sewn with an industrial machine.

Attach the fabric items in this sequence: with the frame in the normal open position, insert the small hem of the pouch through the inside slot of the front crosspiece from the bottom up and secure with a dowel. Next, insert the small hem of the headrest into the inside slot of the back crosspiece and slide a dowel into one of the hems; there are four to allow for adjustment.

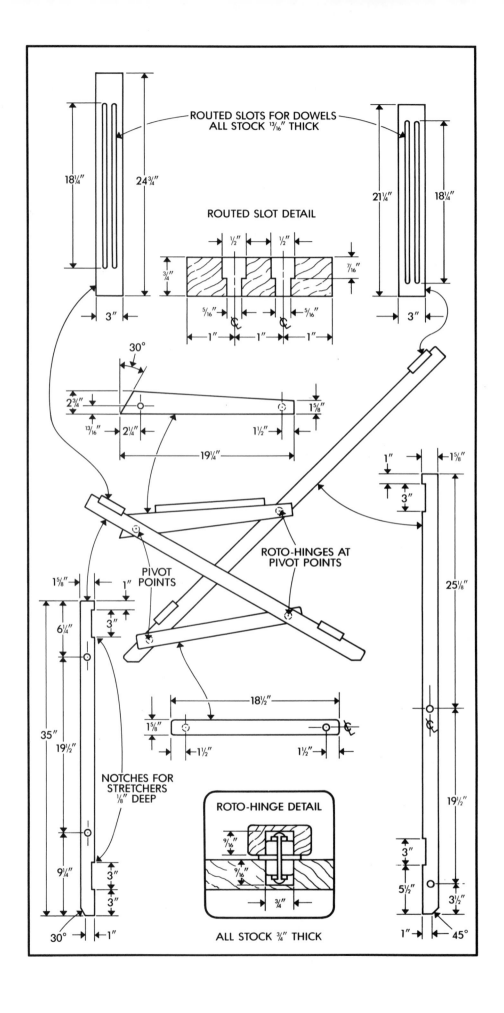

ROUTED SLOTS FOR DOWELS
ALL STOCK 13/16″ THICK

ROUTED SLOT DETAIL

ROTO-HINGES AT
PIVOT POINTS

PIVOT
POINTS

NOTCHES FOR
STRETCHERS
1/8″ DEEP

ROTO-HINGE DETAIL

ALL STOCK 3/4″ THICK

Now drape the sling over the chair so that the end with a single hem extends over the front crosspiece and the other end (triple hem) extends over the back crosspiece. Wrap each end around its respective crosspiece and, from the bottom up, insert the hems through the outside slots and secure with dowels.

Roto-Hinges are manufactured by Abra, Inc., Dept. WN, P.O. Box 1086, Bloomington, IN 47402. Write to them for more information. The hinges are available in hardware stores and mail order catalogs, but if you have trouble finding what you want, they can be ordered direct from Abra, Inc. They also sell plans for a Folding Foot Stool (free) which matches the folding rocking chair shown here, and for the Kradle, a portable reclining swing.

Sewing Instructions

Sling: Sew double-fold ½-in. hems (with raw edges hidden) along both long sides. On "wrong" surface draw two stitch guidelines from hem to hem; one at 3½ in. from one raw edge and the other at 7½ in. from the opposite raw edge. At the 3½-in. end, fold the raw edge in ½ in. and butt this folded edge up to the 3½-in. line to sew a 1½-in. hem. Repeat this procedure at the opposite end to make the 3½-in. hem. Both hems should be double stitched. The 3½-in. hem then is

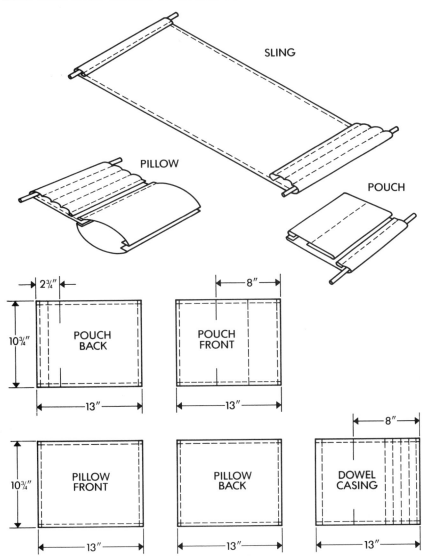

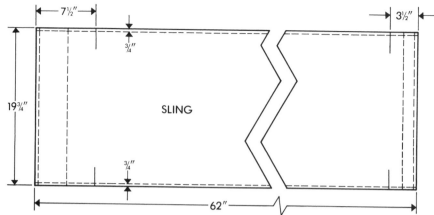

divided into three equal sections lengthwise by two long stitch lines. Each of these sections should be large enough to allow a ⅜-in. dowel to be inserted easily (see drawing).

Pillow: Eliminate all raw edges on all three pieces with a tight zigzag stitch. Join the three pieces lengthwise end to end with two ½-in. seams. Fold one end piece back onto the middle piece at the seam (with the seams on the outside). Stitch both sides to make a pocket and then turn the right side out. Stitch down the ½-in. hems on both sides of the flap. Fold the flap and stitch a 4¼-in. hem. This 4¼-in. hem then is divided into four equal sections lengthwise by three long stitch lines. Each of these sections should be large enough to allow a ⅜-in. dowel to be inserted easily. Stuff the pocket of the pillow with batting and stitch closed.

Pouch: Eliminate all raw edges on both pieces with a tight zigzag stitch. Stitch a 4-in. hem on one piece. Stitch both pieces together inside out with a ½-in. seam on three sides. Then turn right side out. Stitch down the ½-in. hems on both sides of the flap. Fold the flap and stitch a 1¼-in. hem.

Patio Lounge

This attractive wooden patio lounge is a versatile piece of furniture that can serve as a patio lounge, a table or a plant stand, either indoors or out.

It's basically a wooden frame with stationary slats. The movable headrest can be adjusted to prop up in two positions or lie flat.

Begin by cutting the frame from 2 × 6 stock. Legs are cut from 4 × 4 stock to a 10½ in. height.

Assemble the framework with waterproof glue and hex head lag screws. First make the outside framework, then bolt in the four legs.

Next, cut out notched support bars for the headrest, which fit inside the frame at the top and are connected to the sides and legs.

Make the headrest support. Note that the sides of the support have diagonal end cuts.

Now, cut sixteen 1 × 4 slats and one 1 × 3 slat. Sand the rough edges, then glue and screw the slats to the framework sides. The 1 × 3 slat is stationary and fits at the top end of the fixed frame. Slat at bottom of headrest should fit flush. Drive a 4-in. lag bolt through the headrest from the outside frame on each side so that the headrest pivots inside the frame.

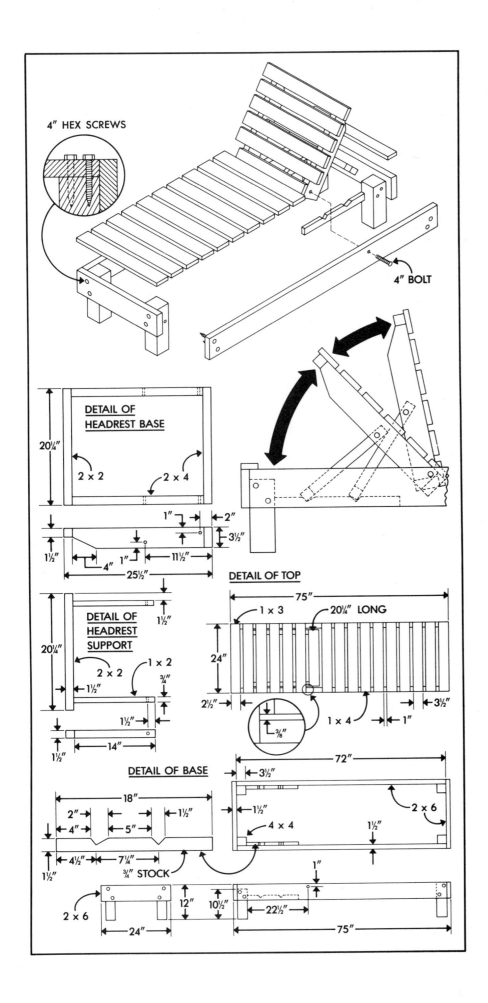

4" HEX SCREWS

4" BOLT

DETAIL OF HEADREST BASE

20¼"

2 × 2

2 × 4

1"

2"

3½"

1½"

4"

1"

11½"

25½"

DETAIL OF HEADREST SUPPORT

20¼"

2 × 2

1 × 2

1½"

¾"

1½"

1½"

14"

1½"

DETAIL OF TOP

75"

1 × 3

20¼" LONG

24"

2½"

3½"

1 × 4

1"

⅜"

DETAIL OF BASE

18"

2"

4"

5"

1½"

4½"

7¼"

1½"

¾" STOCK

72"

3½"

1½"

4 × 4

1½"

2 × 6

1"

2 × 6

12"

10½"

22½"

24"

75"

Child's Gym

When we shopped for a backyard gym set we found that prices ranged from $250 to $400 and the sets were made of light-gauge metal that would deteriorate quickly in rain and weather. I built a gym set that I know would stand up to both weather and rambunctious youngsters, mostly from pressure-treated 4 × 4 lumber. Cost of the set was far less than the least expensive commercial unit.

The first step is to cut six 3-ft. lengths of 4 × 4 for the steps and saw rabbets in each end as shown in the drawing. I did this with multiple passes of my portable circular saw. Next, cut the four 10-ft. lengths of 4 × 4 for the uprights and lag screw the steps to them. Drive two screws through each end of each step, first drilling clearance holes through the step and pilot holes in the uprights. On one pair of uprights I spaced the steps 18, 36 and 54 in. above the ground level mark (3 ft. from the bottoms of the posts, the depth necessary to get below the frost line. On the other pair I located the bottom step 12 in. above the ground line so smaller children could more easily reach it.

Next I notched two 10-ft. lengths of 4 × 4 as shown and nailed them to the tops of the two pair of uprights with the steps attached, using a couple of 16-penny nails at each joint. The nails held the crosspieces in place until I fitted the 12-ft. lengths between the ladder assemblies. Rabbets are cut in the ends of the pieces as indicated, then blind holes are drilled in each piece to accept the ends of the eleven 1¼-in. dowels (closet poles) that create the horizontal ladder. The dowels are not glued, but simply held by screws as indicated. This assembly now

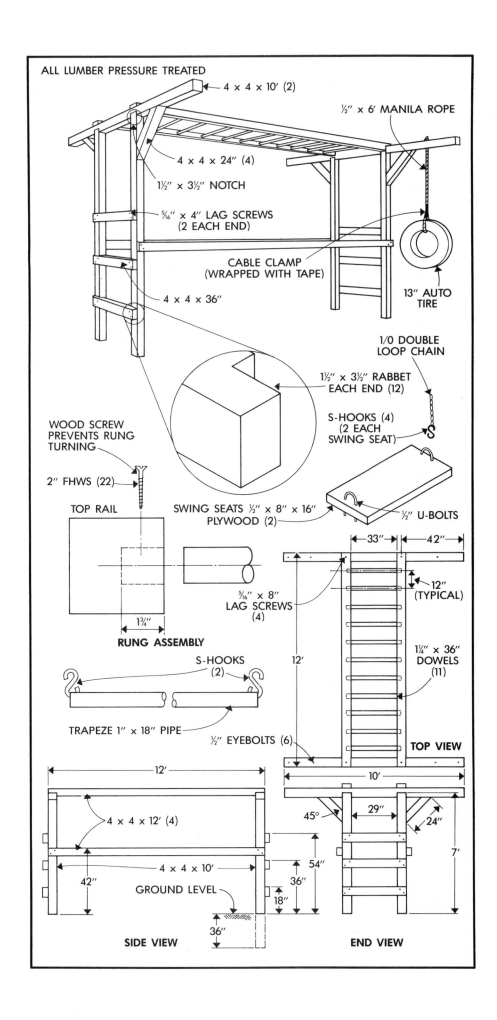

ALL LUMBER PRESSURE TREATED

4 x 4 x 10' (2)

½" x 6' MANILA ROPE

4 x 4 x 24" (4)

1½" x 3½" NOTCH

5/16" x 4" LAG SCREWS
(2 EACH END)

CABLE CLAMP
(WRAPPED WITH TAPE)

13" AUTO
TIRE

4 x 4 x 36"

1/0 DOUBLE
LOOP CHAIN

1½" x 3½" RABBET
EACH END (12)

S-HOOKS (4)
(2 EACH
SWING SEAT)

WOOD SCREW
PREVENTS RUNG
TURNING

2" FHWS (22)

TOP RAIL

SWING SEATS ½" x 8" x 16"
PLYWOOD (2)

½" U-BOLTS

1¾"

RUNG ASSEMBLY

5/16" x 8"
LAG SCREWS
(4)

33"

42"

12"
(TYPICAL)

12'

1¼" x 36"
DOWELS
(11)

S-HOOKS
(2)

TRAPEZE 1" x 18" PIPE

½" EYEBOLTS (6)

TOP VIEW

12'

4 x 4 x 12' (4)

4 x 4 x 10'

42"

GROUND LEVEL

54"

36"

18"

36"

SIDE VIEW

10'

45°

29"

24"

7'

END VIEW

53

is clamped to the vertical ladder assemblies and holes are drilled to allow driving 8-in. lag screws down through them, through the end crosspieces and into the tops of the uprights.

Four holes now were dug to accept the four uprights, with space for concrete around them. The gym frame then was set in the holes and leveled and plumbed. I used one bag of concrete ready mix for each hole, and allowed 24 hours for the concrete to set before I did any more work.

The horizontal side bars that join the two ladder assemblies are 4 × 4s with the ends rabbeted as indicated to create a half lap joint. Depending on the age and size of your children, the bars can be positioned higher or lower than the 36 in. shown in the drawing. These bars are attached with two lag screws at each end.

Any size tire can be used for the swing; ours is from a 13-in. wheel. Manila rope is used to suspend the tire by passing it through a hole in the top crosspiece and tying a knot in the rope. The rope is passed around the tire and held to itself with a wire cable clamp. Plastic electrician's tape is wrapped over the clamp so hands will not contact its sharp edges.

The other two swings have plywood seats and they are suspended on chains. Eyebolts are used at the top, being fitted in holes drilled through the crosspiece. S-hooks are used to join the chains to the eyebolts. The plywood seats are drilled to accept U-bolts, then S hooks are used to connect the chains to the U-bolts.

The trapeze is a length of 1-in. pipe, drilled to accept S-hooks that join it to the chains, while S-hooks at the upper ends of the chains join to eyebolts in holes bored through the top crosspiece. All the S-hooks are clamped shut with a heavy pair of pliers, to eliminate the chance of any of the chains becoming disconnected.

The location and arrangement of the swings and trapeze are strictly arbitrary, and you might want them placed differently on your gym. Lengths of the chains also could be shorter or longer, depending on the ages and sizes of your children. No paint or finish was required for the pressure-treated lumber, and it will weather to a pleasing natural color.

INDOOR FURNITURE

Convertible Table Chair

This charming table/chair delights youngsters and because it folds from table to chair, takes up less space than a straight table.

While the styling shown is sort of "colonial modern" it takes only a change in the shape of the chair back and leg to make it match a particular decor. The photo shows two versions of the back.

The project can be made either from ¾-in. plywood or 1-in. solid stock. In the latter case you will have to edge glue the lumber to make pieces wide enough. Veneer tape can be glued to the edges of the plywood to hide the grain.

Joinery is plain but strong, with glue and screws being used. You might prefer dowel joints, or mortise and tendon. Note that the chair back has a tenon on it that fits in an open mortise in the chair seat/table top. The leg could be handled in the same manner, if you wish.

Start construction by enlarging the squared drawings to make patterns. If you might make more than one of the units, make the patterns of ⅛-in. hardboard so they can be traced many times without the edges becoming worn and fuzzy as would be the case with paper or cardboard.

Cut the various pieces to size and shape, then cut the mortise for the chair back. It's a good idea to cut the mortise a bit undersize and the tenon a bit oversize. Cut and fit the two components until you get a nice snug fit.

The chair back is reinforced by a cleat glued and screwed to the chair seat behind the back as detailed. The bottom of the chair (table) has two individual legs that are glued and screwed to a cleat, which then is glued and screwed to the underside of the top.

The larger individual leg also is reinforced by being glued and screwed to a cleat that also is glued and screwed to the underside of the top. Space the two single and the one individual leg by fitting the short, shaped stretcher between them when attaching them to the underside of the chair/table bottom.

Recess the hinges as indicated; these can be rounded-end sewing-machine cabinet hinges, and you might want to use three or four rather than the two indicated. Active youngsters can put considerable strain on hinges, especially in a situation like this where changing the chair to a table and back can be half the fun.

Be sure to round all sharp edges and remove any splinters. Stain and varnish with several coats of polyurethane or paint the table/chair bright colors to match other furniture in the child's room.

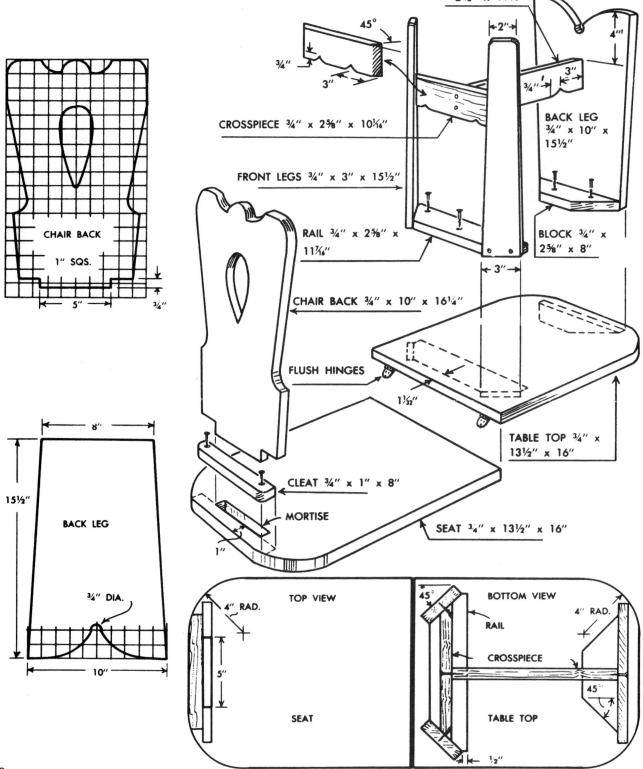

Video Game Console

You can never be too rich, too thin or have too many video games. But this wealth of electronic wizardry can become a tangled mess and, if not properly stored, cartridges can be damaged.

The solution is this easy-to-build video game storage cart. Construction is fast since KD-type (knock down) fittings (called connector bolt and cross dowel) are used to hold the hardwood plywood panels together. The smoked acrylic doors are held in place with self aligning hinges and kept closed by concealed spring-actuated, self-opening magnetic latches.

Lay out the panel dimensions (next page) on the oak (or other hardwood) plywood panels so you rip the sides and back to the 17-in. width with a single cut. Next, rip the top/bottom to a 16-in. width and cut all panels to length. Cut the shelves to size individually.

Apply ¾-in. self-adhering veneer tape with a hot iron (or use non-

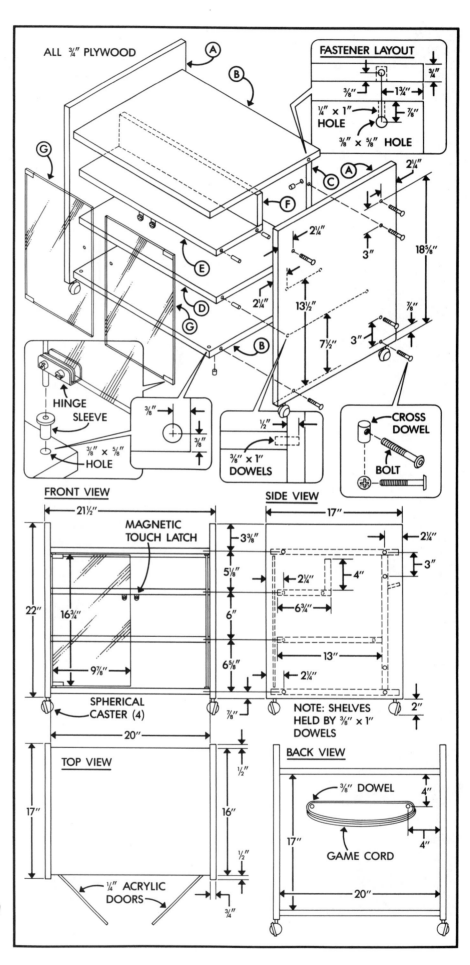

MATERIALS LIST

¾″ hardwood plywood:
  A, Side, 17″ × 22″ (2)
  B, Top/bottom, 16″ × 20″ (1 each)
  C, Back, 17″ × 20″ (1)
  D, Lower shelf, 13″ × 20″ (1)
  E, Upper shelf, 6¾″ × 20″ (1)
  F, Shelf back, 4″ × 20″ (1)
  G, Door, ¼″ acrylic plastic, 9⅞″ × 16¾″ (2)
  H, Cord holder rack, ⅜″ × 2″ dowel (2)
  I, Shelf peg, ⅜″ × 1″ dowel (8)
Hardware:
  Joint connector bolt and cross dowel #D6600 (12)
  Hinge, black, #D3521 (2)
  Casters, spherical, 1⅝″ dia. (4)

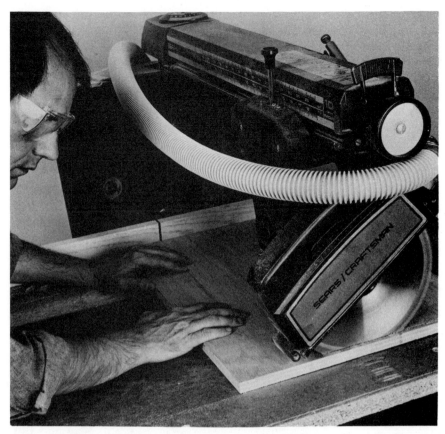

Rip to width the side panels "A" and back panel "C," then the top and bottom "B" panels. Finally, cut all panels to their finished length. Use plywood cutting blade.

self-adhering tape and contact adhesive) to all four edges of sides "A" and to the front and back edges of the top and bottom "B" panels. Sand the tape smooth and slightly round all edges and corners to prevent lifting.

Apply veneer tape, either self adhering or the type that requires contact adhesive, to all edges. Smooth edges and corners when glue is dry.

The KD fasteners require a ¼-in. hole for the screw shaft and a
⅜ × ⅝-in. hole for the steel cross dowel. First lay out the shaft holes
1¾ in. from the edges of both "B" and "C." Then clamp a doweling jig
in place and drill ¼ × 1-in. holes through the layout lines.

Use a square to transfer the edge layout line to the underside of the
top "B." Measure ⅞ in. from the edge and mark the locations of steel
dowel holes on the face. Drill a ⅜ × ⅝-in. hole through each of your
layout marks. The fastener layout is the same on back "C."

Use square to accurately lay out holes for KD fasteners. Locate 1/4 in. edge shaft hole 1-3/4 in. from edge. Dowel hole, 3/8 x 5/8 in. deep, 7/8 in. from edge.

Transfer hole locations in upper shelf assembly ("E" and "F") to sides by placing shelf directly on side, using sharp pencil to transfer the locations.

Hardwood dowels are used to support shelves "D" and "E." Locate these ⅜ × ⅝-in. holes 1 in. from front and rear.

Mark the fastener layout lines for the top, bottom, shelves and back on the inside surface of side "A." Use a square to draw these lines across the width of "A" ⅞, 7½, 13½ and 18⅝ in. from the bottom edge. Mark additional lines ½ in. from the front edge to guide the setback, and 2¼ in. from the rear edge to position the back panel.

Transfer the fastener hole locations in the top, bottom and back to the sides "A." Start with the bottom panel "B" and place it in alignment with the ½ in. setback line and parallel with the layout line ⅞ in. from the bottom. Transfer the hole locations to the side "A." Transfer the remaining fastener and dowel locations to the sides: note the shelves are set back 1¼ in. from the front edge of "A."

Use your doweling jig as a guide while drilling the ¼-in. holes completely through the side for the fasteners. Drill ⅜ × ⅝-in. holes for the shelf dowels. Drill two ⅜ × ⅝-in. holes in the rear of the back for the wire rack dowels. Place the holes 4 in. from the top and side of the back panel.

Use stop on drill bit to limit depth of holes bored to accept the 3/8 in. dowels that are used as shelf supports. Drill press also can be used to control depth.

The hinge pin bushings are located in four ⅜ × ⅝-in. holes set back ⅜ in. from the front and the end of the underside of top "B" and the upper side of the bottom "B."

Check the instructions for installing the spherical casters. Most require a ⅜ × 1¼ in. hole. Drill these holes in the bottom edges of the sides 1 in. from the vertical edges.

"Dry assemble" the video console and check the fit of all parts, then test fit the acrylic doors.

Some plastic suppliers will cut the door panels "G" to size, or you can cut the material with a sharp, fine-tooth blade on a table, radial-arm or band saw. Smooth the edges with fine sandpaper until all saw marks are gone, then "flame polish" the edges with a propane torch. You do this by "brushing" the flame along the edges, watching closely to see when the plastic flows and loses the milky look caused by cutting and sanding.

Plastic hinge pin bushing fits in 3/8 x 5/8 in. deep hole drilled 3/8 in. from front and sides in top and bottom. Plastic door panel is easily adjusted to fit in opening.

Position the magnetic catches on the underside of the top shelf. Rather than mounting the standard plate that comes with the catch, cut down the length of a pan head sheet metal screw to less than ¼ in. Put a drop of black paint on the end of the shaft before you screw it into the pilot hole you drilled in the door, and it will be almost invisible in the semi-transparent plastic door.

Disassemble the console for finishing. Sand all surfaces with 120-grit followed by 220-grit paper. To highlight the natural grain of the oak used for the unit shown, we applied Minwax Golden Oak No. 210B, wiping it on with a soft cloth. After the stain dried overnight, several coats of easy-to-apply Antique Oil were applied. Between coats of oil all surfaces were lightly burnished with 4/0 steel wool to ensure a smooth finish.

Insert steel dowel of KD fastener in hole, align with screw, use allen wrench to tighten the fitting. Heads of dowels are quite flat and unobtrusive, add to contemporary styling.

Video Recorder/TV Stand

While stock 2 × 3 Douglas fir lumber was used for this attractive stand of contemporary design, hardwood also could be used. For a special effect, you might use two different kinds of lumber, alternating every other strip. Note that a 2 × 3 measures a true 1½ × 2½ in., so the boards in the various shelf assemblies are offset 1½ in. as indicated to join with adjacent assemblies.

Vertical assemblies are spaced with larger offsets that determine the levels of the shelves, as shown in the photo and drawings (next page).

Start by cutting the various strips to length. I found that 8-ft. lengths of lumber produced the least waste. Edge glue and clamp the assemblies, using glue sparingly to avoid excess mess. Some craftsmen might want to use dowels or splines to reinforce the glued-up assemblies.

Be accurate with the alignment of the various parts of the shelves so the vertical supports fit neatly and tightly when assembled.

When joining the vertical supports to the shelves, work with the assemblies positioned on their back edges on the floor. Use a 2-ft. square to keep all corners at right angles. Glue the joints between the uprights and shelves, then clamp the assembly until the glue sets.

MATERIALS LIST

(all 2 × 3 lumber)
Top shelf:
  21" (4)
  24" (3)
Middle shelf:
  22½" (4)
  48" (3)
Bottom shelf:
  45" (4)
  48" (3)
Vertical panels:
  D, 12" (3)
  D, 27" (4)
  E, 12" (3)
  E, 18" (4)
  F, 10½" (4)

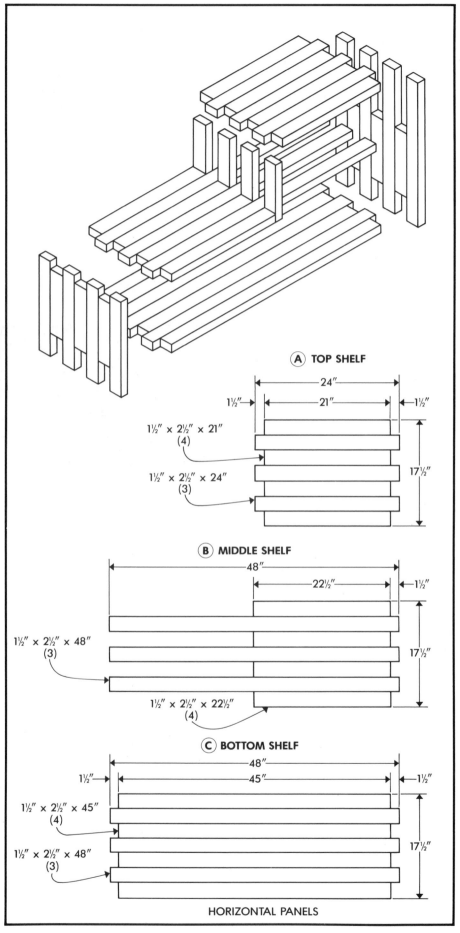

A TOP SHELF

1½" × 2½" × 21" (4)
1½" × 2½" × 24" (3)
24"
21"
1½" 1½"
17½"

B MIDDLE SHELF

48"
22½"
1½"
1½" × 2½" × 48" (3)
1½" × 2½" × 22½" (4)
17½"

C BOTTOM SHELF

48"
45"
1½" 1½"
1½" × 2½" × 45" (4)
1½" × 2½" × 48" (3)
17½"

HORIZONTAL PANELS

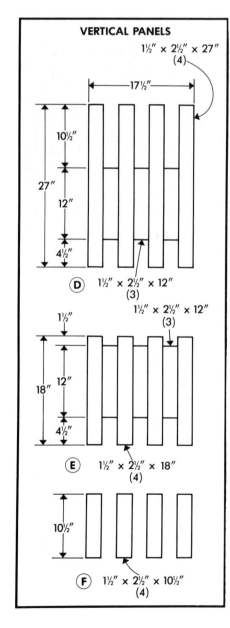

VERTICAL PANELS

1½" × 2½" × 27" (4)
17½"
10½"
27"
12"
4½"

D 1½" × 2½" × 12" (3)

1½" × 2½" × 12" (3)
1½"
18"
12"
4½"

E 1½" × 2½" × 18" (4)

10½"

F 1½" × 2½" × 10½" (4)

An alternative method of joinery would be to make a jig that would allow accurate drilling of the ends of uprights and shelves so a long dowel could be inserted in the joints between the "fingers" of the uprights and shelves.

It is easier to sand the various pieces before assembly, then do a final sanding when the stand is glued together. Stain and finish to suit. The wood can be left natural and sealed with tung oil or a Danish oil if you prefer.

TV Stand

This clear pine TV stand is quite strong and capable of supporting a 25-in. set.

Begin making the stand by assembling the four notched pieces for the top frame. Glue each joint, then clamp the frame while you counterbore for the screws and attach the corner braces. The screws are covered with wood buttons, or may be concealed with dowels glued into place and sanded flush.

Now, cut the legs to length and chamfer as indicated. Glue and screw the legs to the top frame. Add the chamfered bottom rails to the legs, then attach the stretcher between the rails. Sand the entire structure and finish as desired.

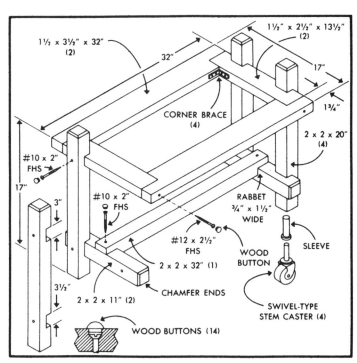

Stereo and Lamp Stand

Besides being starkly functional, this stand features an open frame with no large panel surfaces, so it appears to be smaller than it actually is. This makes it ideal for small rooms, where more "standard" furniture designs would create a crowded, cramped feeling.

Standard 2 × 4 stock is used throughout. When you get the lumber, be sure you hand select, so all pieces are straight, as free of knots as

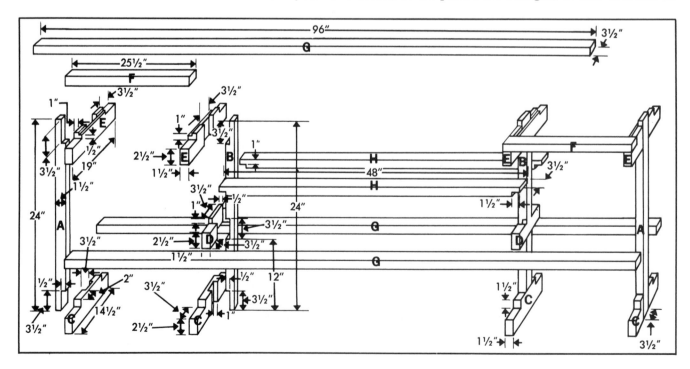

possible and those that are present are tight and solid. Avoid splits and heavy streaks of sap.

Cut all pieces to size. It would be a good idea to line up your stereo components on the floor and measure the length needed to accommodate them all. You then can make the stand longer or shorter, or reposition the vertical members to provide the required length of shelf.

Also note that the stand is assembled from a number of matching pieces. For example, there are three "G" pieces, four "E" pieces, and so on. Clamp these sets of pieces together when you mark and machine them so they are identical. Do your work accurately, and the pieces should be interchangeable, so future disassembly and reassembly will be simple.

The original stand was simply glued and nailed together with 16-penny spikes, but an alternative assembly method with bolts and Teenuts provides a means of easy disassembly for moving or storage.

Although the drawing shows space for a piece of ⁵⁄₁₆-in. plate glass 12 × 24 in. fitted in the tops at each end of the stand, we suggest you do not order the glass or heavy plastic until after you have assembled the stand. Then measure the space between the "F" and "G" pieces and the projecting ends of the "A" and "B" members. The glass should be an easy fit inside the four members.

Child-size Desk

Sized for youngsters from about two to six years old, this easy-to-build desk will be used for everything from eating lunch to doing homework to coloring pictures and for just fun and games. And it's a fun project to build for father or grandfather to give to a favorite child or grandchild.

The original desk was built completely from no. 2 pine in stock lumber sizes, so no ripping was required. Each side, for example, is glued and doweled from lengths of 1 × 10, while the inner sides are assembled from lengths of 1 × 3 and 1 × 10. Some draftsmen might prefer to make these four panels, as well as the rest of the desk, from plywood (drawing on next page).

The desk top is assembled from 28½ in. lengths of 1 × 4 and 1 × 10 (the actual net widths of the lumber are shown in the chart in the drawing). The top is attached to the inner sides by driving screws down through counterbored holes that are plugged with wooden buttons, or use wooden plugs and sand them flush with the desk top.

The lower stretcher is cut to length from 1 × 3 stock and glued and screwed to the back edges of the sides. Cut the tray from a 28½ in. length of 1 × 6 and glue and screw it to the underside of the desk top at the rear as shown. Assemble the back from lengths of 1 × 4 and 1 × 10 to create a panel 12¾ in. high. It is glued and screwed to the back edges of the sides, and also to the back edge of the tray.

Assemble the shelf and its four supports, using glue and screws. Supports are cut from 1 × 4 stock, the shelf is a length of 1 × 6. This assembly is freestanding, and can be removed as a unit for easier cleaning.

The upper top of the desk also is a length of 1 × 6 and it has lengths of 1 × 3 fitted across the back, on top, and two shorter pieces of 1 × 3 at the ends. Shape the latter as in the detail.

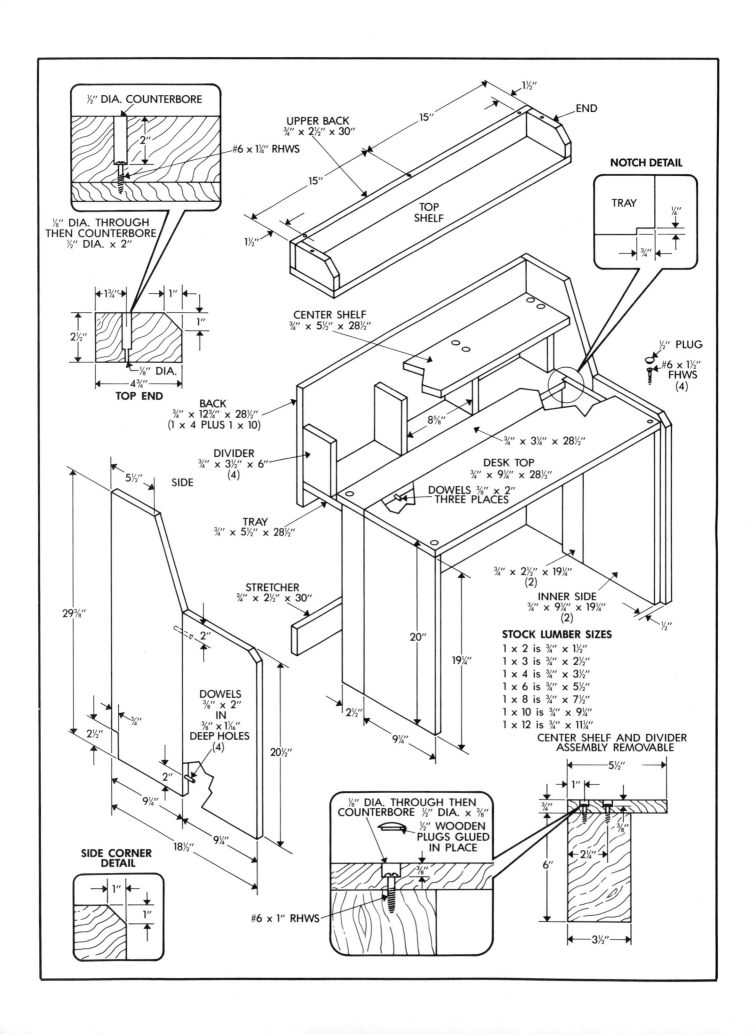

½" DIA. COUNTERBORE

2"

#6 × 1¼" RHWS

⅛" DIA. THROUGH
THEN COUNTERBORE
½" DIA. × 2"

1¾"
1"
2½"
1"
⅛" DIA.
4¾"

TOP END

1½"

UPPER BACK
¾" × 2½" × 30"

15"

END

15"

TOP
SHELF

1½"

NOTCH DETAIL

TRAY

¼"

¾"

CENTER SHELF
¾" × 5½" × 28½"

½" PLUG

#6 × 1½"
FHWS
(4)

BACK
¾" × 12¾" × 28½"
(1 × 4 PLUS 1 × 10)

8⅝"

¾" × 3¼" × 28½"

DIVIDER
¾" × 3½" × 6"
(4)

DESK TOP
¾" × 9¼" × 28½"

DOWELS ⅜" × 2"
THREE PLACES

SIDE

5½"

TRAY
¾" × 5½" × 28½"

29⅜"

STRETCHER
¾" × 2½" × 30"

20"

¾" × 2½" × 19¼"
(2)

INNER SIDE
¾" × 9¼" × 19¼"
(2)

½"

19¼"

STOCK LUMBER SIZES
1 × 2 is ¾" × 1½"
1 × 3 is ¾" × 2½"
1 × 4 is ¾" × 3½"
1 × 6 is ¾" × 5½"
1 × 8 is ¾" × 7½"
1 × 10 is ¾" × 9¼"
1 × 12 is ¾" × 11¼"

2"

DOWELS
⅜" × 2"
IN
⅜" × 1¹⁄₁₆"
DEEP HOLES
(4)

¾"

2½"

2"

20½"

2½"

9¼"

9¼"

9¼"

18½"

**SIDE CORNER
DETAIL**

1"

1"

**CENTER SHELF AND DIVIDER
ASSEMBLY REMOVABLE**

5½"

1"

¾"

⅜"

6"

2¼"

3½"

⅛" DIA. THROUGH THEN
COUNTERBORE ½" DIA. × ⅜"

½" WOODEN
PLUGS GLUED
IN PLACE

⅜"

#6 × 1" RHWS

Bench and Two Stools

This fireside bench and two smaller stools are simple projects that can be made on a weekend, or an evening or two. They are practical for spare seating, and children will find them extremely useful for reaching sinks and washbasins that are too high to use comfortably otherwise.

They all basically are variations of the common "five-board bench," although the fireside bench requires more than five pieces.

Both the kitchen stool and child's stool are cut from 1-in. (¾-in. net) stock, and pine shelving 1 × 12s can be used for even the larger pieces. For the child's stool, first enlarge the squared drawings to make patterns for the two legs and the two stretchers. As we often suggest, make them from heavy cardboard or thin hardboard so they can be used a number of times. The benches and stools are popular items and you just might get requests for a number of them. They also should sell well in gift and novelty shops.

Trace and cut out two (or more) of the ends and stretchers for the child's stool and cut the ¼ × ¾-in. dadoes in the stretchers as detailed. As shown in the squared drawing (next page), the dadoes are ¾ in. from each end of each stretcher.

Glue and screw or nail the stretchers to the legs, keeping the upper edges of the stretchers flush with the tops of the legs. Center the top on the legs/stretcher assembly and use glue and nails or screws to attach it. On the original, finishing nails were used, and they were recessed with a nailset and covered with wood putty.

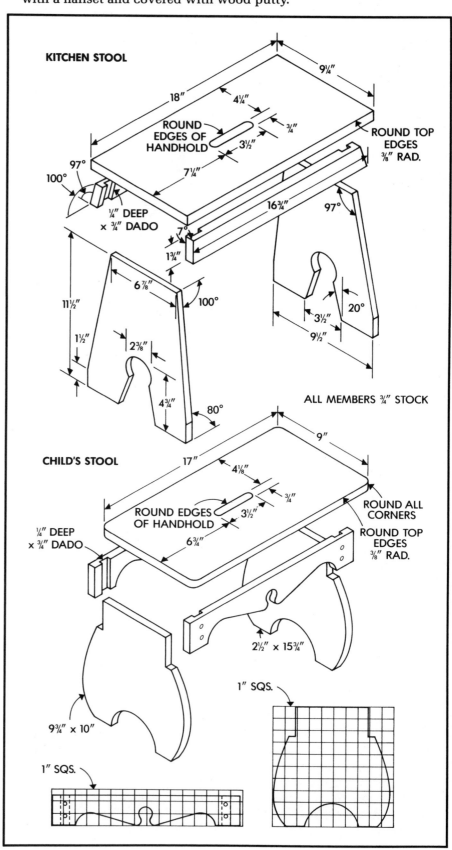

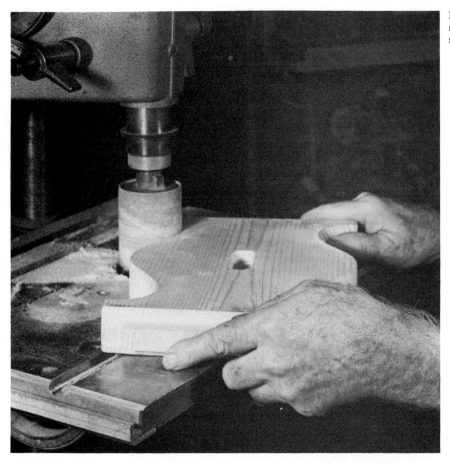

Drum sander in drill press speeds smoothing curved legs of the benches and stools. Do all sanding before assembly.

Dowel jig used with portable electric drill ensures holes are truly vertical. Tape on bit is depth stop.

The kitchen stool is similar in construction, except that the legs are splayed at an angle of 100 degrees and the stretchers are angled 97 degrees to match the edges of the legs.

Lay out the legs as dimensioned. It would be a good idea to make a pattern of cardboard or hardboard, so you could use it for making duplicate stools rather than laying out the leg each time.

The stretchers are cut to size and shape and the ¼ × ¾-in. dadoes are cut parallel to the angled ends, and ¾ in. from each end. Nail or screw the stretchers to the legs and use glue. Be sure the upper edges of the stretchers are flush with the tops of the legs.

The top for the kitchen stool is just a bit bigger than the one on the child's stool, as dimensioned, but the handhold is the same size. This opening can be made by boring two ¾-in. holes, then sawing between them. Use a router with a rounding-over bit on both top and bottom of the handhold, or round it with rasp, file and sandpaper.

The top edges of the tops of the stools can be rounded over with a router before or after assembly, although before might be easier.

The fireside bench is cut from 2-in. (1½-in. net) lumber and most 2 × 12s will be closer to 11¼ in. wide than 11½ in. shown for the top. The ¼ in. should make no real difference in construction.

Enlarge the squared drawings for the legs and the feet (depending on which method of joinery you use). One method has a "foot" at the top and bottom of each leg, the other requires tenons on the ends of the legs. Note that the tenons are not included on the squared drawing and must be added to the length of stock used for the legs.

For the legs without the tenons, the bottom foot is attached by glue and dowels and the top one is attached to the leg with no. 10 wood screws. Dowels in the upper surface of each top foot fit in holes drilled in the underside of the top. A doweling jig will aid in keeping the dowel holes properly spaced and at right angles to the various surfaces.

The stretcher is cut to size and shaped as detailed. Drill holes in each end positioned so they will be partially inside the outside sur-

Tenons on bench stretcher are rasped with rounded ends to fit open mortise in legs. Fit should be snug.

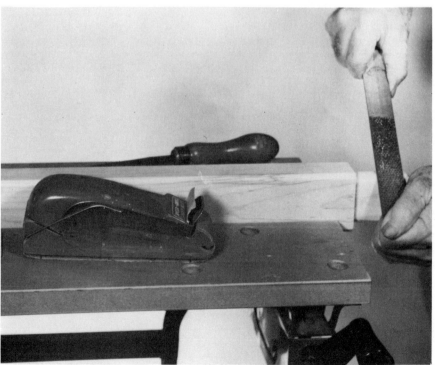

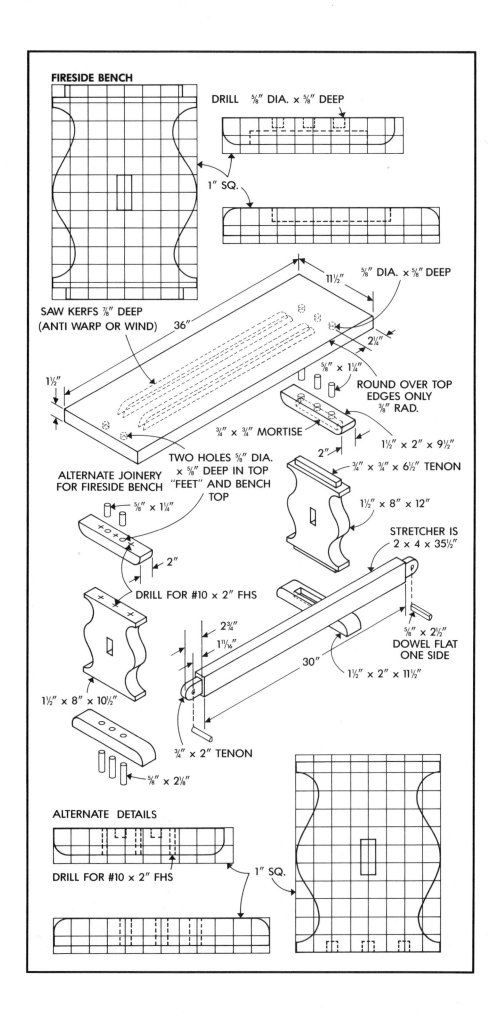

FIRESIDE BENCH

DRILL ⅝″ DIA. × ⅝″ DEEP

1″ SQ.

11½″

⅝″ DIA. × ⅝″ DEEP

SAW KERFS ⅞″ DEEP
(ANTI WARP OR WIND)

36″

2¼″

1½″

⅝″ × 1¼″

ROUND OVER TOP
EDGES ONLY
⅜″ RAD.

¾″ × ¾″ MORTISE

TWO HOLES ⅝″ DIA.
× ⅝″ DEEP IN TOP
"FEET" AND BENCH
TOP

1½″ × 2″ × 9½″

2″

¾″ × ¾″ × 6½″ TENON

1½″ × 8″ × 12″

STRETCHER IS
2 × 4 × 35½″

ALTERNATE JOINERY
FOR FIRESIDE BENCH

⅝″ × 1¼″

2″

DRILL FOR #10 × 2″ FHS

2¾″

1¹¹⁄₁₆″

30″

1½″ × 2″ × 11½″

⅝″ × 2½″
DOWEL FLAT
ONE SIDE

1½″ × 8″ × 10½″

¾″ × 2″ TENON

⅝″ × 2⅛″

ALTERNATE DETAILS

DRILL FOR #10 × 2″ FHS

1″ SQ.

faces of the ends. When the tapered pins are driven into the holes they will pull the legs tightly against the shoulders of the tenons on the ends of the stretcher.

The alternate leg assembly has tenons on the top and bottom of each leg. The lower foot is mortised to accept the tenon and is glued to it. The upper foot has a blind mortise in it, with three dowels in the upper surface to fit in holes on the underside of the top.

Because the top is 2-in. lumber, it is kerfed several times, with the kerfs stopped short of the ends. These kerfs will minimize warping or winding of the heavy top.

The original stools and benches were stained a dark color then given several coats of urethane varnish. For the early American buff, the items lend themselves to "distressing" for an antique look.

Colonial Stool, Chair, Corner Shelf, Letter Holder

These four pieces of early American furniture and accessories are cut from a half sheet of ¾-in. AD plywood. Hardwood plywood can be used, but ordinary fir plywood can be stained to have an "antique" look, or can be painted.

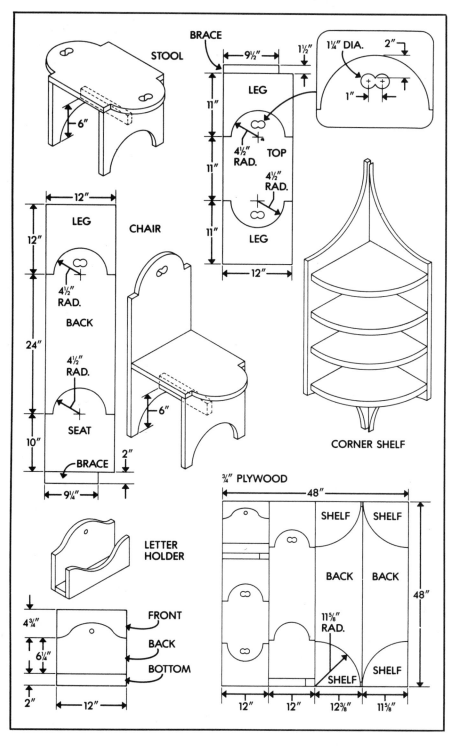

STOOL

BRACE

STOOL

1¼" DIA. 2"

9½"   1½"

LEG

11"

4½" RAD.   TOP

4½" RAD.

11"

LEG

11"

12"

12"

LEG

4½" RAD.

BACK

24"

4½" RAD.

SEAT

10"

BRACE   2"

9¼"

CHAIR

6"

CORNER SHELF

LETTER HOLDER

FRONT

4¾"

6¼"   BACK

BOTTOM

2"   12"

¾" PLYWOOD

48"

SHELF   SHELF

BACK   BACK

48"

11⅝" RAD.

SHELF   SHELF

12"   12"   12⅜"   11⅝"

Start by cutting the 4 × 4-ft. piece of plywood into two 2 × 4-ft. pieces. Lay out the various pieces as per the cutting diagram and cut each 2 × 4-ft. piece into two 1 × 4-ft. strips. Cut out the various pieces.

For the handholes, drill two 1¼-in. holes that overlap ¼ in. You can leave the holes "as is," with just a bit of sanding, or you can file between the holes to make a straight opening with half-round ends.

Assemble all four projects with glue and finishing nails. Sand all the projects to remove any rough edges or corners, then stain or paint to suit. The corner shelf is held in place by screws driven into the wall studs through the back.

Colonial Shelf

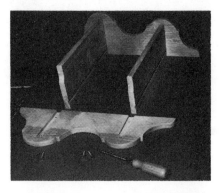

Shelf consists of four pieces, two dadoed sides, two shelves with plate groove. Shelves are notched for stopped dado.

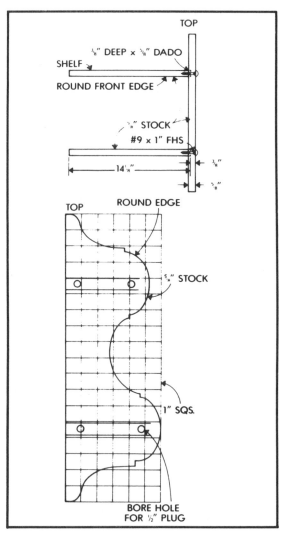

Cricket Stool

This simple stool is made of common ¾-in. lumber assembled with butt joints, glue and screws. Any straight-grained wood will work. We suggest it be relatively knot free, as stools, at times, are expected to support quite a bit of weight.

The design is flexible. You can follow it exactly (enlarge the squared drawings for the design), or it an be simplified by making square cuts and/or making the legs vertical. Dimensions can be altered to meet a specific need. Or you can make it more complicated by using mortise-and-tenon or dowel joints for assembly.

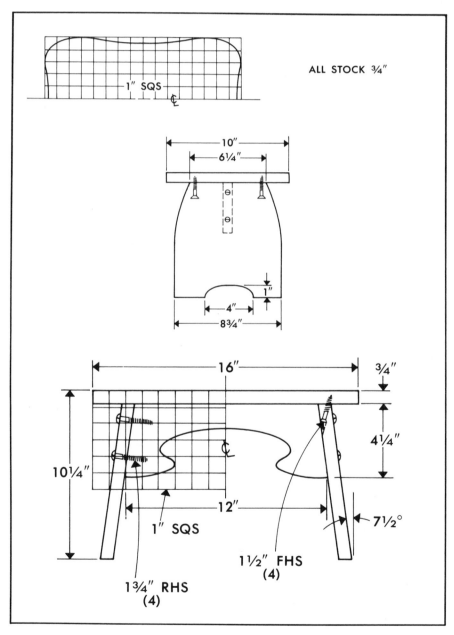

ALL STOCK ¾"

1" SQS

10"
6¼"

1"
4"
8¾"

16"
¾"
4¼"
10¼"
12"
7½°
1" SQS
1½" FHS
(4)
1¾" RHS
(4)

Conductor's Stool

This stool can be cut completely from a 6-ft. length of 1 × 10 shelving. Cut the top to size, then the two ends and sides. Bevel the vertical edges 42½ degrees; tops and bottoms 17 degrees. Assemble with glue and finishing nails.

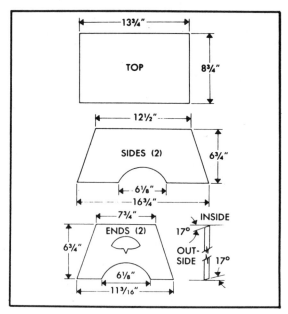

Kiddie Step Stool

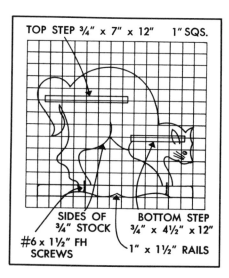

If there is one thing a youngster likes, it's being able to reach things around the house without the help of anyone else. This "kitty cat" step stool will give any child the extra height he needs.

The sides of the original were made of 1-in. stock glued up to a rough size of 12 in. square, but ¾-in. plywood can be used as an alternative. Tack two pieces together with nails through the waste portions and cut out the shape of the cat. Before separating the pieces, mark the positions of the steps by boring a small hole through the sides. Separate them and sand smooth, slightly rounding all corners and edges.

Cut and sand the steps and attach them to the sides with no. 8 × 1½-in. flathead wood screws in counterbored holes. After cutting the bottom rails, attach them as shown.

Stand-up Desk

For many situations, a stand-up desk is more convenient than a sit-down type that can cause fatigue and lower back pains. Also, alternating between sitting and standing often will alleviate problems produced by constantly sitting. The higher desk is especially handy in a workshop where you can check a drawing or instructions quickly when building a project, simply by walking to the desk, rather than sitting or leaning over as with a standard-height desk.

The desk is cut from stock 1-in. (¾ in. net) lumber, and requires just four 10-ft. lengths of 1 × 12. I rough cut all the pieces as indicated on the cutting diagram, then finish cut them afterward. Legs were made by gluing up three strips. I cut the mortises after the glue set, but an alternative method would be to glue shorter pieces between the outer pieces to create the mortises as detailed. Stretchers that join the legs can be glued up from two short and one long piece to create tenons.

When the glue has set, glue and clamp the legs and stretchers to-

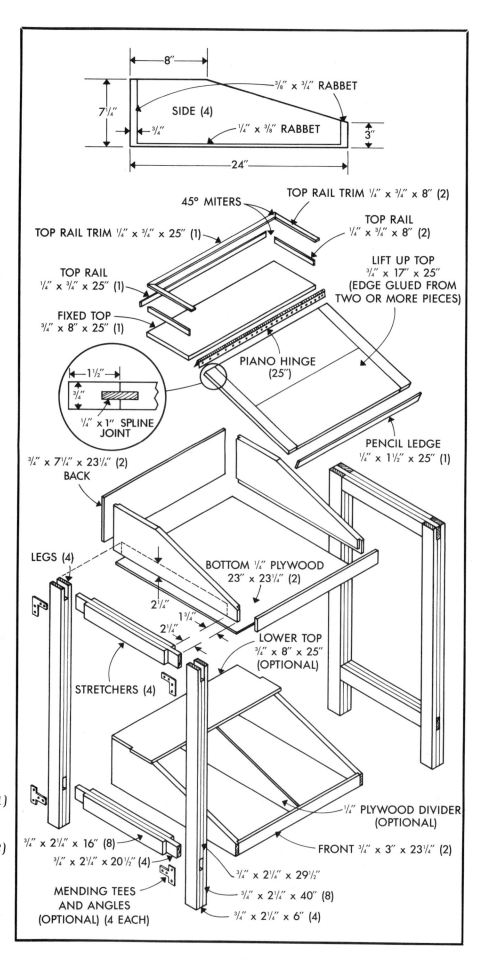

MATERIALS LIST

(All 1 in. stock except as noted)

Legs:
 2¼" × 6" (4)
 2¼" × 29" (4)
 2¼" × 40" (8)

Stretchers:
 2¼" × 20½" (4)
 2¼" × 16" (8)

Desks:
 Side, 7¼" × 24" (4) (2 pairs)
 Front, 3" × 23¼" (2)
 Back, 7¼" × 23¼" (2)
 Fixed top, 8" × 25" (2) (lower top optional)
 Lift-up top,
  17" × 22" (1) (edge glued from 2 or more pieces)
  1½" × 17" (2)
 Pencil rail, ¼" × 1½" × 25" (1)
 Top rail, ¼" × ¾" × 8" (2)
 Top rail, ¼" × ¾" × 25" (1)
 Top rail trim, ¼" × ¾" × 8" (2)
 Top rail trim, ¼" × ¾" × 25" (1)
Optional hardware, mending angles and tees (4 each)

SIDE (4)
8"
7¼"
¾"
⅜" × ¾" RABBET
¼" × ⅜" RABBET
24"
3"

TOP RAIL TRIM ¼" × ¾" × 8" (2)
45° MITERS
TOP RAIL TRIM ¼" × ¾" × 25" (1)
TOP RAIL ¼" × ¾" × 8" (2)
TOP RAIL ¼" × ¾" × 25" (1)
LIFT UP TOP ¾" × 17" × 25" (EDGE GLUED FROM TWO OR MORE PIECES)
FIXED TOP ¾" × 8" × 25" (1)
1½"
¾"
¼" × 1" SPLINE JOINT
PIANO HINGE (25")
PENCIL LEDGE ¼" × 1½" × 25" (1)
¾" × 7¼" × 23¼" (2) BACK
BOTTOM ¼" PLYWOOD 23" × 23¼" (2)
LEGS (4)
2¼"
1¾"
2¼"
LOWER TOP ¾" × 8" × 25" (OPTIONAL)
STRETCHERS (4)
¼" PLYWOOD DIVIDER (OPTIONAL)
¾" × 2¼" × 16" (8)
¾" × 2¼" × 20½" (4)
FRONT ¾" × 3" × 23¼" (2)
MENDING TEES AND ANGLES (OPTIONAL) (4 EACH)
¾" × 2¼" × 29½"
¾" × 2¼" × 40" (8)
¾" × 2¼" × 6" (4)

80

gether, making the two assemblies as close to identical as possible. While the glue is setting, cut out the four desk sides and rabbet them according to the drawing. Be sure to make two pairs, with the rabbets facing inward. Cut the fronts and backs and glue and clamp the two assemblies together. If you have cut the two ¼-in. plywood bottoms accurately, they can be bradded and glued into the bottom rabbets to help keep the two desk assemblies square.

The two desk assemblies are joined to the legs with glue and flathead screws driven through from the inside of the desk sides. Make sure that both desks are at right angles to the leg assemblies. Next, glue and screw or attach with finishing nails the fixed top on the upper desk. The top for the lower desk is optional, as is the plywood divider.

Legs and stretchers are joined by through mortise and tenons. This makes neat, strong construction, and is not difficult.

It may be necessary to clamp diagonally to get leg/stretcher assembly absolutely square. Both assemblies should be identical.

The lift-up lid for the top desk requires edge gluing two or more pieces. I added the 1½-in. strips to each end with a spline joint to prevent the top from warping. The lift top is attached to the fixed top with a 25-in. length of piano hinge. Some craftsmen might want to also hinge a lid to the lower desk, if the unit will be in a workshop where sawdust would quickly fill up the uncovered lower desk.

The pencil rail on the lift-up top is necessary for obvious reasons. The rail around the fixed top could be left off, but I find it keeps items from rolling or sliding off when I stack them up there. Stain and finish, or paint, the desk to suit. The mending angles and tees are optional. I bought them at a local hardware store, then worked over their surfaces with a ball-peen hammer to create a "wrought-iron" look. I painted the distressed metal flat black and it does have an early American look.

Piano hinge is used to join lift-up lid to fixed lid at the top. Note optional fixed lid on bottom unit that provides storage shelf.

Lap Desk

It's fun to sit in the warm sunshine of a spring day to write personal letters or work on the monthly budget, but not if you try to use a flexible magazine or book as a writing surface, one that usually slides off your lap.

This lightweight lap desk is the answer to the problem. It holds a generous supply of stationery and pens and pencils, has a large writing surface, yet is ready to carry and store.

Except for the trim cut from solid stock, all parts of the desk are made from ¼-in. plywood with two good sides. Use glue and brads to join the various components (drawing on next page).

Construction is quite basic, with the front, back and sides joined with butt joints. The bottom is simply glued and bradded to the frame of sides, front and back. The top consists of a narrow fixed section, with a larger top hinged to it. We used fancy strap hinges, but other types could be used. Narrow strips of solid stock are used to trim the top, and the strip at the front of the hinged top also provides a finger grip for lifting the top.

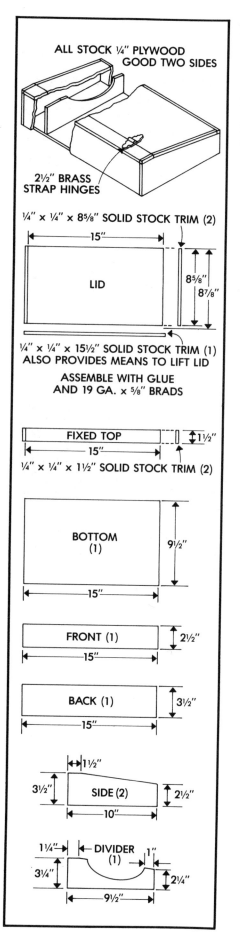

ALL STOCK ¼" PLYWOOD GOOD TWO SIDES

2½" BRASS STRAP HINGES

¼" × ¼" × 8⅝" SOLID STOCK TRIM (2)

|←——— 15" ———→|

LID

8⅝"
8⅞"

¼" × ¼" × 15½" SOLID STOCK TRIM (1)
ALSO PROVIDES MEANS TO LIFT LID

ASSEMBLE WITH GLUE
AND 19 GA. × ⅝" BRADS

FIXED TOP

1½"

|←——— 15" ———→|

¼" × ¼" × 1½" SOLID STOCK TRIM (2)

BOTTOM
(1)

9½"

|←——— 15" ———→|

FRONT (1)

2½"

|←——— 15" ———→|

BACK (1)

3½"

|←——— 15" ———→|

1½"

3½"   SIDE (2)   2½"

|←——— 10" ———→|

1¼"   ←DIVIDER   1"
(1)

3¼"   2¼"

|←——— 9½" ———→|

The partition is an option, but it does keep pens, pencils and the like from rolling around over the paper, envelopes and other materials.

Stain and finish the desk to suit. A mechanical or magnetic latch could be used to keep the lid shut, and a suitcase handle on the narrow front would then be handy for carrying the desk. If the desk is to be used indoors on occasion, it would be a good idea to attach four rubber feet to the corners of the bottom to protect any finished surface on which the desk is placed.

Contemporary Parsons Table

This versatile Parsons table features rounded legs to give it a contemporary character. Its smooth lines and plastic laminate covering make it appropriate for many decors. The table shown measures 18¼ × 40 × 40 in., but the size can be varied by changing the length of the apron pieces and the size of the top.

Cut out the pieces for the legs and the apron as shown in the drawing (next page). The leg pieces each have a notch ¾ × 4¼ in. in one corner to receive the apron pieces. The apron pieces are notched at each end to fit between the leg segments.

The legs and apron are made from ¾-in.-thick stock and the top is cut from ¾-in. plywood. The joints are assembled with glue and finishing nails. Cut the head off a finishing nail and chuck it in a drill to bore pilot holes for the nails. This will help prevent the wood from splitting.

Lay out the leg segments. The segments, and the smaller apron segments, each have a 2¾-in. radius cut on one corner. Use a compass or a template to mark the radius and cut the segments with a hand-held jig saw or a band saw. Sand off any rough edges.

Fasten the apron segments to four of the leg segments and assemble each leg. When the glue is dry, insert the apron pieces and test the fit. When you assemble the legs to the apron pieces, make sure that the assembly is square and the legs are perpendicular to the apron.

Cut the four ⅛-in. hardboard covers for the outside surfaces of the legs and the two hardboard pieces to cover the apron. It's a good idea to cut them a little oversize since it is hard to calculate exactly the distance around the corners.

Let all of the hardboard pieces set overnight between layers of wet newspaper. The next day they will be flexible enough to bend around the corners of the table. Use brads and water-based white glue to fasten them to the table frame. You might want to use strips of inner tube to hold them in place while the glue is drying. A day or two should pass for the glue to harden completely.

Trim off any hardboard that projects beyond the edges of the frame. Then cut out the top to fit flush with the outside edge of the hardboard. A little sanding here will ensure a smooth surface for the plastic laminate where the plywood top meets the hardboard. Use 1/30-in. laminate so it will bend easily around corners.

Cover one inside surface of each leg with plastic laminate. Again, it is a good idea to cut the covering a little oversize and trim the excess later. Cover the other inside surface of each leg and trim the edges.

Next, cut the plastic laminate for the outside surface of each leg. This time, test the fit and precut the plastic to fit exactly around each leg. This way, the joint on the apron will line up with the edge of the leg and result in a professional-looking job. Start with one leg and work your way around the table, cutting the pieces for the legs and the apron as you go. These pieces can be a bit long in the vertical dimension and be trimmed later on the top and bottom edges.

When attaching the plastic to the outside of the legs, you might want to use the inner tube strips or a strap clamp again while the contact cement is hardening. As always, when using contact cement, work in a well-ventilated area and follow all warnings on the label. Glue on the top, trim the edges and enjoy your table.

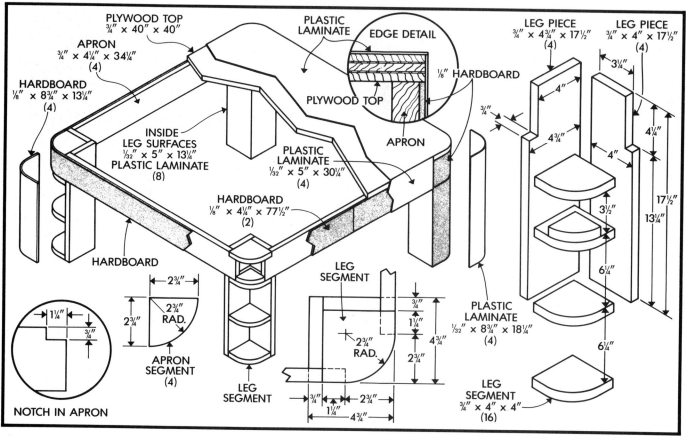

Poker Table

When the fellows in our neighborhood formed a poker club, I got the job of designing and building a table. The finished project is easily made and with the addition of a round or square auxiliary top, also can be used for dining or hobbies.

The sturdy folding legs require no fancy hardware and total cost of the table was under $50. The table readily disassembles if the felt on the top needs to be replaced.

Make the top from a 4 × 4-ft. piece of ½-in. plywood with one good side, cutting off the corners to make an octagon. Each of the eight sides will be 19⅞ in. Note that the tray fronts are just 19½ in., because the top fits in dadoes in the fronts (drawing on next page).

Cover the top with felt or vinyl, adhering it with white or yellow (carpenter's) glue. I sprayed the felt with "Scotch Guard" to protect it from staining.

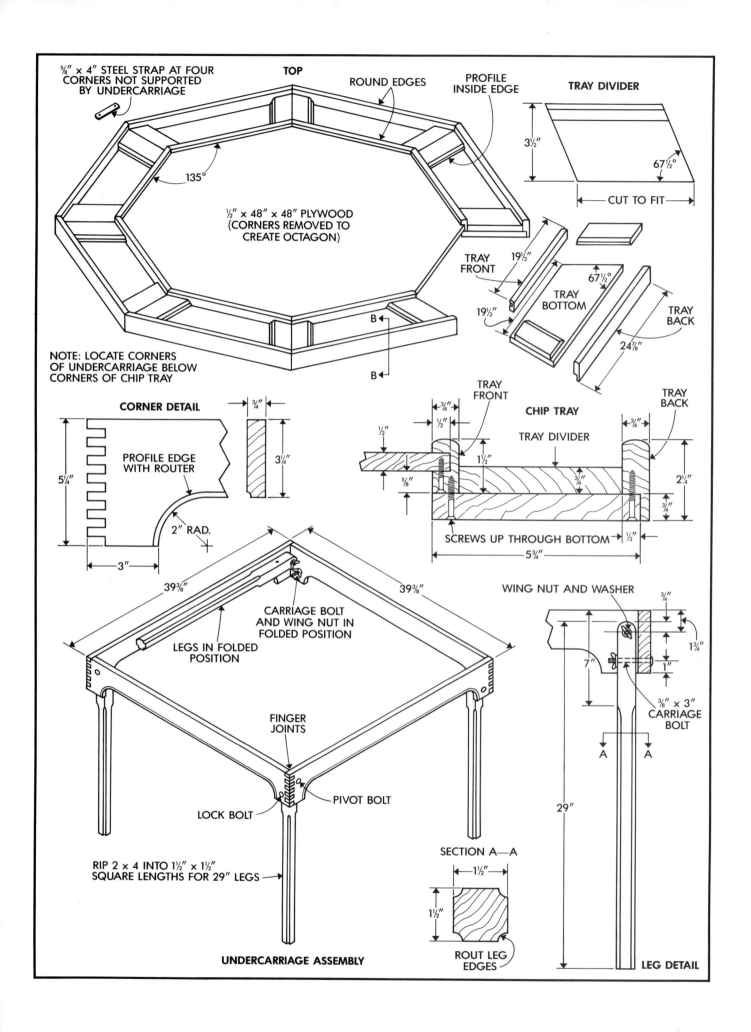

⅝" × 4" STEEL STRAP AT FOUR CORNERS NOT SUPPORTED BY UNDERCARRIAGE

TOP

ROUND EDGES

PROFILE INSIDE EDGE

135°

½" × 48" × 48" PLYWOOD (CORNERS REMOVED TO CREATE OCTAGON)

B

B

NOTE: LOCATE CORNERS OF UNDERCARRIAGE BELOW CORNERS OF CHIP TRAY

TRAY DIVIDER

3½"

67½°

CUT TO FIT

TRAY FRONT

19½"

19½"

TRAY BOTTOM

67½°

TRAY BACK

24⅞"

CORNER DETAIL

¾"

PROFILE EDGE WITH ROUTER

3¼"

5¼"

2" RAD.

3"

CHIP TRAY

TRAY FRONT

TRAY DIVIDER

TRAY BACK

½"

¾"

½"

1½"

¾"

⅝"

¾"

2¼"

SCREWS UP THROUGH BOTTOM

½"

¾"

5¾"

39⅜"

39⅜"

CARRIAGE BOLT AND WING NUT IN FOLDED POSITION

LEGS IN FOLDED POSITION

FINGER JOINTS

PIVOT BOLT

LOCK BOLT

RIP 2 × 4 INTO 1½" × 1½" SQUARE LENGTHS FOR 29" LEGS

UNDERCARRIAGE ASSEMBLY

SECTION A—A

1½"

1½"

ROUT LEG EDGES

WING NUT AND WASHER

¾"

1¾"

7"

1"

⅜" × 3" CARRIAGE BOLT

A   A

29"

LEG DETAIL

Make the chip trays next. Cut the dadoes in the tray fronts to provide a snug fit for the top with the felt or vinyl attached. The tray fronts are screwed to table top from below, using no. 9 × 1-in. wood screws. Do not use glue for this assembly, as the trays then can readily be removed in the event that the felt must be replaced because of soiling or wearing.

Cross section of tray shows how top, with felt, is inserted in dado in tray front. Back of tray is rabbeted for bottom.

Tray dividers shaped somewhat like arrowheads cover miter joints in trays, so any slight misalignment is not seen.

I found it best to cut the various tray parts a bit long, then to fit each one to the table top. If the miters are not exact, don't fret about it, as the 67½-degree miters are covered by the arrowhead shape dividers.

Before installing the tray backs, fit the dividers at each of the eight corners. Cut them to fit snugly. Openings to hold glasses can be cut in each of the dividers, and lined with felt for a neat appearance. My experience, however, has been that the glasses or cups end up on the table surface, and elbows of the card players end up resting on the dividers.

In any event, don't attach the tray dividers to the tray bottom at this point in construction.

The table "undercarriage" is assembled by cutting finger joints at the ends of the aprons. If you can't make finger joints, then use rabbet or butt joints. It is possible to reinforce the corners with thin glue blocks, but they must be positioned above where the folded legs will be when the table is in the stored configuration.

Finger joints in apron of undercarriage make neat, strong connections. Leg corners are chamfered or profiled with router.

Position the table top on the undercarriage so that the corners of the undercarriage fall under four of the tray miters. Attach the top by driving no. 9 × 1½-in. screws down through the tray bottoms into the undercarriage. Locate the screws so they will be hidden by the tray dividers when they are installed.

Install the tray dividers, then attach the tray backs. Steel support straps can be used on tray miters not supported by the undercarriage. (See Editor's note.)

The last step is to add the legs. The design allows the legs to be easily folded without the need for expensive hinge hardware. The legs are shaped from 2 × 4 stock ripped to 1½ × 1½ in. Cut the 2 × 4 stock into 29-in. lengths, then rip it to size. A router can be used to shape the four corners of each leg, or they can simply be chamfered with rasp, file and sandpaper.

Each leg is clamped in position and two holes are drilled through each leg and through the undercarriage. One hole is drilled near the

Legs are attached by two bolts and wing nuts. Upper bolt is pivot, lower bolt locks leg in down position. Note round leg top.

upper end of each leg, the other about 3 in. below the first. The top hole serves as a pivot, while the lower hole provides a means of locking the legs in the vertical position by a carriage bolt and wing nut.

When the table is to be stored, remove the lower wing nut and carriage bolt and swing up the leg. Replace the lower bolt and wing nut for storage.

The poker table can double as a game table or dining table by making an auxiliary top of ⅝- or ¾-in. plywood, particleboard or wafer board. Make the top a bit bigger in diameter than the maximum diameter of the poker table. This ensures there will be no projecting corners to cause problems.

Keep the auxiliary top in position by gluing and nailing four cleats on the underside, positioned to fit inside every other tray.

Because of the required size of the top, it will be necessary to join two pieces of plywood or other material together with screws and cleats.

Editor's note: Instead of using steel straps to reinforce the tray assembly, you may glue and screw the tray dividers in place. This greatly strengthens the miter joint, but still allows easy disassembly of the tray assembly.

Because each tray assembly is made separately, you will have a problem with the miter joints on the table backs.

Assembly of the table can be simplified by completing each tray section with glue and nails or screws, then fitting the sections to the edges of the top. A couple of screws at each end of each tray section that fits over the undercarriage corners are used to make the final assembly of the top and undercarriage. When disassembling the table you remove each two tray sections as a unit, as the dividers are glued and screwed to two sections.

Our final test, as shown in the photo, was to test the playing quality of the table. It passed all tests.

TV Tray

We've had many requests for plans for a TV tray made of wood, so we designed the one shown here. The frame is made of ¾-in. hardwood stock and the tray is ¼-in. hardwood plywood (we used birch). The top also could be made using hardboard or cheaper plywood covered with plastic laminate.

Begin by cutting the legs, braces and the frame for the tray. Cut the leg braces slightly long. We made patterns out of heavy cardboard for the legs, suitably labeled, so the holes for the blind pivot hinges (Roto-Hinges) would be drilled on the correct sides of the legs. You can drill the holes and check the leg assembly for fit, but do not do the final

Tray is assembled first, legs fitted before final assembly. Roto-Hinges were glued to outer legs, then to center section and support rail.

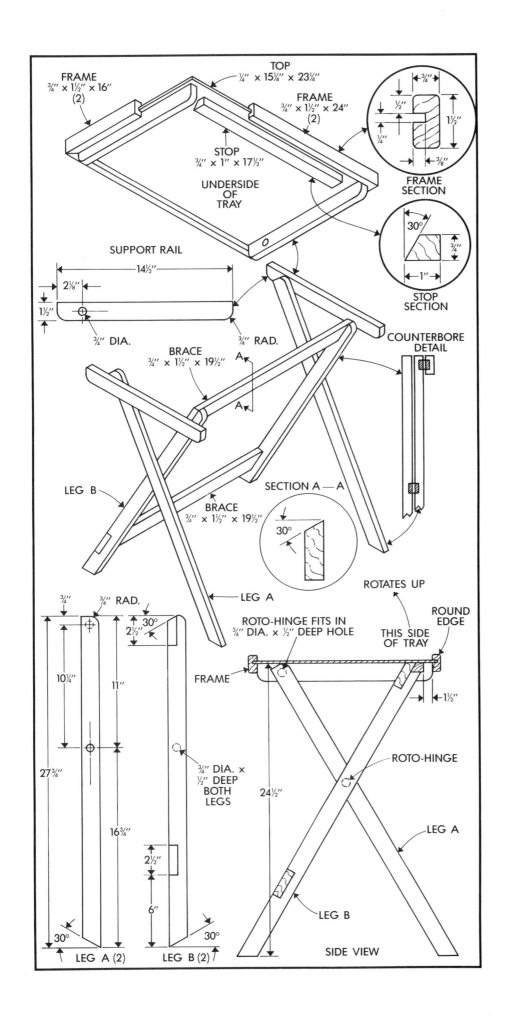

FRAME
¾" × 1½" × 16"
(2)

TOP
¼" × 15¼" × 23¼"

FRAME
¾" × 1½" × 24"
(2)

STOP
¾" × 1" × 17½"

UNDERSIDE
OF
TRAY

¾"
½"
¼"
1½"
⅜"

FRAME
SECTION

30°
¾"
1"

STOP
SECTION

SUPPORT RAIL

14½"
2⅛"
1½"
¾" DIA.
¾" RAD.

COUNTERBORE
DETAIL

BRACE
¾" × 1½" × 19½"

A
A

LEG B

BRACE
¾" × 1½" × 19½"

SECTION A — A

30°

LEG A

ROTATES UP

ROTO-HINGE FITS IN
¾" DIA. × ½" DEEP HOLE

THIS SIDE
OF TRAY

ROUND
EDGE

FRAME

1½"

ROTO-HINGE

LEG A

¾"
¾" RAD.
30°
2½"

10¼"
11"

27¾"

¾" DIA. ×
½" DEEP
BOTH
LEGS

16¾"

2½"

6"

30°
30°

LEG A (2)
LEG B (2)

24½"

LEG B

SIDE VIEW

93

assembly of the center leg section at this time. Remember, when drilling for the hinges, the holes will be on opposite faces of the legs. If you make a mistake (we have), you can fill the hole with a dowel or wood plug, and then redrill from the opposite side, but the flaw will always show, of course.

You may note that the bottom leg brace is located higher in the drawing than is shown in the photo. This was a design error which we discovered when we tried to use the tray. This brace was located too low and got in the way of our feet and we have repositioned it since taking the photo.

Make the tray next. We made a frame from ¾ × 1½-in. stock, dadoed as shown and with mitered corners. You may prefer to use molding or leave the top flat. The top was cut slightly undersize and was not glued in the frame, so it could expand and contract with differing humidity and conditions. The leg stop was glued and screwed into position; blind holes were drilled in the support rails and they, too, were glued and screwed into place.

At this point, we recommend making a dry assembly of the leg sections, with the Roto-Hinges in place. This will permit making an accurate length adjustment of the braces for the center leg section. Any slight variation in the size of the top may otherwise cause the legs to bind or be too loose. Now cut the leg braces to the correct length and assemble the center leg section by gluing and screwing the braces to the legs. We counterbored the screws and plugged the holes with short pieces of dowel.

Do the final sanding and finishing at this time. We used Minwax Early American stain and polyurethane varnish. Final assembly consists of gluing the Roto-Hinges in the blind holes, first coating the inside of the hole with white glue, then inserting the hinge, wiping away any excess glue with a damp cloth. Clamping is not required other than to be sure the hinge is fully seated. We first glued the hinges in the legs, then into the support rails and center leg section as shown in one photo.

High and Low Bookcases

These two sturdy bookcases are built from stock 1-in. lumber (¾ in. net) that can be cut to length with a handsaw. The small case does require notches to be cut in the upper ends of the sides and the ends of the top, to provide a half-lap joint.

For the tall bookcase (drawing below) you'll need four 5-ft. 1 × 12s for the sides and back, two 24½-in. 1 × 12s for the top, one 24½-in. 1 × 2 for the back edge of the top, six 23-in. 1 × 10s for the shelves, and ten 8½-in. ¾ × ¾-in. cleats.

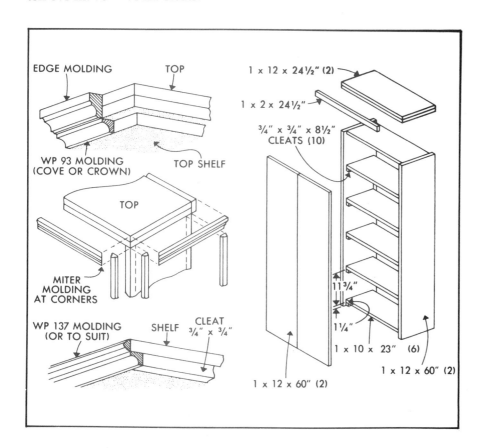

You also will need six 5-ft. lengths of WP137 molding for corner trim, five 22½-in. lengths of WP137 molding for shelf facing, six 22½-in. lengths of WP93 molding for trim under the shelves, one 28-in. length of edge molding for the top front trim and two 14-in. pieces of edge molding for trimming the sides of the top.

Glue and nail the cleats to the inner surfaces of the sides, spaced as indicated, and 1¼ in. from the back edges of the sides. Glue and nail together the top pieces, then glue and nail the top assembly to the sides. Square up the assembly with a 2-ft. square, then insert and glue and nail the shelves to the cleats. Toenail the nails, driving them at an angle so they center both the cleats and the sides. Glue and nail in the two back pieces.

The smaller bookshelf (drawing below) is assembled in a similar manner, after you notch the top and sides. For the smaller unit you need two 32-in. 1 × 12s for the sides, one 28½-in. length of 1 × 2 for the bottom brace, two 28½-in. lengths of 1 × 12 for the shelves, one 30-in. 1 × 12 for the top and two 10¼-in. ¾ × ¾-in. cleats.

Both cases are assembled with white glue and 4- to 6-penny finishing nails. If you have bar clamps, use them to hold the assembly square until the glue sets.

Use a nailset to countersink all nail heads, fill the depressions with wood putty and sand smooth when dry.

Molding of different profile than that specified can be used, of course.

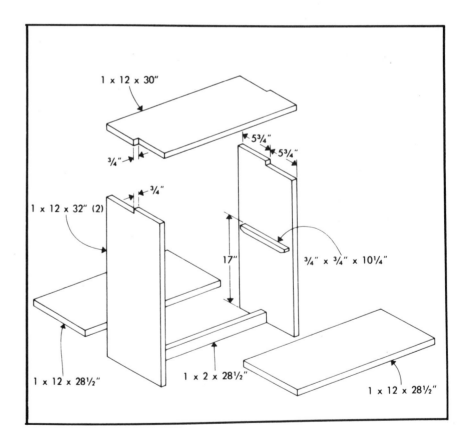

Floor Mirror

Despite its antique look, this floor mirror is assembled from stock lumber and molding. The molding used on the mirror shown is a purchased spiral turning that was ripped in half lengthwise. Another type molding could be used, and it would make your mirror more individualized.

Start construction by enlarging the squared drawings for the legs and pediment (on next two pages). Make the patterns and cut out the two legs from 2 × 12 stock. The pediment also can be cut from 2-in. lumber, or you might prefer somewhat thinner stock.

Join the two legs with the crosspiece cut from 2 × 12 stock, using glue and two no. 10 × 3-in. flathead wood screws in each end. Assemble the 2 × 4 mirror frame as shown, using two no. 10 × 3-in. flathead wood screws at each corner. You might also want to drive a corrugated fastener across the back of each miter joint. Be sure the frame is square and flat, with no twist. Clamping the assembly to a flat surface while the glue sets would be one way to ensure it would not twist.

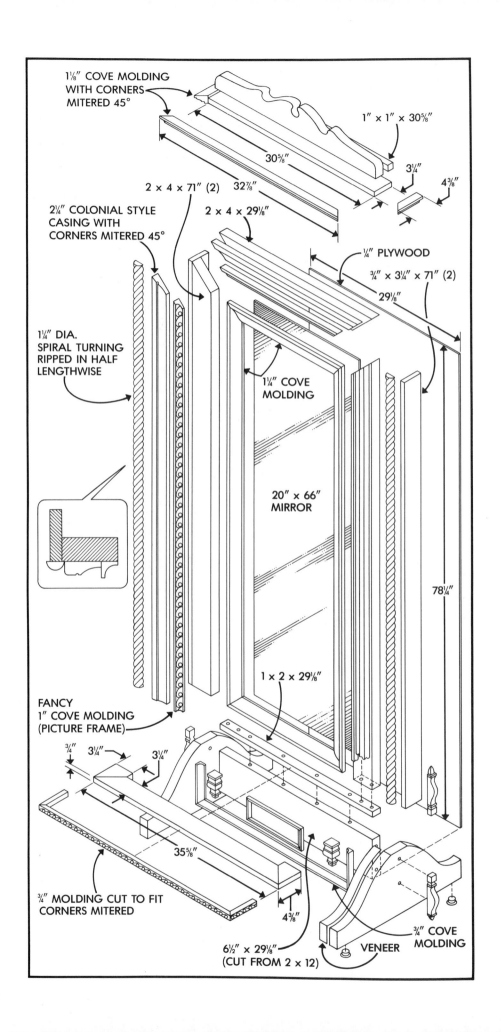

1⅛" COVE MOLDING WITH CORNERS MITERED 45°

1" × 1" × 30⅝"

30⅝"

3¼"

4⅜"

2 × 4 × 71" (2)   32⅞"

2 × 4 × 29⅛"

2¼" COLONIAL STYLE CASING WITH CORNERS MITERED 45°

¼" PLYWOOD

¾" × 3¼" × 71" (2)

29⅛"

1¼" DIA. SPIRAL TURNING RIPPED IN HALF LENGTHWISE

1¼" COVE MOLDING

20" × 66" MIRROR

78¼"

FANCY 1" COVE MOLDING (PICTURE FRAME)

1 × 2 × 29⅛"

¾"   3¼"   3¼"

35⅝"

¾" MOLDING CUT TO FIT CORNERS MITERED

4⅜"

¾" COVE MOLDING

6½" × 29⅛" (CUT FROM 2 × 12)

VENEER

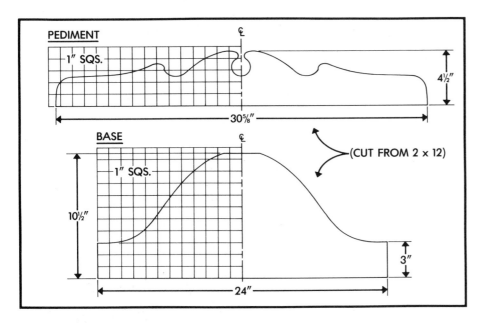

PEDIMENT
1" SQS.
4½"
30⅝"

BASE
1" SQS.
(CUT FROM 2 x 12)
10½"
3"
24"

The 1-in. crosspiece at the bottom of the mirror frame is attached with glue and two no. 8 × 2-in. screws driven into the lower end of each 2 × 4 leg of the frame. Cut the three pieces of cove molding for the C-shape frame that fits at the bottom of the mirror frame, join them with glue and 4-penny finishing nails and attach to the frame with the same size nails and glue.

Cut the two side and top strips 3¼ in. wide and attach them to the frame with glue and 4-penny finishing nails. Set all nails when the assembly is complete and cover the heads with wood putty.

The cornice that sits on top of the frame is assembled from three pieces of 1⅛-in. cove or other type molding. Corners are mitered as indicated and the assembly is joined with 4-penny finishing nails and attached to the frame top with glue and the same size nails.

We ripped a spiral turning lengthwise and applied it to the outside edges of the face of the mirror frame, again using glue and 4-penny finishing nails. You might want another type of turning for this application.

Inside the ripped turning, we glued and nailed 2¼-in. colonial-style door and window casing. This three-sided assembly has mitered corners.

Molding on the inner edges of the frame is cut from 1-in. picture frame molding, and the molding around the front edges of the base is ¾ in. These moldings can vary from those shown, as previously stated, so your mirror has an individual styling.

Attach the pediment to the top of the frame using glue and flathead screws driven up through the frame into the pediment, reinforcing the attachment with a 1 × 1-in. cleat.

We further decorated the front of the mirror base by cutting in half a decorative spindle top and gluing and nailing the halves to fit up under the bottom shelf. A decorative plain or fancy wood or pressed wood plaque is glued and bradded to the center of the bottom crosspiece. For an added touch, we applied walnut veneer to the edges of the feet.

Measure the mirror opening and have a glass shop cut a mirror ⅛ in. shorter in each dimension than the opening. Fit the mirror in the opening and hold it by nailing the plywood back to the frame. To hold it while attaching the plywood, use wooden cleats to hold the mirror snugly to the 1¼-in. cove molding. Alternately, place the frame face down, fit the mirror, then attach the back.

If the mirror is to be placed on a finished floor, attach a floor glide to each end of each leg before installing the mirror.

Finish is up to the builder. We applied a dark walnut stain and two coats of low-gloss varnish, steel-wooling between each coat. Over this we applied paste wax, buffing it, but leaving some in depressions and crevices to create an "antique" appearance.

The original of this floor mirror is used in a room with high ceilings, so its height is no problem. In a room with normal 8-ft. ceilings, you might want to shorten the frame and mirror 6 in. or so to prevent the mirror from looking too high. Alternately, keep the mirror the same size and shorten the two legs.

Doll Display Case

This octagonal doll display case began as a simple project, but evolved into a rather complex piece of cabinetmaking.

The case need not have shelves, depending on the size of the dolls to be displayed, but the shelves were requested and the lazy-Susan bearing permits rotating the shelves to remove or replace dolls.

There are three basic subassemblies: the legs, the center section and the top. The legs are mortised to fit tenons on the crosspieces that are half lapped. Tenons are created on the ends of the braces by cutting recesses $5/16$ in. deep, dimensioned as detailed. Because the legs are splayed at an angle, the recesses must be angled also. The recesses were marked on the braces, then a router was hand held and a straight bottom bit was used to remove the waste.

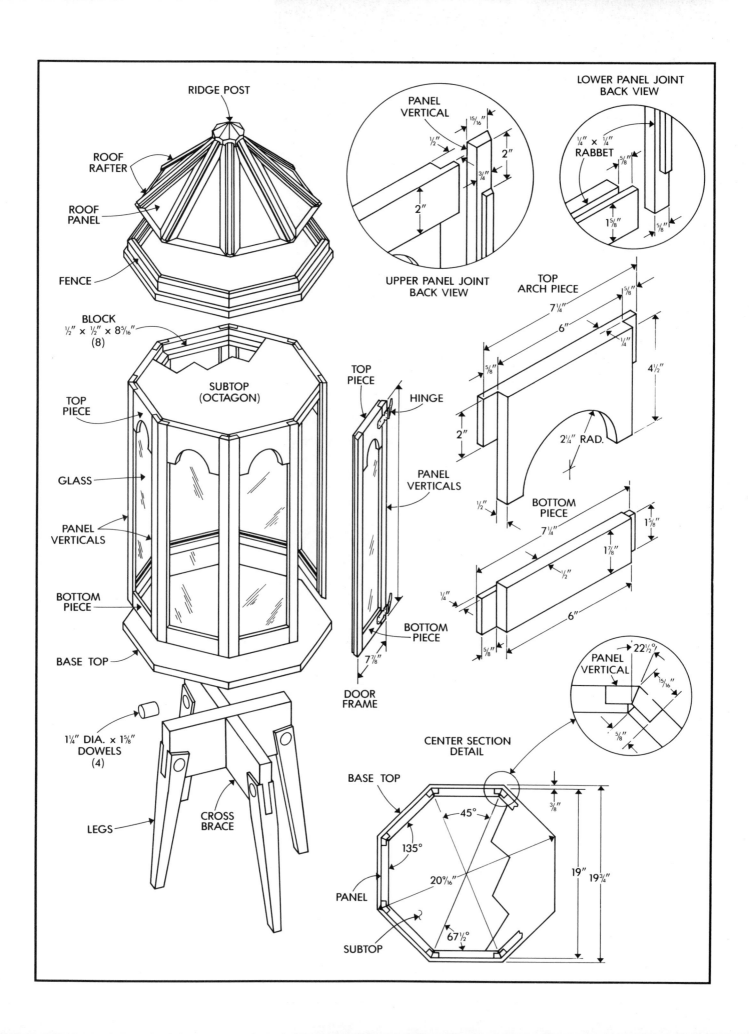

RIDGE POST

ROOF RAFTER

ROOF PANEL

FENCE

BLOCK
½″ × ½″ × 8⁵⁄₁₆″
(8)

TOP PIECE

GLASS

PANEL VERTICALS

BOTTOM PIECE

BASE TOP

1¼″ DIA. × 1⁵⁄₈″
DOWELS
(4)

LEGS

CROSS BRACE

SUBTOP
(OCTAGON)

PANEL VERTICAL

½″

¹⁵⁄₁₆″

2″

¾″

2″

UPPER PANEL JOINT
BACK VIEW

LOWER PANEL JOINT
BACK VIEW

¼″ × ¼″
RABBET

⁵⁄₈″

1⁵⁄₈″

⁵⁄₈″

TOP PIECE

HINGE

PANEL VERTICALS

BOTTOM PIECE

DOOR FRAME

7⁷⁄₈″

TOP ARCH PIECE

7¼″

6″

⁵⁄₈″

¼″

4½″

⁵⁄₈″

2″

2¼″ RAD.

BOTTOM PIECE

½″

7¼″

1⁵⁄₈″

1⁷⁄₈″

½″

¼″

6″

⁵⁄₈″

PANEL VERTICAL

22½°

⁵⁄₁₆″

⁵⁄₈″

CENTER SECTION
DETAIL

BASE TOP

45°

135°

20⁹⁄₁₆″

PANEL

SUBTOP

67½°

³⁄₈″

19″

19¾″

Ends of cross braces are reduced to create tenons that are angled to accept ends of legs. Can be doweled or screwed.

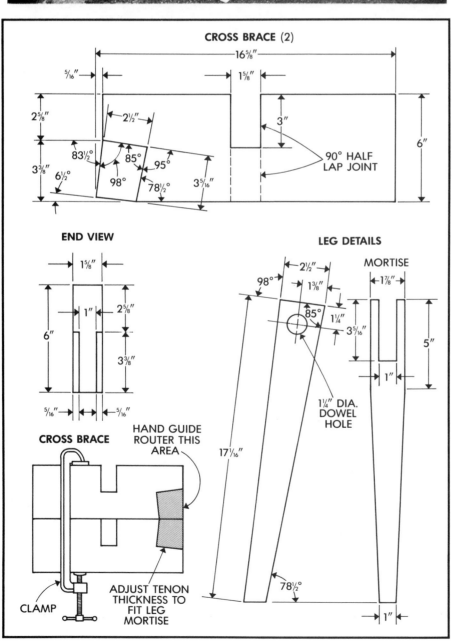

CROSS BRACE (2)

16⁵/₈″

5/16″ 1⁵/₈″

2⁵/₈″ 2½″

83½° 85° 95° 3″

6⁵/₈° 78½° 3⁵/₁₆″

98°

90° HALF LAP JOINT

6″

END VIEW

1⁵/₈″

1″ 2⁵/₈″

6″ 3³/₈″

5/16″ 5/16″

LEG DETAILS

MORTISE

98° 2½″ 1³/₈″ 1⁷/₈″

85° 1¼″

3⁵/₁₆″

5″

1″

1¼″ DIA. DOWEL HOLE

17¹/₁₆″

CROSS BRACE

HAND GUIDE ROUTER THIS AREA

78½°

CLAMP

ADJUST TENON THICKNESS TO FIT LEG MORTISE

1″

Note that both edges of the legs are tapered, then the bottom end is angled at 78½ degrees. This latter angle, like other angles and dimensions, will require some cutting and fitting for your particular project; it is not likely that any two assemblies will be the same.

The top that fits on the legs, which also is the bottom of the center section, is octagonsized as shown. Make an identical octagon to be the main top of the center section.

Eight side frames now are constructed. Cut the vertical stiles with a 22½-degree angle on one edge as detailed. Rabbet the inner edge of each stile to accept the glass, and also rabbet across the upper and lower rails; 2 in. at the top, 1⅝ in. at the bottom.

Outer edges of the panel stiles (verticals) are angled 22-1/2 degrees, half lapped into ends of top and bottom rails.

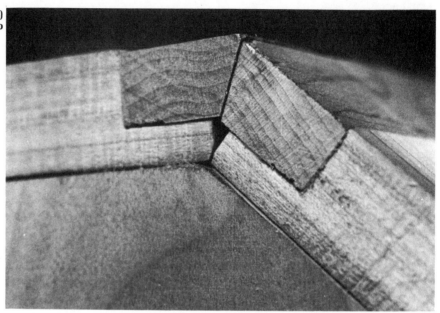

Bottom rails are rectangular pieces rabbeted on the inside upper edge, and across each end. The upper rails are arch shaped and are rabbeted as indicated at each end and on the inside up past the arch. The glass then will fit in the rabbets in the rails and stiles.

Blocks screwed inside frames near top provide cleats to support the octagon shape subtop that fits inside the panels.

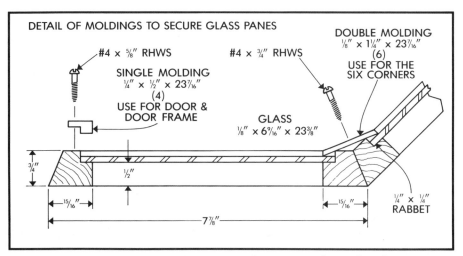

DETAIL OF MOLDINGS TO SECURE GLASS PANES

DOUBLE MOLDING
$\frac{1}{8}$″ × $1\frac{1}{4}$″ × $23\frac{7}{16}$″
(6)
USE FOR THE
SIX CORNERS

#4 × $\frac{5}{8}$″ RHWS   #4 × $\frac{3}{4}$″ RHWS

SINGLE MOLDING
$\frac{1}{4}$″ × $\frac{1}{2}$″ × $23\frac{7}{16}$″
(4)
USE FOR DOOR &
DOOR FRAME

GLASS
$\frac{1}{8}$″ × $6\frac{9}{16}$″ × $23\frac{3}{8}$″

$\frac{3}{4}$″

$\frac{1}{2}$″

$\frac{15}{16}$″ $\frac{15}{16}$″

$\frac{1}{4}$″ × $\frac{1}{4}$″
RABBET

$7\frac{7}{8}$″

Glue and screw 1 × 1-in. cleats near the upper edges of each assembled glass panel, then cut an octagon shape for the subtop and assemble the seven panels to the subtop with screws, driving the screws down into the cleats.

The subtop/panel assembly now is inverted and the bottom is centered on the panels (they should be held with a strap clamp to maintain the same dimension at top and bottom) and screws are driven through the bottom into the lower edge of each panel assembly. If you are a fairly skilled woodworker, we suggest you cut a groove in each panel stile, then glue and join the seven panels with thin splines.

At this point you can check the size of the opening for the door that is the eighth panel assembly. Quite likely the door will have to be trimmed and fitted like any door. Use hinges of your choice and hang the door.

You now can fasten the finished center section to the legs by driving screws down through the bottom into the cross braces.

The top assembly comes next, and starts with the octagon you made to match the bottom. Make a "fence" to go around the top, with a cross section as in Section B–B. The groove accepts the lower ends of the roof panels, and the tenons on the lower ends of the "rafters."

Cut the ridge post from a 12-in. length of a 4 × 4 and bevel the corners to create an octagon with sides $1\frac{5}{8}$ in. Fasten the post to the center of the top, using glue and screws driven from the underside. Position the post so its flats are opposite an angle of the top as shown in the roof assembly detail (next page).

Main top is slightly larger octagon that has grooved "fence" around it. Grooves accept lower ends of roof panels.

Lower ends of roof panel frames (rafters) have "tongues" that fit in dadoes cut into the angled bottom pieces that fit roof.

Cut the rafters to the profile shown, then cut them into 12-in. lengths. Shape the ends as indicated and reduce the overall length to about 10⅞ in. as shown on the drawing. We say "about," because each rafter will have to be individually fitted and this length may vary. Better make a few extra rafters because you may spoil a couple.

When you get one rafter to fit well, with the upper end positioned as indicated, try it in other locations. You might get lucky and have one length fill all locations. Just make the other rafters the same length.

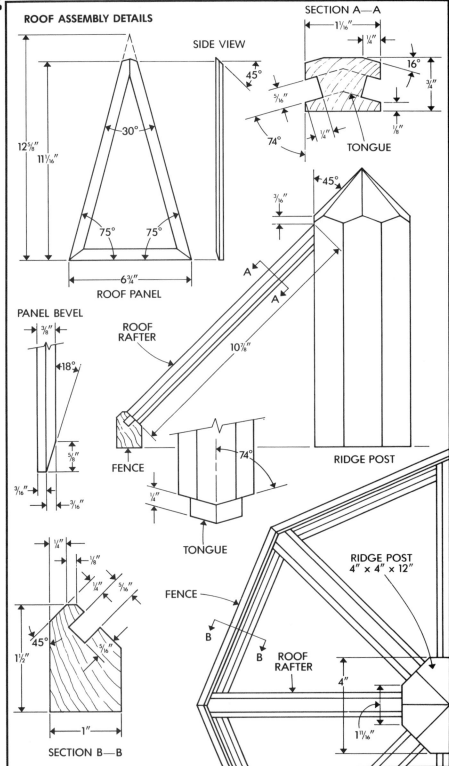

ROOF ASSEMBLY DETAILS

SECTION A—A

SIDE VIEW

ROOF PANEL

PANEL BEVEL

ROOF RAFTER

RIDGE POST

FENCE

TONGUE

FENCE

RIDGE POST 4" x 4" x 12"

ROOF RAFTER

SECTION B—B

Upper ends of rafters fit just below angled top of the 4 x 4 ridge post. Roof assembly requires considerable "cut and try."

Roof panels are ⅜-in. stock, with the edges beveled to reduce to 3/16 in. The upper point of each triangular roof panel will have to be cut and shaped to fit against the ridge post. It also may be necessary to do a little whittling on the beveled edges to get the triangles to fit into the dadoes in the rafters. Glue the panels into the grooves and drive a small finishing nail through the upper end of each triangle into the ridge post.

The finished top can be attached to the subtop by driving screws up through the subtop into the top.

Before making this assembly, remove the subtop and install the rotating shelf unit. Some craftsmen will want the post to be one piece, and the shelf spacing also may be varied depending on the dolls to be displayed. You also can display other items in the cabinet.

The cabinet shown was painted white to match other furniture in the young lady's room. You might prefer a hardwood that could be stained and finished.

If the octagonal roof will give you too much trouble, you can top off the cabinet with a simple or fancy fence or gallery. This might even

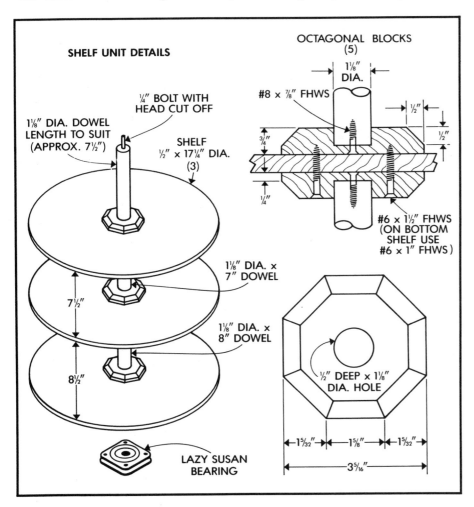

look better than the roof in some decor, and would be more period. The cabinet shown is of fairly contemporary design, again to go with existing furniture.

Make the L-shape glass retainers, have 8 pieces of glass cut to size, then install the glass. Reinstall the shelves, replace the subtop, then the main top.

Nautical-style Bunk Beds

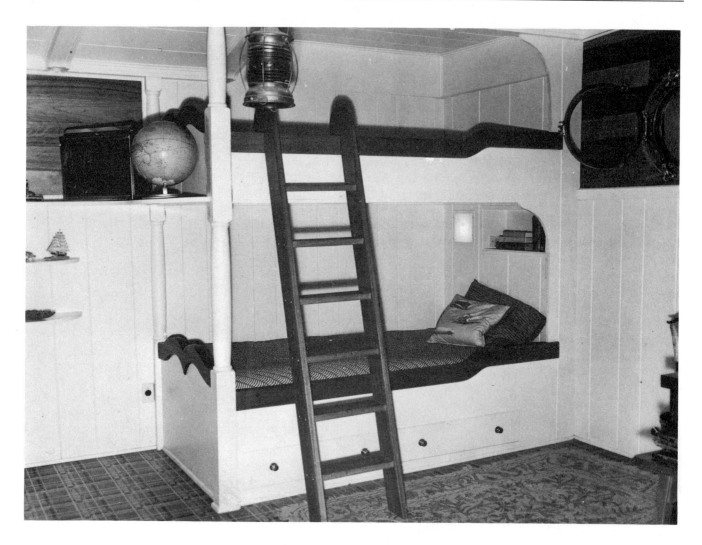

Complete utilization of every square foot of space is necessary when a bedroom is small. These built-in bunk beds not only conserve space, but give the room a truly "aboard-ship" atmosphere. Two generous-size drawers beneath the lower bunk provide storage for bedding and other items, and a shelf at the end of the lower bunk holds a radio and books that otherwise would require room space.

Two lathe-turned posts are required at the end of the bunks; the one against the wall is split lengthwise to make a "half post." Use stock 3½ in. square for the turnings. Ends and sides of the bunks are assembled from 1-in. pine (¾ in. net), with cap rails of mahogany. The rails are grooved so they fit over the end and side members of the bunks. Slat rails cut from 2 × 2 stock are glued and screwed to the inner faces of the end and side members of the bunks to provide support for single bed box springs and mattresses. To prevent dust and debris from dropping on the lower bunk from the upper, and from the lower bunk into the drawers, a piece of ⅜-in. plywood is secured to the lower edges of the slat rails.

The drawers are of conventional construction, and the fronts can be overlapping, as in the photo, or flush, as in the drawing. Mahogany pulls are used to match the caps. Note that the shelf at the head of the lower bunk also includes a flush-mounted light with frosted glass. This setup can be duplicated in the upper bunk if space allows.

Ladder treads are mortised into the side members, and a length of flat steel holds together the hook pieces at the top. The ladder assembly is of mahogany stock, but also can be pine. Paint the bunks white, or a light color, to contrast with the dark tone of the mahogany cap rails and the ladder.

To give the room a more completely nautical decor, shop at a marine supply store or ships' chandler for lights, portholes and other accessories.

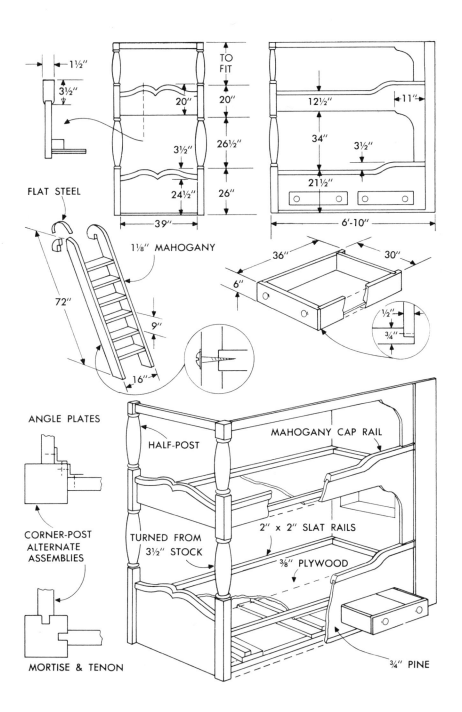

FLAT STEEL

1⅛" MAHOGANY

ANGLE PLATES

CORNER-POST ALTERNATE ASSEMBLIES

MORTISE & TENON

HALF-POST

TURNED FROM 3½" STOCK

MAHOGANY CAP RAIL

2" x 2" SLAT RAILS

⅜" PLYWOOD

¾" PINE

Sleeper "75" Bed Combo

This compact one-unit suite is a bed, an 8-drawer chest, a desk, plus a book shelf. The "75" in the title refers to the fact that a standard twin bed mattress is used, measuring 39 × 75 in.

Because there are drawers on both sides, the Sleeper "75" should be away from a wall, which might present a problem in a small room. In such case, the construction could be modified so the drawers would run the full width of the bed, and pull out from either side. Drawer fronts would have to be made to fit inside the openings so they would not stop against the framing as they do in the original design. Trim strips to match the wood of the bed rails could be applied to the faces of the existing framing strips to bring them flush with the faces of the drawer fronts.

Note the drop-down desk shown at the foot of the bed. If the desk top is to be used for hobby work, or will receive considerable abuse, individual hinges could be replaced by a length of continuous (piano) hinge and the single-locking shelf support replaced by two heavy-duty units.

Metal, ball-bearing drawer slides can be used if drawers are half the width of the bed, but it would not be practical (or economically feasible) to use this type drawer slide for drawers that are the full width of the bed.

The basic advantage of making the bed as shown, with two "boxes" construction, is that it readily disassembles for easy transport. Side rails are held to head and footboard with carriage bolts, while the chests of drawers are simply freestanding units.

With a few modifications, the freestanding chests of drawers could be fitted with casters so they could be rolled from under the bed and used separately when more space is available.

It then would be necessary to shorten the chests of drawers by the height of the casters, plus the height of any top that might be added. This probably would be ¾-in. plywood, and it could be covered with plastic laminate to ensure an easily cleaned surface.

One might prefer to eliminate the chests of drawers entirely.

Note also that because both head and footboard are the same, there is an empty space under the headboard. If the bed stands away from the wall, shelves could be installed in the headboard, or doors could be installed to make the space into a cabinet.

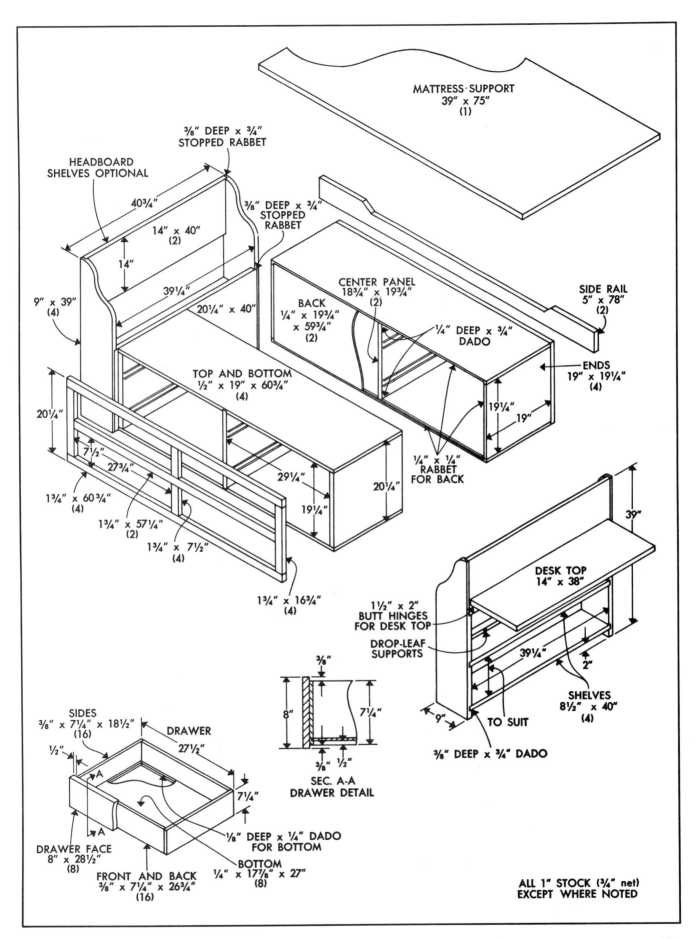

MATTRESS·SUPPORT
39" x 75"
(1)

HEADBOARD
SHELVES OPTIONAL

⅜" DEEP x ¾"
STOPPED RABBET

⅜" DEEP x ¾"
STOPPED RABBET

40¾"

14" x 40"
(2)

14"

9" x 39"
(4)

39¼"

20¼" x 40"

CENTER PANEL
18¾" x 19¾"
(2)

BACK
¼" x 19¾"
x 59¾"
(2)

¼" DEEP x ¾"
DADO

SIDE RAIL
5" x 78"
(2)

ENDS
19" x 19¼"
(4)

TOP AND BOTTOM
½" x 19" x 60¾"
(4)

20¼"

7½"

27¾"

29¼"

19¼"

20¼"

19¼"

¼" x ¼"
RABBET
FOR BACK

1¾" x 60¾"
(4)

1¾" x 57¼"
(2)

1¾" x 7½"
(4)

1¾" x 16¾"
(4)

39"

DESK TOP
14" x 38"

1½" x 2"
BUTT HINGES
FOR DESK TOP

DROP-LEAF
SUPPORTS

39¼"

2"

9"

TO SUIT

⅜" DEEP x ¾" DADO

SHELVES
8½" x 40"
(4)

SIDES
⅜" x 7¼" x 18½"
(16)

DRAWER
27½"

½"

A

A

DRAWER FACE
8" x 28½"
(8)

FRONT AND BACK
⅜" x 7¼" x 26¾"
(16)

⅛" DEEP x ¼" DADO
FOR BOTTOM

BOTTOM
¼" x 17⅞" x 27"
(8)

⅜"

8"

7¼"

⅜" ½"

SEC. A-A
DRAWER DETAIL

ALL 1" STOCK (¾" net)
EXCEPT WHERE NOTED

111

Shaker-style Tot's Bed

This Shaker-style tot's bed takes up no more room than a crib and is suitable for a youngster who feels that he or she is too big to sleep in a crib, yet will get lost in even a twin-size bed.

Not only is the bed attractive and compact, it also has two large storage drawers below that can be pulled out from either side. This means that the bed can be placed wherever it is convenient and there is access to the drawers.

To build the bed, you will need about 25 running feet of clear, straight-grained 1 × 12, 12 running feet of 2 × 6 for the base and a half sheet of ¾-in. plywood with one good side. The total cost should be very reasonable, especially if you use the mattress from the crib the youngster is vacating.

The bed basically is a plywood box, open down the sides, with a divider in the middle to separate the two large drawers. Exposed edges of the plywood box are concealed with strips of pine or other clear, straight-grained softwood.

If you happen to have a piece of ¾-in. plywood on hand large enough to make the top and bottom of the box, which is about a half sheet, you can use lengths of 1 × 12 for the ends and the divider. If not, and you have to buy a full 4 × 8-ft. sheet of plywood for the project, make the divider out of the remaining plywood and cover all exposed plywood edges with strips of solid stock. Use glue and 8-penny finishing nails to assemble the bed.

Cut the headboard, footboard, aprons (that run from the headboard and footboard along the edges of the top) from 1 × 12 stock. Clear pine was used for the original, as it is easy to work, is clear and straight-grained and accepts stain readily. The 1 × 2 trim strips on the edges of the plywood also are pine.

Sand and round over the edges of the aprons, head and footboard to ensure there are no rough edges or splinters.

Drawers are cut from 1 × 12 lumber, and the bottoms are ¼-in. plywood. Rabbets are cut in the edges of each drawer front to accept

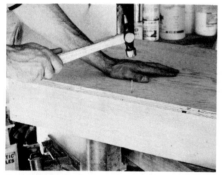

Base of ¾ in. plywood is nailed to frame of 2 x 6s joined with mitered corners. Use glue as well as finishing nails.

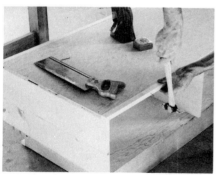

"Box" for drawers is assembled from plywood, edges trimmed with strips of solid stock. Again, use glue, finishing nails.

the sides. A dado across the inner surface of each drawer front accepts the drawer bottom.

Glue and nail two sides to one drawer front, slide in the bottom, then glue and nail on the other front. When both drawers are assembled and the glue has set, recess all nails and cover the heads with wood putty.

Go over the whole bed and set all nails and cover the heads with wood putty. When the putty is dry, sand all surfaces with progressively finer grits of sandpaper, then use a tack rag to remove all dust.

Stain and finish to suit. The original was stained walnut, then two coats of satin finish, clear, nontoxic varnish were applied.

To retain the Shaker styling, no decorations should be applied. No doubt some parents will want to add decals to personalize the bed. It also could be painted to match other furniture in the child's bedroom.

Next come the headboard, footboard and side aprons at headboard end. All these parts are joined with glue, finishing nails.

Drawer bottoms are ¼ in. plywood slipped into dadoes in sides before backs nailed on. Fronts, backs are rabbeted, glued, nailed.

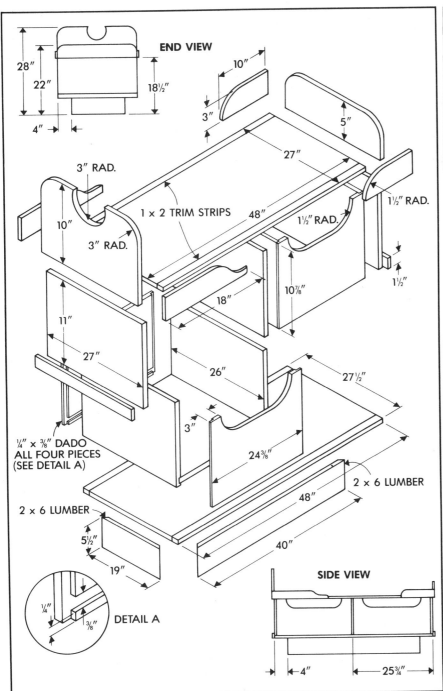

END VIEW

28"
22"
18½"
4"

10"
3"
5"

3" RAD.
3" RAD.
10"
1 × 2 TRIM STRIPS
27"
48"
1½" RAD.
1½" RAD.
1½" RAD.
1½"

11"
18"
10⅞"

27"
26"
27½"

¼" × ⅜" DADO
ALL FOUR PIECES
(SEE DETAIL A)
3"
24⅜"
2 × 6 LUMBER
48"

2 × 6 LUMBER
5½"
19"
40"

¼"
⅜"
DETAIL A

SIDE VIEW
4"
25¾"

113

Basic Bunk Beds

MATERIALS LIST

A, Top cross member, 1 × 6 × 40¾″ (4)
B, Bottom cross member, ¾″ × 2¾″ × 40¾″ (4)
C, Leg, 1 × 6 × 30″ (8)
D, Dowels, ¼″ × 2-916″ (32)
E, Side frame, 1 × 4 × 76¾″ (4)
F, End frame, 1 × 4 × 40¾″ (4)
G, Cleat, ¾″ × 1″ × 75¼″ (4)
H, Cleat, ¾″ × 1″ × 39¼″ (4)
I, Guard rail, 1 × 4 × 76¾″ (4)
J, Guard rail, 1 × 4 × 40¾″ (4)
K, Ladder step, 1 × 3 × 12″ (6)
L, Ladder rail, 1 × 3 × 41⅝″ (2)
M, Dowel, ¼″ × 2″ (24)
N, Ladder hooks, ⅛″ × ¾″ × 5¾″ alum. bar stock (2)
O, Spacer, ¾″ × 4½″ × 23″ (4)
P, Dowels, ¼″ × 3″ (24)
Q, Box side, ¾″ × 6¾″ × 39¾″ (6)
R, Box end, ¾″ × 6¾″ × 23″ (6)
S, Box base, ¾″ plywood 21½″ × 38¼″ (3)
T, Wheel, ¾″ × 2¾″ dia. (12)
U, wheel cover top, ¾″ × 3¾″ × 5″ (12)
V, Wheel cover side, ¾″ × 2¼″ × 5″ (12)
W, Wheel cover end, ¾″ × 2¼″ × 3¾″ (12)
X, Box pull, 1″ × 1⅜″ × 23″ (3)
Bunk bed mattress and spring (2)
White glue, 8 oz.
No. 10 × 1½″ RH wood screws (48)
No. 12 × 2″ FH wood screws (4)
No. 12 × 1¼″ FH wood screws (16)
4d finishing nails
Wood putty
No. 8 × 1½″ RH wood screws (9)
Lag screws, ¼″ × 1½″ (12)
I.D. steel washers, ¼″ (24)

These beds can be used as matching single units or stacked as bunks to save floor space. Roll-out drawers under the bottom bed provide generous storage for blankets, sheets, and even the paraphernalia that youngsters seem to gather. If the beds are used as singles, you can make drawers for both beds.

The mattress and frame set is designed for a standard 39 × 75 in. size, but get the mattress before you start construction, just to make sure the size of your unit does not require some modification.

All assemblies are relatively easy to build, as standard board widths are utilized where possible, to minimize the need for ripping stock. Clear white pine is suggested for the stock, and it can be stained and finished in a number of ways. There is no reason, of course, that hardwood cannot be used and some builders will prefer it. Be sure any stock you use is well seasoned or kiln dried, and that it is flat, straight grained and free of knots, splits and checks.

Shop-made wheels are shown to be used under the storage drawers, but you can substitute casters. We suggest the plate type that can be screwed to the underside of the drawers. Make the drawer bottoms (S) without the notches, and eliminate the boxes that are designed to cover the wheels. If your casters project more than the wheels shown, reduce the overall height of the drawers accordingly. Allow ample clearance; a bouncing youngster can reduce that clearance to zero with only moderate effort.

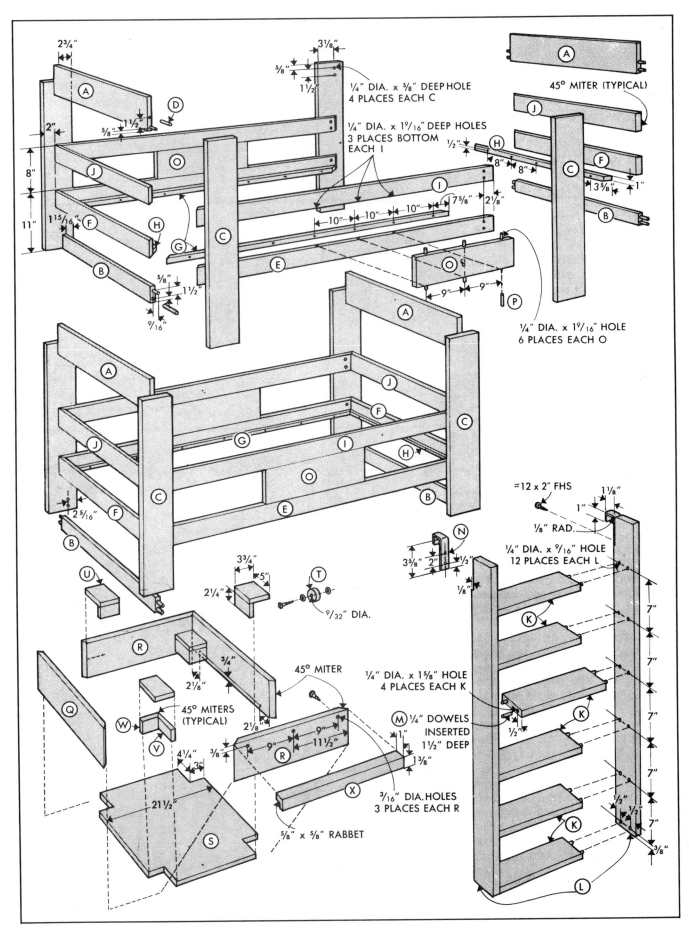

2¾"

¼" DIA. x ⅝" DEEP HOLE
4 PLACES EACH C

3⅛"
⅝"
1½"

¼" DIA. x 1⁹⁄₁₆" DEEP HOLES
3 PLACES BOTTOM
EACH I

45° MITER (TYPICAL)

2"
8"
11"
1¹⁵⁄₁₆"

⅝"
1½"

⅝"
1½"
⁹⁄₁₆"

½"
8"
8"
3⅝"
1"

10" 10" 10" 7⅝" 2⅛"

9" 9"

¼" DIA. x 1⁹⁄₁₆" HOLE
6 PLACES EACH O

2⁵⁄₁₆"

#12 x 2" FHS
1⅛"
1"
⅛" RAD.

¼" DIA. x ⁹⁄₁₆" HOLE
12 PLACES EACH L

3⅝" 2" ½"
⅛"

7"
7"
7"
7"

¼" DIA. x 1⅝" HOLE
4 PLACES EACH K

¼" DOWELS
INSERTED
1½" DEEP

½"

3¾"
5"
2¼"

⁹⁄₃₂" DIA.

¾"
2⅛"

45° MITER

45° MITERS
(TYPICAL)

2⅛"
4¼"
3"
⅜"

9" 9" 11½"

1"
1⅜"

⁵⁄₈" x ⁵⁄₈" RABBET

³⁄₁₆" DIA. HOLES
3 PLACES EACH R

21½

½" ½"
7"
⅜"

Child's Folding Rocker

We were so intrigued by this little folding chair that we built a copy in our model shop. We used hardwood for all the parts except the seat, which we cut from some birch plywood. If the chair is to be painted, we believe a hardwood plywood would be quite adequate, and you would be assured of the strength of the long, slender front legs (side arms) that also create the back posts.

If the chair is to be stained and finished, then all hardwood should be used, including gluing up pieces to create stock wide enough for the seat.

On our first assembly, we found the chair would not fold compactly. A check of dimensions disclosed we had not properly spaced the holes in the rockers. We plugged the holes with dowels, redrilled at the proper spacing and the chair folded quite flat.

Start construction by enlarging the squared drawings to make patterns of the several pieces. (We glued our paper patterns to light cardboard. This makes the patterns easier to use, and we know we'll have to make several after seeing the response of both parents and children.)

Cut out the side arms, the rear bottom side arms and the rockers and clamp the pairs together and sand so they are identical. A disc sander will handle most of the curves, but you may need to use the end of a belt sander, or a drum sander to get some of the inside curves. For sanding on the table of a disc sander, use two or three small finishing nails to hold the pairs together, rather than clamps. This allows easy movement of the pieces across the table; clamps would hang up on the table edges. Drill all holes while the pairs are clamped.

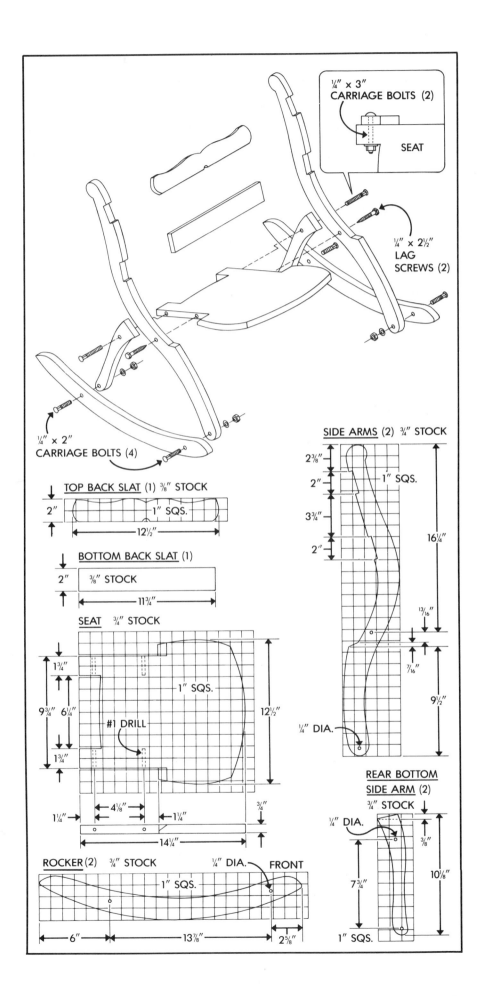

¼" × 3"
CARRIAGE BOLTS (2)

SEAT

¼" × 2½"
LAG
SCREWS (2)

¼" × 2"
CARRIAGE BOLTS (4)

SIDE ARMS (2) ¾" STOCK

2⅜"
2"
3¾"
2"

1" SQS.

16¼"

13/16"

7/16"

9½"

¼" DIA.

TOP BACK SLAT (1) ⅜" STOCK

2"

1" SQS.

12½"

BOTTOM BACK SLAT (1)

2"

⅜" STOCK

11¾"

SEAT   ¾" STOCK

1¾"

9¾" 6¼"

#1 DRILL

1" SQS.

12½"

1¾"

1¼"

4⅛"

1¼"

¾"

14¼"

REAR BOTTOM
SIDE ARM (2)
¾" STOCK

¼" DIA.

⅜"

7¾"

10⅛"

1" SQS.

ROCKER (2) ¾" STOCK   ¼" DIA.   FRONT

1" SQS.

6"

13⅞"

2⅝"

Cut the top back slat with the pattern you made, then cut the bottom back slat to size and shape. Shape the seat with the aid of the pattern you have made, then sand the edges of the three shapes and slightly round all edges.

Be accurate when locating the pilot holes in the edges of the seat into which the ¼ × 2-in. lag screws and ¼ × 3-in. carriage bolts are fitted. Use washers under the nuts; we used both flat and lock washers. It also would be a good idea to upset the threads on the ends of the carriage bolts by lightly hammering on the ends. This would ensure that the nuts would not back off when the rocker is in use.

For easier action you might want to fit flat washers between the various parts that pivot. (When we built our chair in the model shop, we did not use washers between the parts, figuring that a bit of friction would discourage toddlers from folding the chair and getting fingers pinched.)

Mark the top notch in the two side arms, but do not cut them. Do cut the bottom notches and attach the bottom back slat with two no. 6 × 1-in. flathead screws in each end. Make sure the side arms are parallel, then place the top slat in position and mark the upper edge of each notch to match the curved upper edge of the top slat.

Remove the bottom slat, cut the upper notches in the side arms, then assemble the side arms and slats with glue and flathead screws.

When the glue has set, assemble the seat, four side arms and the rockers. Check that the seat folds properly, then disassemble the chair, do final sanding and apply the desired finish. When the finish has dried, reassemble the chair, applying a bit of wax at friction points if you don't use flat washers.

(In our model shop version, we noted that when folding the chair, each rocker and long side arm seemed to move somewhat independently. Our thought is that perhaps a stretcher across the two bottom side arms might reduce the "problem." We'd like to hear from craftspersons who build the chair to see what their ideas might be.)

Child's Playtime Rocker

Sized for children from one to four years of age, this rocker is designed to be safe.

Cut the two rockers, then clamp them together and sand smooth so they are identical. Any good hardwood can be used for making the rocker (drawing on next page).

Join the two rockers with 3 × 11⅛-in. strips of 1-in. hardwood, after first drilling pilot holes for the two screws that hold the handle to the front strip.

Cut pieces for the A-frames from 1 × 3 stock. Note that the top of the rear leg is straight across, while the bottom is cut at 15 degrees. The front leg of the A-frame is ¼ in. longer, with a 45-degree angle at the top and a 30-degree angle at the bottom.

Clamp the sets of legs together, drill and countersink holes for the screws that hold the legs together. Note that the top screw is 1¼ in. long, the lower one 2 in. long. Glue and screw the frames together, clamping the completed pair to ensure they are identical.

Cut the seat to size, then clamp the A-frames to it. Drill pilot holes through the frames into the edges of the seat, then disassemble, apply glue and screw the frames to the seat. Do the same for the back of the seat that fits between the upper ends of the A-frames.

Cut the handle upright to length, radius the top end and bore a hole for the ¾ × 6-in. dowel that is glued and pinned with a finishing nail.

Cut, shape and counterbore the brace block that goes under the seat and connects to the handle upright. Glue and screw it to the underside of the seat, and drive a screw at an angle through the block into the handle upright. Be sure the block is snug against the handle upright and the underside of the seat, which may require clamps. The handle upright is glued and screwed to the front crosspiece between the rockers.

Sand all surfaces smooth. Make sure all screws are countersunk, then cover heads with wood putty. Break all sharp edges.

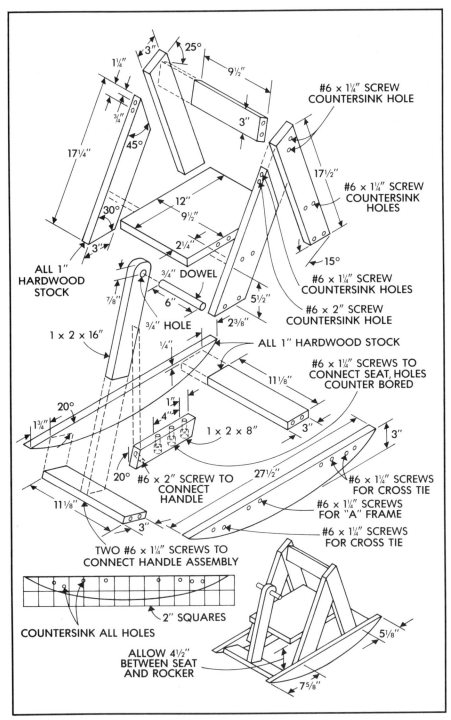

TOYS & GAMES

Custom-made Chessboard

Chess is one of the most popular games in the world, and possibly the most time consuming. Because players spend hours staring at the board, it is small wonder they are willing to invest large sums of money for beautiful chess sets. While fine chess sets can be found in many shops, the same is not true of boards. The board shown is relatively easy to make and very attractive.

The board surface is veneered, but the "veneer" is 3/16 in. thick and is created by resawing 1-in. (3/4-in. net) stock to 3/16 in. thick. This kind of veneer can be sanded vigorously without concern about sanding through it.

Start by resawing enough stock to make four strips of dark wood and five strips of light, 3/16 in. thick and 1 5/8 in. wide. Make the strips at least 15 in. long. Plane or smooth the surfaces and the edges. Edge glue the several strips, using the hold-down arrangement pictured to prevent them from buckling. A good selection of bar clamps or pipe fixtures is a big help for this kind of project.

When the glue has set, rip the glued-up assembly into strips the width of the original squares and edge glue again, offsetting the squares to form a large square of 64 alternating light and dark squares. There will be four extra light squares on each side of the board that are removed after the glue has set.

The core is next, and it can be a square of ⅝-in. plywood, or assembled from five layers of ⅛-in. poplar crossbanding veneer as I did. I used a paint roller to apply the glue, then clamped the sheets under a piece of ¾-in. plywood. A sheet of paper between the core and plywood prevented them from being glued together.

I trimmed the core lamination to within ½ in. of finished size, then glued on the squares, with the grain of the squares at a right angle to the grain of the top layer of veneer. Two sheets of ¾-in. plywood were used to sandwich the core and squares when they were clamped and glued. Paper again was used to prevent the assembly from being glued to the plywood-clamping boards.

Strips of dark and light colored wood are edge glued, clamped. Note heavy pieces of stock under clamps to prevent buckling.

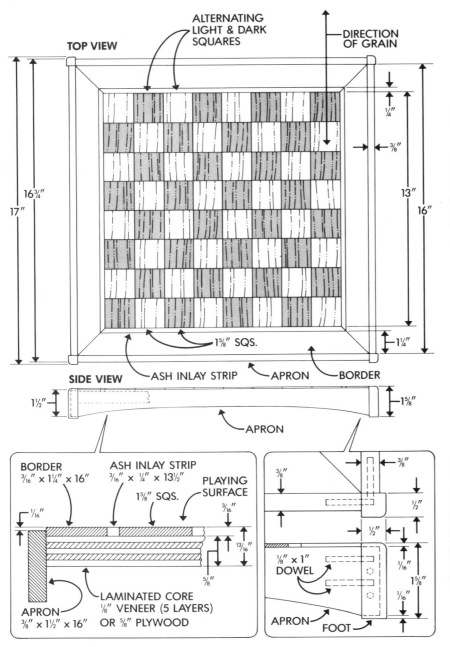

When glue has set, strip assembly is scraped smooth. Scraper is better than sandpaper that will stain light wood.

If you do not use 5/8 in. plywood, make up laminated core by gluing together five 1/8 in. sheets of poplar crossbanding veneer.

After strips are crosscut and reglued to form board, clamp and glue the assembly to the core you assembled, or plywood.

The core/squares assembly was trimmed to final size after the glue set. A layer of mahogany veneer was glued to the underside of the core to ensure "balanced construction" for the core/square assembly.

Next, cut the aprons to size and shape and dowl them to the corner posts (feet). The aprons can be simple rectangles or you can make them with a gentle curve as shown. For a more "colonial" design, the aprons can be scalloped or shaped in a variety of ways.

Fit the board assembly inside the leg/apron assembly and glue and clamp it. Note that the board is positioned to be ⅟₁₆ in. above the bottoms of the legs.

When the glue has set overnight, scrape all surfaces smooth, then apply a coat of paste wax, burnishing it in with fine steel wool. Alternately, apply a clear sealer, then wax when it is dry.

Dollhouse Furniture

All the pieces of furniture for the living room, dining room, bedroom and kitchen shown and described can be made from scraps of hardwood. Additionally, you will need glue, brass escutcheon pins and some brass wire. Clamps will be required, plus some ⅛-in. dowels to reinforce the butt joints of the various items.

Dining Room

Make patterns for the chair sides as detailed on page 124, then clamp two pieces of wood together with two patterns traced on the top piece. Cut out the two outlines and you will have four chair sides with the matching pieces identical.

The table requires turning the pedestal, with the bottom left square so the four feet can be doweled to the pedestal. We used dowel centers to align the holes. The table top is a faceplate turning. Assemble as shown on page 126.

For the hutch, cut the two side pieces, the top, bottom, back and shelf and glue them together. When the glue sets, drill and insert dowels to reinforce the butt joints. Cut the pieces for the false door and drawer fronts from ¹⁄₁₆-in. stock to the sizes shown, and glue them to the front of the hutch. Drawer and door pulls are ⅝-in. brass escutcheon pins. Drill pilot holes for the pins ½ in. deep.

Cut the parts for the buffet-chest and assemble it in the same manner as the hutch.

DINING ROOM TABLE

TOP ¼″ × 3½″ DIA.

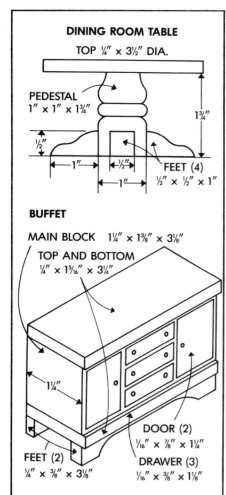

PEDESTAL
1″ × 1″ × 1¾″

1¾″

½″

1″ ½″

1″

FEET (4)
½″ × ½″ × 1″

BUFFET

MAIN BLOCK   1¼″ × 1⅜″ × 3⅛″

TOP AND BOTTOM
¼″ × 1⁵⁄₁₆″ × 3¼″

1¼″

FEET (2)
¼″ × ⅜″ × 3⅛″

DOOR (2)
¹⁄₁₆″ × ⅞″ × 1¼″

DRAWER (3)
¹⁄₁₆″ × ⅜″ × 1⅛″

KITCHEN TABLE AND BENCH

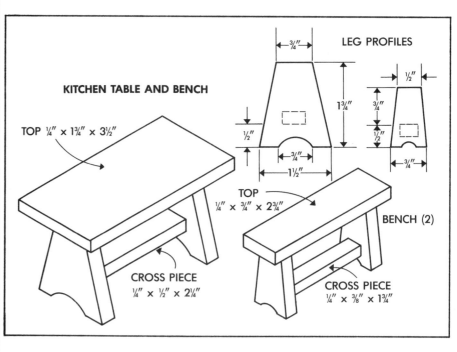

TOP ¼″ × 1¾″ × 3½″

LEG PROFILES

¾″

1¾″

½″

¾″

1½″

½″

¾″

½″

¾″

TOP
¼″ × ¾″ × 2¾″

BENCH (2)

CROSS PIECE
¼″ × ½″ × 2¼″

CROSS PIECE
¼″ × ⅜″ × 1¾″

HUTCH

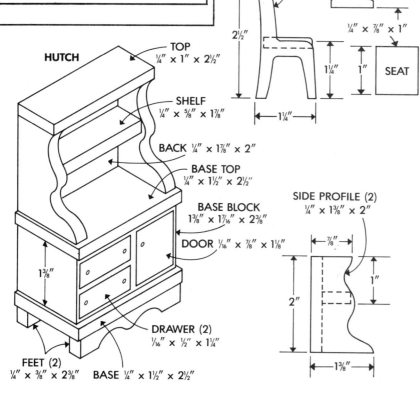

TOP
¼″ × 1″ × 2½″

SHELF
¼″ × ⅝″ × 1⅞″

BACK ¼″ × 1⅞″ × 2″

BASE TOP
¼″ × 1½″ × 2½″

BASE BLOCK
1⅜″ × 1⁷⁄₁₆″ × 2⅜″

DOOR ¹⁄₁₆″ × ⅞″ × 1⅛″

1⅜″

DRAWER (2)
¹⁄₁₆″ × ½″ × 1¼″

FEET (2)
¼″ × ⅜″ × 2⅜″   BASE ¼″ × 1½″ × 2½″

DINING ROOM CHAIR

¼″ STOCK

BACK (2)

⅞″

¼″

¼″ × ⅞″ × 1″

2½″

1¼″

1″

SEAT

1¼″

SIDE PROFILE (2)
¼″ × 1⅜″ × 2″

⅞″

1″

2″

1⅜″

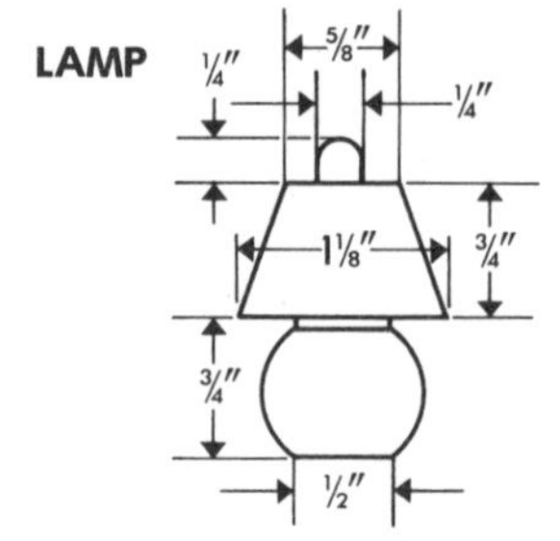

LAMP

¼″   ⅝″   ¼″

1⅛″   ¾″

¾″

½″

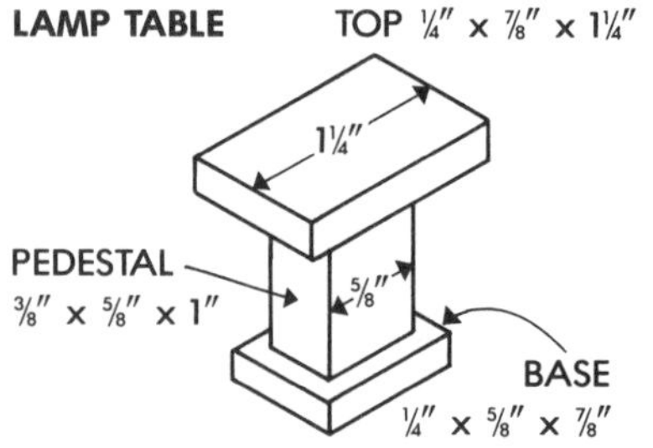

LAMP TABLE

TOP ¼″ × ⅞″ × 1¼″

1¼″

PEDESTAL
⅜″ × ⅝″ × 1″

⅝″

BASE
¼″ × ⅝″ × ⅞″

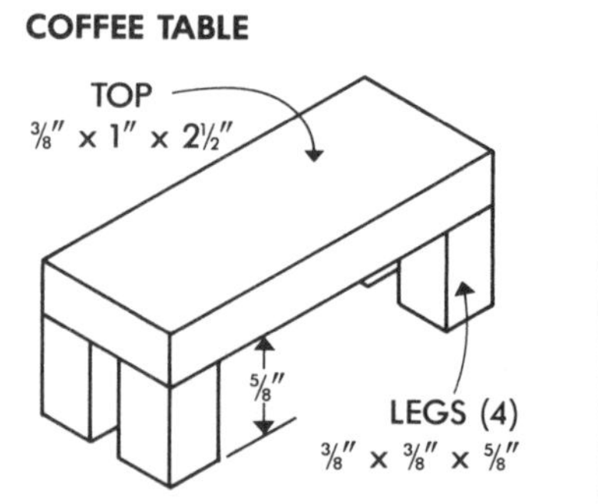

COFFEE TABLE

TOP
⅜″ × 1″ × 2½″

⅝″

LEGS (4)
⅜″ × ⅜″ × ⅝″

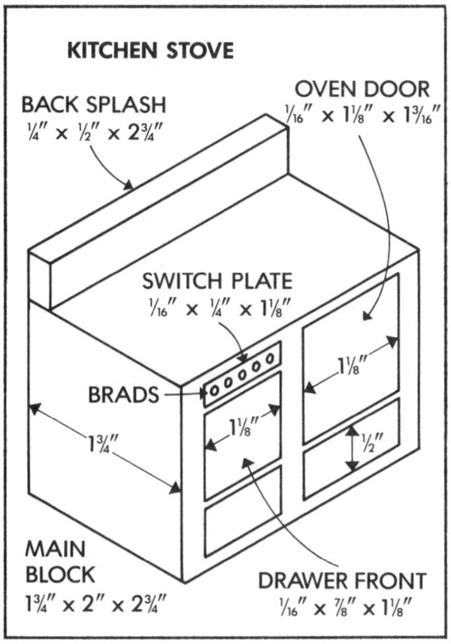
KITCHEN STOVE
BACK SPLASH
1/4" x 1/2" x 2 3/4"
OVEN DOOR
1/16" x 1 1/8" x 1 3/16"
SWITCH PLATE
1/16" x 1/4" x 1 1/8"
BRADS
1 1/8"
1 1/8"
1/2"
1 3/4"
MAIN
BLOCK
1 3/4" x 2" x 2 3/4"
DRAWER FRONT
1/16" x 7/8" x 1 1/8"

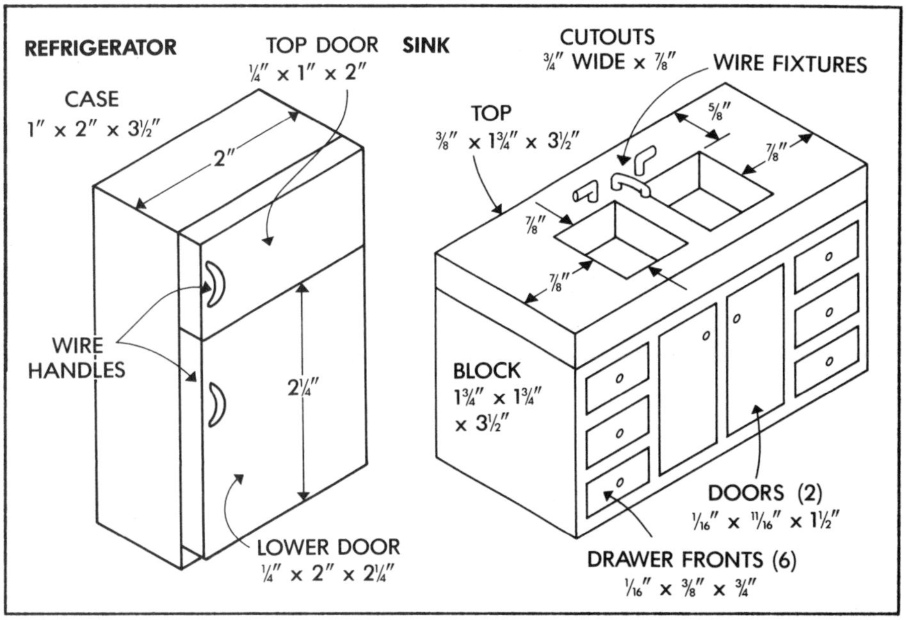
REFRIGERATOR
TOP DOOR
1/4" x 1" x 2"
CASE
1" x 2" x 3 1/2"
2"
WIRE
HANDLES
2 1/4"
LOWER DOOR
1/4" x 2" x 2 1/4"
SINK
CUTOUTS
3/4" WIDE x 7/8"
WIRE FIXTURES
TOP
3/8" x 1 3/4" x 3 1/2"
5/8"
7/8"
7/8"
7/8"
BLOCK
1 3/4" x 1 3/4"
x 3 1/2"
DOORS (2)
1/16" x 11/16" x 1 1/2"
DRAWER FRONTS (6)
1/16" x 3/8" x 3/4"

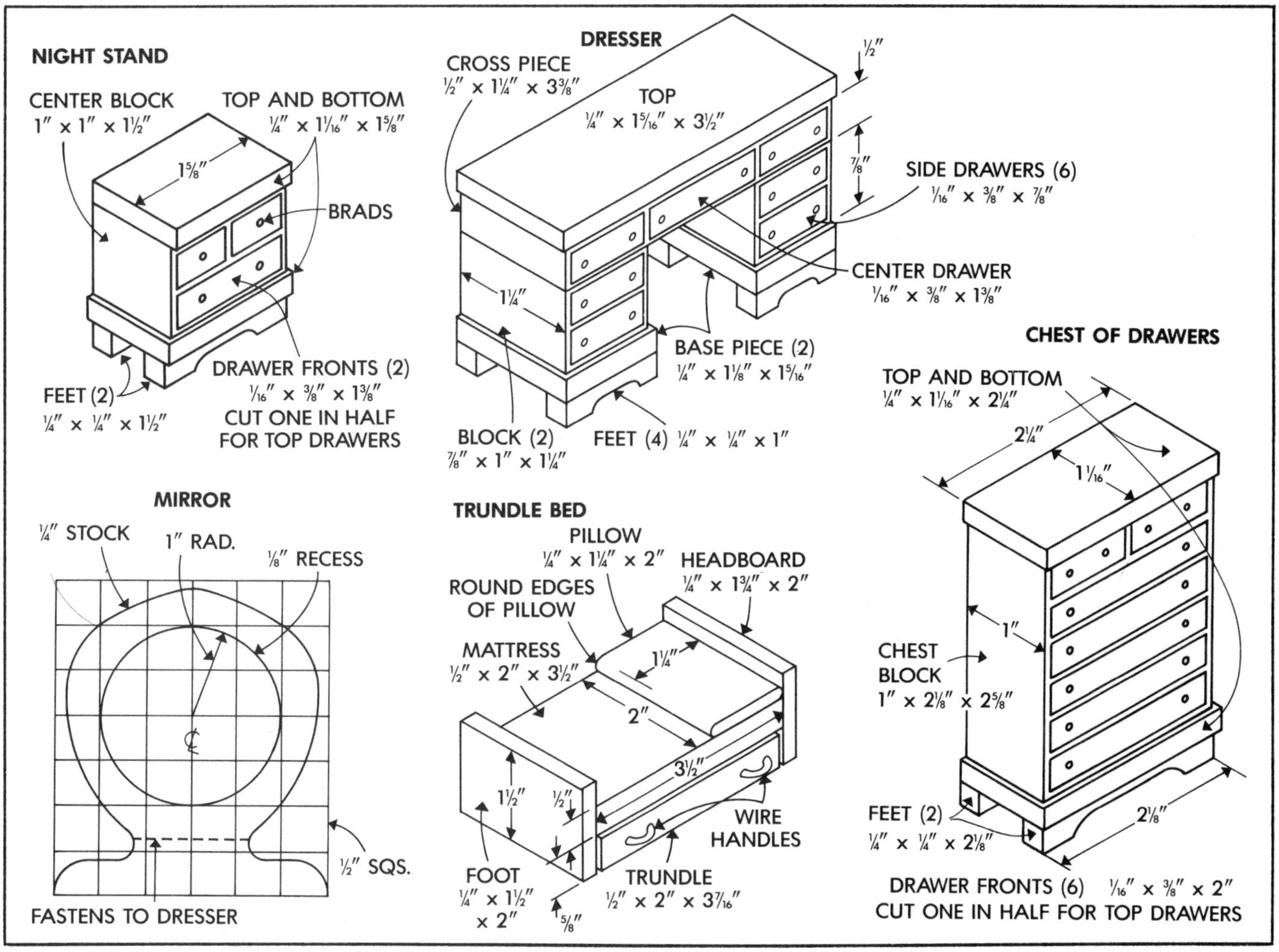
NIGHT STAND
CENTER BLOCK
1" x 1" x 1 1/2"
TOP AND BOTTOM
1/4" x 1 1/16" x 1 5/8"
1 5/8"
BRADS
FEET (2)
1/4" x 1/4" x 1 1/2"
DRAWER FRONTS (2)
1/16" x 3/8" x 1 3/8"
CUT ONE IN HALF
FOR TOP DRAWERS
DRESSER
CROSS PIECE
1/2" x 1 1/4" x 3 3/8"
TOP
1/4" x 1 5/16" x 3 1/2"
1/2"
7/8"
SIDE DRAWERS (6)
1/16" x 3/8" x 7/8"
CENTER DRAWER
1/16" x 3/8" x 1 3/8"
1 1/4"
BASE PIECE (2)
1/4" x 1 1/8" x 1 5/16"
BLOCK (2)
7/8" x 1" x 1 1/4"
FEET (4) 1/4" x 1/4" x 1"
CHEST OF DRAWERS
TOP AND BOTTOM
1/4" x 1 1/16" x 2 1/4"
2 1/4"
1 1/16"
1"
CHEST
BLOCK
1" x 2 1/8" x 2 5/8"
2 1/8"
FEET (2)
1/4" x 1/4" x 2 1/8"
DRAWER FRONTS (6) 1/16" x 3/8" x 2"
CUT ONE IN HALF FOR TOP DRAWERS
MIRROR
1/4" STOCK
1" RAD.
1/8" RECESS
1/2" SQS.
FASTENS TO DRESSER
TRUNDLE BED
PILLOW
1/4" x 1 1/4" x 2"
HEADBOARD
1/4" x 1 3/4" x 2"
ROUND EDGES
OF PILLOW
MATTRESS
1/2" x 2" x 3 1/2"
1 1/4"
2"
3 1/2"
1 1/2"
1/2"
WIRE
HANDLES
FOOT
1/4" x 1 1/2"
x 2"
5/8"
TRUNDLE
1/2" x 2" x 3 7/16"

Tack nail in the waste portion of two strips, then saw out two sets of sides for the chair; they will be identical.

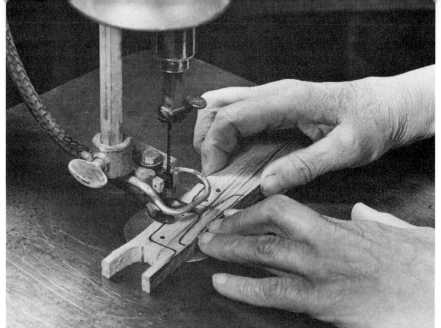

Assemble chairs with glue, clamp until dry. For added strength, use small dowels between various components, also gluing.

Dowels are used to join feet to pedestal of dining room table. Dowel points are real aid in aligning dowel holes.

Bed with trundle beneath. U-shape handles for trundle are pieces of brass wire bent to shape, glued into holes.

Bedroom

For the bedroom, the trundle bed is assembled from the pieces as detailed on page 125. Handles for the trundle are bent from 16-gauge brass wire.

Chest of drawers for the bedroom is assembled from the parts detailed, then assembled like the hutch bottom.

Night stand is assembled from parts cut to the sizes shown. Assemble the same as the chest of drawers.

The dresser is cut and assembled in a similar manner to the other pieces. A small round mirror is inserted in a recess turned to accept it so it is flush with the face. The mirror probably will have to be removed from a plastic frame. Turn the recess in stock ¾ in. thick, then resaw it to ¼ in. thick after turning the recess. Finish the dresser before gluing the mirror into the recess.

After turning mirror recess, saw the stock for the frame so that it is 1/4 in. thick. Fence clamped to table will help.

Kitchen

Tables and benches for the kitchen are assembled from pieces cut to the shape and dimensions given on page 124. When the glue sets, drill and insert dowels in the joints.

The refrigerator/freezer is cut from a block as detailed on page 125, then two pieces are glued onto the block to represent the doors. Handles for the two doors are U-shape pieces bent from brass wire, as for other items.

The stove (range) is a block to which the back strip at the top is glued, as well as the pieces to represent the four doors. Indicate burners by making two concentric circles and a center dot with soft pencil. The oven door handle is shaped from wire, other pulls are brass escutcheon pins.

Stove burners are marked with soft pencil, brass escutcheon pins are used for knobs, drawer, door handles. Oven handle is wire.

For the sink, cut the base block to size, then make the two basin holes in the top piece and glue it to the base block. Glue on the several doors and drawer fronts, add escutcheon pins for pulls. The faucet and faucet handles are escutcheon pins driven partway, then bent to shape.

Living Room

Start the living room with the couch. Cut the various parts to the dimensions given on page 129, then glue the arms to the base with the back between the arms at a slight angle, and raised ¼ in. above the base. Glue the seat cushions in place, then the back cushions. When the glue sets, reinforce the joints by drilling and gluing in dowels.

The chair is cut and assembled much the same as the couch.

Coffee table for the living room is cut and assembled, then the joints are reinforced by running dowels through the top into the legs.

Cut the parts for the lamp table as dimensioned on page 124, glue together and dowel the joints between top, base and pedestal.

Turn the living room lamp in one piece from a turning block 1¼ in. square and about 3 in. long. Trim the ends so the lamp is 1¾ in. high.

Desk/bookcase is cut and assembled in the same manner as other pieces. Glue and clamp, then drive in brass escutcheon pins for the drawer pulls, after drilling pilot holes.

We finish all pieces of furniture with polyurethane varnish, but you might want to paint some of the items, especially for the kitchen.

BOOKCASE/DESK

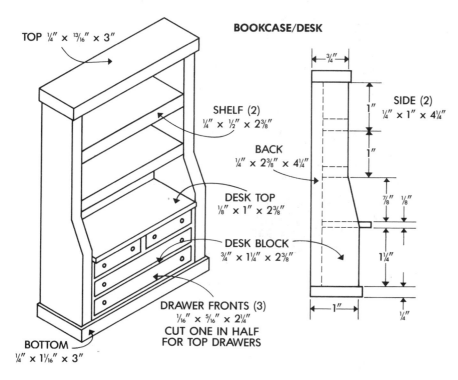

TOP ¼″ × ¹³⁄₁₆″ × 3″

SHELF (2) ¼″ × ½″ × 2⅜″

BACK ¼″ × 2⅜″ × 4¼″

DESK TOP ⅛″ × 1″ × 2⅜″

DESK BLOCK ¾″ × 1¼″ × 2⅜″

DRAWER FRONTS (3) ¹⁄₁₆″ × ⁵⁄₁₆″ × 2¼″ CUT ONE IN HALF FOR TOP DRAWERS

BOTTOM ¼″ × 1¹⁄₁₆″ × 3″

SIDE (2) ¼″ × 1″ × 4¼″

COUCH AND CHAIR

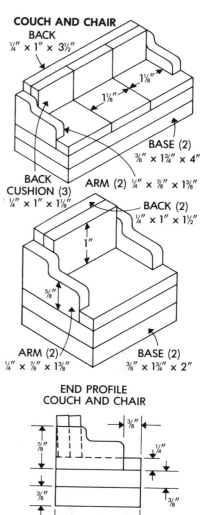

BACK ¼″ × 1″ × 3½″

BASE (2) ⅜″ × 1¾″ × 4″

BACK CUSHION (3) ¼″ × 1″ × 1⅛″

ARM (2) ¼″ × ⅞″ × 1⅜″

BACK (2) ¼″ × 1″ × 1½″

ARM (2) ¼″ × ⅞″ × 1⅜″

BASE (2) ⅜″ × 1¾″ × 2″

END PROFILE COUCH AND CHAIR

Assemble couch base, arms and back with glue and dowels. Note back is set 1/4 in. above base so seat cushions slip under.

Old-fashioned Building Logs

For years, one of the most popular toys has been building "logs." Most children seem to be born construction experts and can spend hours building various structures. Not only are these logs fun for the builder, but they are also simple and economical for the woodworker.

About 7 ft. of standard white pine 1 × 1 (without any knots) will make enough logs to keep even the most industrious young builder happy for hours. First, sand the surface of the stock as smooth as possible. Then cut it into various lengths. Three pieces 12 in. long, three pieces 9 in. and three pieces 6 in. plus some 2-in. pieces for spacers should provide enough material for almost any builder. Cut pieces for roofing, according to the drawing. To prevent splintering, make all cuts using a fine-toothed saw blade. Then sand the ends of the cut pieces on a belt sander and lightly round the edges. For the roofing pieces, carefully sand by hand.

Cut four triangles for the gables, two of them 9 in. on each side and two 6 in. on each side. Then make a cut on two sides, as shown in the drawing, so a lip is left to hold the roofing panels.

Although the notches for the logs can be cut in a number of ways, including using a router, the best method is to use a table saw or radial-arm saw and dado blade. Set the dado head for a ¾-in.-wide cut and if using a table saw, move the fence to allow a ½-in. space between the notch and the end of the stock. Then push the stock over the dado head using the miter gauge and push stick. The notch should be cut ¼ in. deep. If making the notches on a radial-arm saw, position a stop block so the stock is held with the end ½ in. past the dado head.

After all notches have been cut, use a piece of stock just a bit under

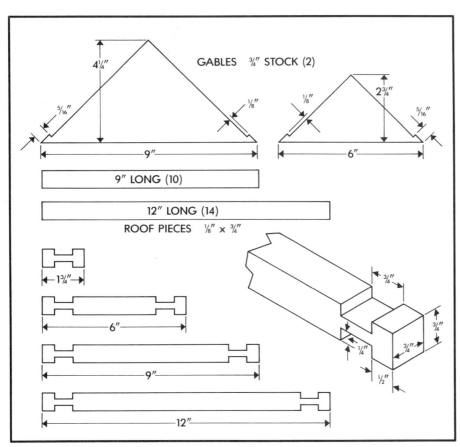

GABLES ¾″ STOCK (2)

4¼″   9″

5/16″   ⅛″

2¾″   6″

⅛″   5/16″

9″ LONG (10)

12″ LONG (14)

ROOF PIECES ⅛″ × ¾″

1¾″

6″

9″

12″

¾″

¾″

¾″

¼″

½″

¾ in. thick and wrapped with sandpaper to lightly sand the inside of all notches. Rip the dadoed stock into ¾-in. strips, then lightly sand surface. Using a non-toxic stain or paint, finish to suit.

For long logs, make dadoes on each end and both sides, then cut lengthwise into ¾ in. wide strips.

Model 1915 Chevrolet

While this model is quite large—about 5 in. wide, 10½ in. high and over 20 in. long—it is not a toy for children. Rather it is an "adult's toy" that is for display, not play.

The only parts of the project that might cause problems are the wheels. You can make them with a wood-turning lathe, or a modified fly cutter can be utilized in a drill press to shape them. Hubs can be turned in a lathe or shaped with the aid of a drill press that is used as a "vertical lathe."

Start construction by making the chassis from a piece of stock 1⅛ in. thick. Hardwood is best, as the "pierced" areas at the back and front of each side create a very thin cross section that will break easily. You can plane 1¼-in. stock to produce the chassis material; gluing up stock can be done, but care is required at the pierced areas.

Cut the notches at the ends of the chassis to shape the "springs." Drill through and make the cutouts that further shape the springs. Make the hood and cowl; they can be separate pieces glued together. The radiator is cut separately, the outer "shell" being ¼ in. wide. Screen wire is glued between the shell and the hood to give the look of a radiator.

Lay out the seat block, then cut out the inside in one pass with a scroll, jig or band saw. Remove this waste piece, reduce the height and round the front edge for the seat cushion. Finish shaping the seat by cutting the curved ends, per the squared drawing, then round over the top edge.

Make the fuel tank and tool box as detailed in the drawing on page 134. Make patterns for the front and rear fenders and cut them to shape. Note that the back ends of the front fenders and the forward ends of the back fenders are square, while the running-board ends are cut at 45 and 55 degrees. Because of this, the ends of the fenders that contact the running board are ⅜ in. thick, while the running board itself is ¼ in. These angles may have to be adjusted a bit in your

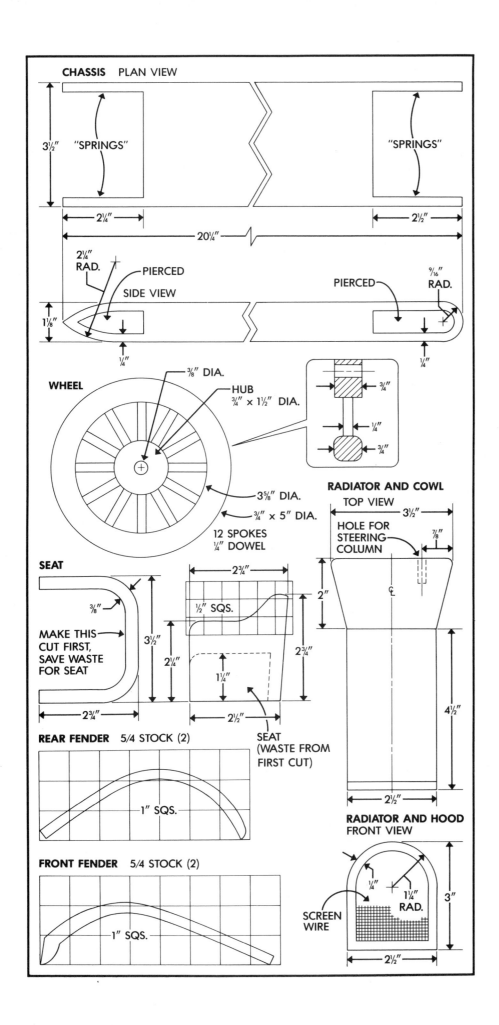

CHASSIS PLAN VIEW

3½″

"SPRINGS"

"SPRINGS"

2¼″

2½″

20¼″

2¼″ RAD.

PIERCED

SIDE VIEW

PIERCED

9/16″ RAD.

1⅛″

¼″

¼″

WHEEL

⅜″ DIA.

HUB ¾″ × 1½″ DIA.

¾″

¼″

¾″

3⅝″ DIA.

¾″ × 5″ DIA.

12 SPOKES ¼″ DOWEL

RADIATOR AND COWL

TOP VIEW

3½″

HOLE FOR STEERING COLUMN

⅞″

2″

4½″

2½″

SEAT

⅜″

MAKE THIS CUT FIRST, SAVE WASTE FOR SEAT

3½″

2¼″

2¾″

½″ SQS.

2¾″

2½″

1¼″

SEAT (WASTE FROM FIRST CUT)

REAR FENDER 5/4 STOCK (2)

1″ SQS.

FRONT FENDER 5/4 STOCK (2)

1″ SQS.

RADIATOR AND HOOD
FRONT VIEW

3″

¼″

1¼″ RAD.

SCREEN WIRE

2½″

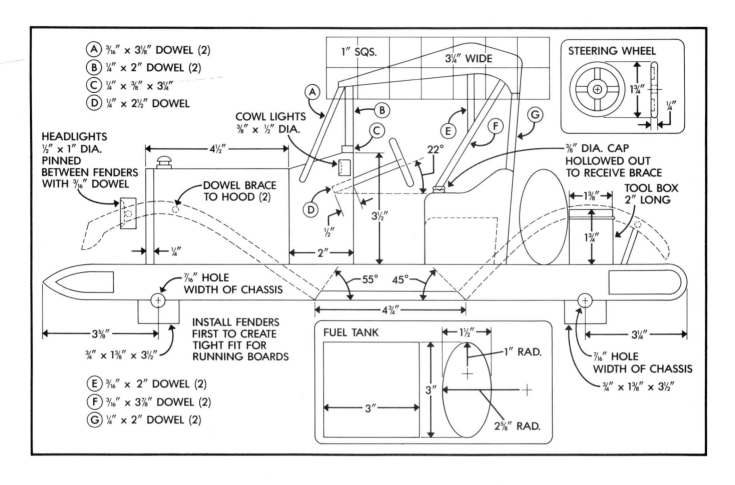

assembly and you may have to blend fenders and running board together for best appearance.

Make the steering wheel and center drill for the ¼-in. dowel that is the steering column. Drill a ¼-in. hole about ½ in. deep in the cowl as detailed to accept the steering column at an angle of about 22 degrees. Glue in the wheel/column assembly in the cowl, then glue cowl and hood to the chassis.

Fit screen wire inside the radiator shell and glue it to the front of the hood. A few small brads will help hold it. Glue on the seat, fuel tank and tool box. Shape the roof, using a pattern made by enlarging the squared drawing. Join the roof to the seat and cowl with the four vertical dowels. This will be a bit tricky and you may want to lengthen the dowels about ¼ in. to fit in holes ⅛ in. deep in roof, cowl and seat back.

When the glue has set, finish installing the other dowels. You might want to pin some of the dowels with small brads or escutcheon pins. Drill pilot holes for them by cutting off the head of one and using it as a bit in your drill motor.

Fit on the fenders, gluing them and perhaps driving small fishing nails through the edges into the chassis as reinforcement. They will look like the ends of bolts or rivets as used on early model cars.

Incidentally, if you glue up stock to make the fenders, remember that ⁵⁄₄ stock is so-called 1¼-in. lumber, but actually measures 1⅛ in. thick. Yes, it is confusing, but the fenders and running boards are 1⅛ in. wide.

Cut and fit a ³⁄₁₆-in. dowel between the front fenders to both support the fenders and hold the headlights. Holes for the dowel can be predrilled in the fenders, as can the holes for the two dowel braces between the front fenders and hood. Vertical braces are run from the back fenders down to the chassis as indicated. You can, with care, drill down through the fenders into the chassis and insert the dowels. When the glue sets, cut off the portion of the dowels that projects above the fenders and sand smooth.

To make the wheels, I modified a fly cutter and shaped the tires with a drill press, cutting just one side first, then mounting the rims in the lathe on a face plate with a plywood disc to back them up, also using a bolt to center the wheel blanks.

No matter how you shape the wheels, you want to create a flat surface ¼ in. wide around the inside against which the spokes are glued. The wheels are ¾ in. thick, so cutting in ¼ in. from each side, in a curve to simulate a tire, will produce the flat surface.

The wheel hubs are cylinders ¾ in. in diameter, 1½ in. long, center drilled ⅜ in. for the axle. You could use pieces of ¾-in. dowel if you can accurately center drill the dowel.

Use the simple jig shown at right to assemble the hub, tire and spokes. The center ⅜ in. dowel is glued in a hole in a scrap of wood about 6-in. square, with spacer blocks glued and nailed at the four corners exactly 5 in. from the center of the dowel. The hub is slipped over the dowel and the tire is fitted inside the blocks. Dowels then are cut to fit snugly between the inside of the tire and the hub. Use glue on the ends of the spokes, tap them in until they are centered in the width of the tire and the hub, then let the assembly sit overnight to make sure the glue sets solidly.

When all four wheels are assembled, glue one on one end of each axle, pass the axles through the chassis, then glue on the other wheels.

Cowl lamps now are attached, and the radiator cap and cap for the fuel tank are made and attached. These can be short pieces of dowel, or you can hand carve to suit. During the assembly you may want to add your own touches, such as louvers on the sides of the hood, and some kind of material on the running boards.

The front of the hood can be painted a dark color to aid in creating the look of a radiator when the screen and shell are attached. Ink or paint lines can be drawn to delineate the separation of the hood parts and its separation from the cowl. A look in a book on antique cars may give you other ideas for authentic touches, such as pin striping along the edges of fenders.

It is your model and you can make it as realistic or fanciful as you wish.

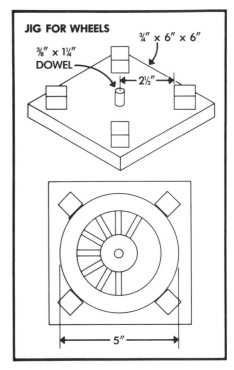

JIG FOR WHEELS

¾″ x 6″ x 6″

⅜″ x 1¼″ DOWEL

2½″

5″

Dovetail-Joint Puzzle

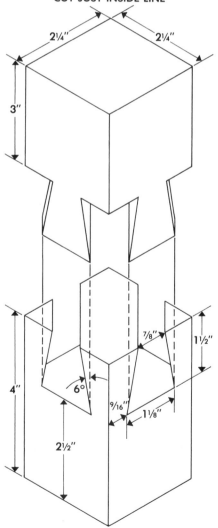

MARK ON ALL FOUR FACES
CUT JUST INSIDE LINE

2¼" 2¼"

3"

7⁄8" 1½"

6°

4" 9⁄16" 1⅛"

2½"

It's an old, "traditional" puzzle that probably has been around since the first woodworker made a dovetail joint, but it's still an interesting project that will baffle nonwoodworkers and even some of those craftsmen who had not had much experience in joinery.

The puzzle can be made almost any size. The two pictured in the photograph are about 7 in. tall. While using the same kind of wood for both parts of the puzzle makes it more difficult to solve, the use of contrasting-color woods makes the puzzle a more interesting item to display. Invariably, someone will pick it up and try to figure out how it is assembled.

Craftsmen who are skilled in the use of hand tools will go that route, while others will use a table saw to more accurately cut the angles. In the latter case, use pieces of stock long enough, say, 8 or 10 in., so your fingers are well clear of the blade. It is quite likely you will have to make several puzzles before you get one that has joinery tight enough to create the "impossible to solve" appearance that will fool the eye.

The flat puzzle in the photograph has a "locking pin" that prevents pulling the two pieces apart until it is removed.

Jigsaw Puzzles

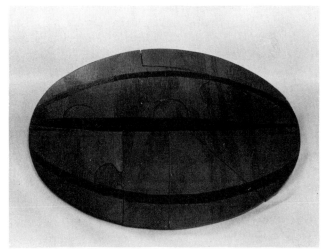 

Watermelon puzzle is cut to represent slices of the fruit and rind. Paint the two sides in appropriate colors. Could this be a football?

Children love puzzles and these games also can help hand and eye coordination. Jigsaw puzzles also are fun for the woodworker to make, and the material required can be picked out of the scrap box. The puzzles shown were cut from 1-in. stock, but lumber up to 2 in. thick can be utilized. Be sure that any material is splinter free, and sand all edges and surfaces, as well as "breaking" any sharp edges with sandpaper.

Almost any shape can be transformed into a jigsaw puzzle, so the four patterns shown on the next page should be considered only the beginning for your selection. Your imagination is the only barrier to creating an infinite number of shapes.

Cutting lines for the various pieces of a puzzle are arbitrary, with the only restriction being that you want to avoid very sharp turns. A fine-blade scroll saw, of course, will make sharper turns and angles than a jig or saber saw.

You also want to make sure that the pieces of a puzzle are different enough so each can be fitted into a puzzle in only one way. Otherwise a child can become frustrated by not being able to assemble a puzzle. Also, too complex a puzzle will discourage a child, while too simple a challenge will cause him or her to quickly lose interest.

For the puzzles shown, start by enlarging the squared drawings to make patterns. Keep in mind that you do not have to follow exactly the cutting patterns shown. I do try to make the various parts appropriate to the shape. For example, the center portion of the apple puzzle somewhat resembles an apple core.

The watermelon demonstrates the inclusion of familiar shapes; basically pieces of watermelon and a piece of the rind. Paint the watermelon in a natural way, with the outside green with dark green stripes and the "inside" red with black seeds. A 1-in. band of green around the edge represents the rind.

The truck is an appealing puzzle as it represents a familiar toy or vehicle seen every day. The wheels are two pieces of the puzzle, but note that each of the wheel pieces has a different shape so they cannot be interchanged.

Animals are another favorite of children and the duck shape has that appeal. You might want to add legs and feet to this puzzle shape. For other animal shapes, you might leaf through a child's coloring book that has large-size drawings of various creatures.

Be sure to use nontoxic paint or enamel on the puzzles. The label on the paint container should state whether or not it is safe for children. Toxic paints have been banned by Federal law for some years, but there may still be old containers of paint on workshop shelves. Even modern finishes, however, may be toxic until they are dry. Again, check instructions on the paint container.

For older children, you can paint the puzzles all one color to add to the challenge of assembling them. For younger children, paint the separate pieces different colors so they are more easily identified.

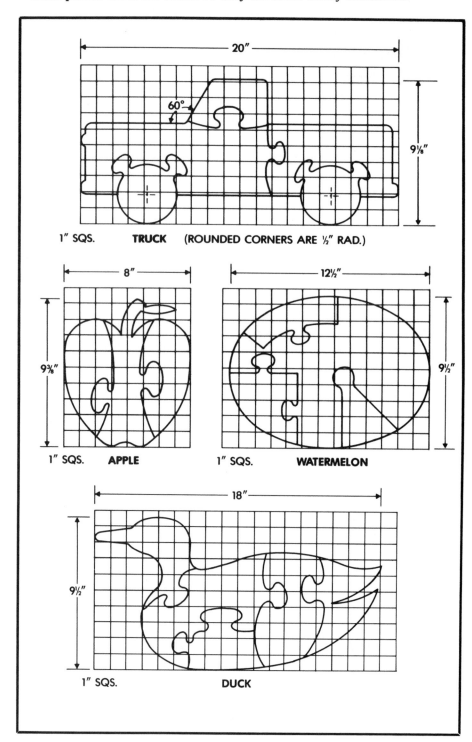

Woodblock Furniture Puzzle

Differing versions of this furniture block puzzle have been around for perhaps 100 years or more. This version possibly has a different number of pieces than others, and one low table requires two smaller shapes to support the top.

Start by enlarging the squared drawings to make full-size patterns. The basic block from which the puzzle is cut measures 2½ × 3 × 5½ in. The wood should be straight grained and free of knots and other defects. Heartwood redwood, for example, is a good choice. It also is soft enough to cut and sand easily.

Follow the step-by-step drawings on the next page, starting by cutting on the 3-in. side to produce pieces 1 and 2, with piece 2 being removed and temporarily put aside.

Piece 1 now is placed on end and cut 2 is made to create piece 3. Note that piece 3 is cut so a table, complete with top, is created.

Piece 2 is positioned as it was when cut from the original block, as in drawing 3, and cuts 3, 4 and 5 are made. This produces pieces 4, 5 and 6, the latter two being pushed out of the block as indicated.

Piece 2 now is rotated 90 degrees, as in drawing 4, and cuts 7 and 8 are made to create chairs 9 and 10, and the two foot stools 7 and 8.

The two chairs, pieces 9 and 10, now are cut as in drawings 5 and 6, after rotating them 90 degrees. These cuts produce the two end tables and the supports for the table top, piece 4.

The various pieces may require a light sanding to remove saw marks, but don't overdo it or the pieces will not fit snugly together when the puzzle is assembled.

Making the puzzle requires a scroll saw with at least a 5½ in. depth of cut, or a band saw with a narrow blade. No finish is recommended,

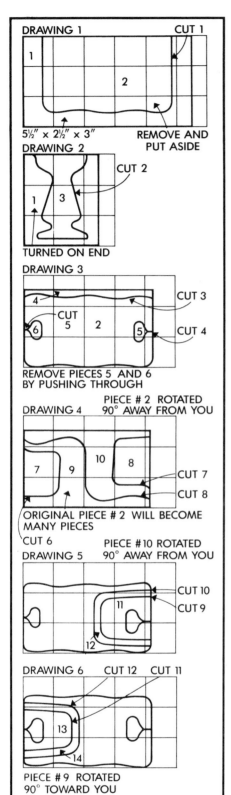

DRAWING 1   CUT 1

1

2

5½″ × 2½″ × 3″   REMOVE AND PUT ASIDE

DRAWING 2   CUT 2

1   3

TURNED ON END

DRAWING 3

4   CUT 3

CUT 5   2   5   CUT 4

6

REMOVE PIECES 5 AND 6 BY PUSHING THROUGH

PIECE # 2 ROTATED
DRAWING 4   90° AWAY FROM YOU

7   9   10   8   CUT 7

CUT 8

ORIGINAL PIECE # 2 WILL BECOME MANY PIECES

CUT 6

PIECE #10 ROTATED
DRAWING 5   90° AWAY FROM YOU

11   CUT 10

CUT 9

12

DRAWING 6   CUT 12   CUT 11

13

14

PIECE # 9 ROTATED
90° TOWARD YOU

Various pieces of furniture are replaced in the block to restore it to its original dimensions.

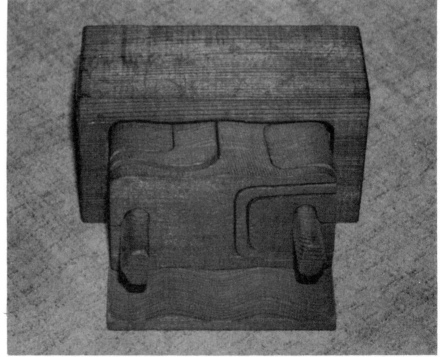

but a penetrating sealer could be used to minimize soiling of the various pieces that will be handled frequently as the puzzle is assembled and disassembled.

Checkerboard Puzzle

Puzzles are always interesting and fun, particularly when there is more than one solution. The challenge then is to find all the possible solutions. This checkerboard puzzle has several.

The puzzle can be made of ⅛-in. plywood, hardboard or even cardboard, and there is no reason that thicker plywood or solid stock cannot be used.

The easiest way to make the puzzle is to cut a piece of ⅛-in. hard-

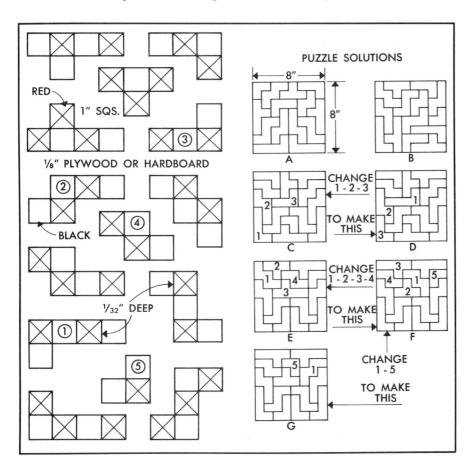

board 8 in. square. With a table or radial-arm saw, cut grooves, 1/32-in. deep on 1-in. centers in both directions so the hardboard has a checkerboard face. Using one of the solutions shown, mark where the cuts should be made. The individual pieces then can be cut out.

When all the pieces are cut, sand the edges. Use a sealer, then paint the squares red and black.

Game of Hearts Cubes

While the basic game of "hearts" played with cubes is quite simple, the fun involved is contagious for young and old alike. The game is simple to make and would be a fine gift for any time of the year.

Make the box as detailed, using 1/2-in. stock for the bottom, sides and ends, with 3/8-in. stock for the lid. A through dado is cut in the one end piece, while stopped dadoes are cut in the sides. Use a stop block on your saw to cut the stopped dadoes, then square up the round end with a wood chisel.

If a router is used for the dadoes, you still will have to square up the stopped ends, or round the end of the lid to fit.

To make the cubes, rip the stock to 1/2 in. square, then use a stop block or gauge on your saw to cut the strip into ½-in. cubes. Use a fine-tooth blade for cutting the cubes, then polish each cube with fine sandpaper. Use a lint-free cloth to wipe a coat of clear urethane finish on each of the six faces of each cube.

When the finish is dry, print one letter of the word "hearts" on each face using a black felt-tip pen.

Assemble the box with glue, then finish it with the same urethane finish as used on the cubes. The box is sized to hold 30 cubes, and this number is sufficient for six cubes each at five tables.

For safety, rip strip to size for cubes, then use stop and push stick to create cubes on table or radial arm saw.

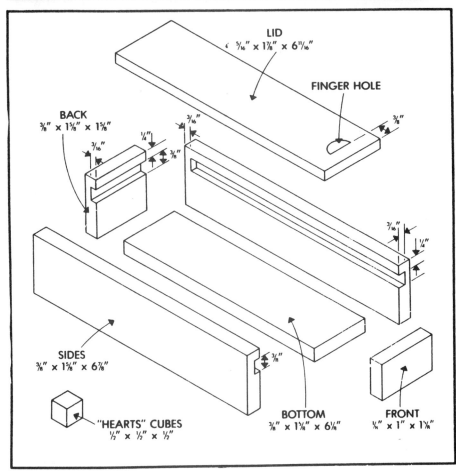

LID
5/16" × 1⅞" × 6¹¹/₁₆"

FINGER HOLE

BACK
⅜" × 1⅝" × 1⅝"

SIDES
⅜" × 1⅝" × 6⅞"

"HEARTS" CUBES
½" × ½" × ½"

BOTTOM
⅜" × 1⅝" × 6¼"

FRONT
⅛" × 1" × 1⅝"

143

Rules For The Game

The game may be played by two, three, five or more players individually, four as partners of two each, or by progressive tables as with some card games.

Six cubes per table are needed, each cube being marked with six letters from "hearts" as previously described. Beginning with the leader, each player in rotation to the left throws the set of cubes only once. Scoring is by the following method, as these combinations are found on the cubes: HE is 5 points, HEA is 10 points, HEAR is 15 points, HEART is 20 points and HEARTS is 25.

If three "H's" turn up, the entire score of the player or partners is cancelled. A player rolling the complete word "hearts" immediately calls out "hearts!" and play at all tables ceases immediately for that round. When playing individually, the score is 100.

When playing as progressive tables, partners (facing each other) talley their scores, each individually. Partners with the highest score move to the next higher table, changing partners so that each person who is moving plays with one of the partners remaining at the next table. The losing couple at the head table moves to the lowest table. Playing continues for a specified number of rounds or for a set period of time. Partners at the top table do not change.

People who play games will see at once that there can be all kinds of variations on the basic "hearts." For example, you can provide more or fewer than six cubes for each player. Winners might get one less cube each game as they move up or, conversely, the losers could get fewer cubes.

Each of the six faces of each cube could be painted a different color for quicker recognition of the letter marked on that color. Colors would be especially useful for younger children.

If the game is made as a gift, lining the box with felt, velvet or flocking would make it rather special for the recipient.

Cribbage and Checkerboard Tables

These two tables have everything needed for playing either checkers or cribbage except chairs and players. Sliding drawers hold the playing materials. Designed for two players, the tables are small and can be easily moved and are convenient to store.

The method of construction is basically the same for both tables, differences being in the size of the top and layout of the drawers. Oak was used throughout except for dark squares of the checkerboard which are walnut. Other species of hardwood also could be used and some interesting effects could be obtained by alternating light and dark woods in the butcher-block top.

Begin construction by cutting the strips for the top, making them a little longer than the finished size. After the strips are glued together, the ends are sawed to the desired dimension. Note that the individual strips are wider than the table thickness. The rough oak varied from 1⅞ to 2 in. and after all the strips were glued, the top was planed to 1½ in. thick.

Drill ½-in. holes in each end and the middle, centered in each strip. It is best to drill these on a drill press using a jig, so all the holes are

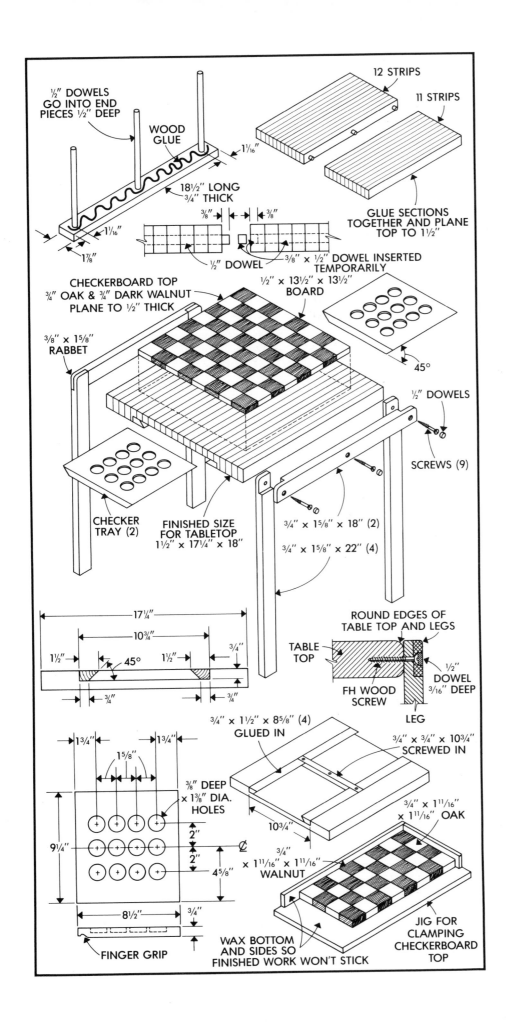

½″ DOWELS GO INTO END PIECES ½″ DEEP

WOOD GLUE

12 STRIPS

11 STRIPS

1¹⁄₁₆″

18½″ LONG
¾″ THICK

1¹⁄₁₆″

1⅞″

GLUE SECTIONS TOGETHER AND PLANE TOP TO 1½″

⅜″   ¾″

½″ DOWEL   ⅜″ × ½″ DOWEL INSERTED TEMPORARILY

CHECKERBOARD TOP
¾″ OAK & ¾″ DARK WALNUT
PLANE TO ½″ THICK

½″ × 13½″ × 13½″
BOARD

45°

⅜″ × 1⅝″ RABBET

½″ DOWELS

SCREWS (9)

CHECKER TRAY (2)

FINISHED SIZE FOR TABLETOP
1½″ × 17¼″ × 18″

¾″ × 1⅝″ × 18″ (2)

¾″ × 1⅝″ × 22″ (4)

17¼″

10¾″

1½″   45°   1½″   ¾″

¾″   ¾″

ROUND EDGES OF TABLE TOP AND LEGS

TABLE TOP

FH WOOD SCREW

½″ DOWEL ³⁄₁₆″ DEEP

LEG

¾″ × 1½″ × 8⅝″ (4) GLUED IN

¾″ × ¾″ × 10¾″ SCREWED IN

¾″ × 1¹¹⁄₁₆″ × 1¹¹⁄₁₆″ OAK

1¾″   1¾″

1⅝″

⅜″ DEEP × 1⅜″ DIA. HOLES

9¼″

2″
2″
4⅝″

8½″   ¾″

FINGER GRIP

10¾″

¾″ × 1¹¹⁄₁₆″ × 1¹¹⁄₁₆″ WALNUT

WAX BOTTOM AND SIDES SO FINISHED WORK WON'T STICK

JIG FOR CLAMPING CHECKERBOARD TOP

spaced the same. In one strip, drill the holes only ½ in. deep. This will serve as one of the end pieces for the top.

The top is assembled in two sections which later are glued together. Glue ½-in. dowels into the end piece described above. Apply glue to the face of this strip, then drive the second strip onto the dowels, apply glue to it and continue until all the strips for that section are in place. Pound the boards down tight with a wood mallet, then clamp

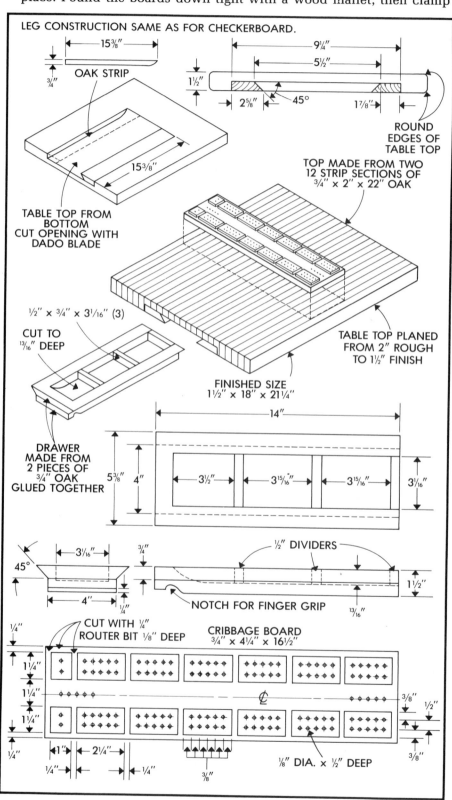

the unit with several clamps. Remove excess glue with a damp rag and let set overnight.

The other section is assembled in the same way with this exception: In the first strip put ⅜-in. lengths of ½-in. dowel flush with one face. Do not glue them as they will be removed later. Insert the ½-in. dowels and assemble the section. When the glue in both sections has set, pry out the short lengths of dowel placed temporarily in the one section, then glue and clamp the two sections together to make the table top.

Once the top is assembled, the ends can be trimmed to size and the top planed. There are several ways the top can be smoothed but I found the easiest and quickest way was to take it to a local woodworking firm and have the top planed on a 24-in. planer to a thickness of 1½ in. The cost was $5.00 and well worth it to me.

Both table tops have a sliding tray or drawer to hold either 12 checkers or two decks of cards and cribbage pins. To make the tray for the checkers, first cut a dado ¾ in. deep × 10¾ in. wide. Tray holders are cut from ¾-in. material with a 45-degree bevel, as shown, which are glued along the edges of the dado. A drawer stop in the center of the opening is held in place with screws. Make two checker trays to fit the opening, sanding as necessary for a smooth fit. Drill holes for the checkers. If the checkers used are larger than the standard 1¼ in. diameter, hole size and spacing will need to be changed. The hole made by the point of the expansion bit used was filled with wood putty. Cut a groove along the bottom of the outer edge to make a finger pull.

The cutout for the cribbage drawer is a stopped dado cut by making repeated passes on a table saw. A stop was mounted on the saw so all the cuts were even. The dado is made longer than the drawer so it is not necessary to chisel out any of the wood.

The drawer is made from two pieces of ¾-in. oak cut to size. Note that the top piece has a 45-degree bevel on each side. These then are glued together and a ¾-in. dado is cut in a manner similar to that used for cutting the dado in the bottom of the top. Dividers are added to provide spaces for cards and cribbage pins.

Oak strips with a 45-degree bevel hold the tray in place. These strips are rounded on one end to conform to the curve left by the saw blade. Here again, sand as necessary to fit the drawer.

Legs for the table are glued to side supports with lap joints. The leg sections then are glued and screwed to the top with countersunk flathead wood screws and the holes filled with wood plugs, glued and sanded flush. Before attaching the legs, round the corners of the top and legs. A rounding bit in a router was used here, but you could merely smooth the corners with sandpaper.

The checkerboard is made from oak and walnut squares. The dimension shown is 1¹¹⁄₁₆ in. Maintaining this precise measurement is not as important as being sure that all squares are exactly the same. If they are not, they will not fit evenly and there will be spaces between them that will need to be filled. A jig for clamping the checkerboard is very convenient, but coat the bottom and sides with automobile wax to prevent the squares from sticking to the jig. I had the checkerboard planed down to ½ in. before gluing it to the top.

Spacing for holes in the cribbage board is as shown in the drawing. The raised effect is made by removing ⅛ in. of surface with a ¼-in. straight face bit in a router. I drilled the holes for the cribbage pins after the top had been sanded and finished. First make a full-size paper pattern for the holes, tape the paper to the cribbage board, then use a drill press for accuracy. Finish the tables as desired.

HOUSE & GARDEN ACCESSORIES

Bluebird House

Simple homes from rough lumber are fine for the bluebird. Bluebird scouts will find the houses and lead the flock to them.

Where possible, as in rural areas, put up a whole "trail" of these houses. They can be close to a road, but put them on posts and trees facing away from the road, or over a hill so they are not visible from the road. Place the houses 5 to 10 ft. above the ground, facing an open space.

There should be a couple of drain holes in the floor of a bluebird house, so that windblown rain will drain away. The hinged roof permits easy removal of the old nest and cleaning for the following year.

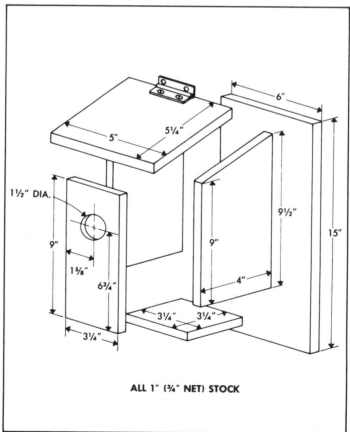

ALL 1" (¾" NET) STOCK

Decorated Bird Feeder

Less than half of a sheet of ⅜-in. exterior-grade plywood is required for this unique bird feeder that is decorated with peasant art. If you want to make more than one, figure about 3½ feeders per full 4 × 8-ft. sheet of ⅜-in. plywood.

Start by cutting the various pieces to size and shape (drawing on next page), and joining them with strips of solid stock as indicated. The peak of the roof is sealed with a strip of do-it-yourself sheet aluminum.

The feeder shown was mounted on a 7-ft. length of 1½-in. pipe, threaded on one end to accept a pipe flange. Wood screws are driven through the flange into the bottom of the feeder. The pipe is set in concrete 12 in. deep. Because squirrels can get into the feeder and eat all the sunflower seeds before the birds do, I had a sheet metal shop make up the squirrel guard shown.

(Editor's Note: We worked up a pattern for the squirrel guard, and it can be made from any lightweight gauge of sheet metal. A piece at least 22 in. square is required, and the L-shape brackets to fasten the guard to the pipe are cut from the waste sheet metal after cutting out the guard.)

When it comes to decorating the feeder, some imagination and creativity can be used, even with the squared drawings shown on page 151. On the original, fast-drying enamel was used for the decorations applied over the base coat. Spar varnish then was applied to all exposed surfaces. The inside of the feeder was left natural, but a clear sealer could be used if you wish.

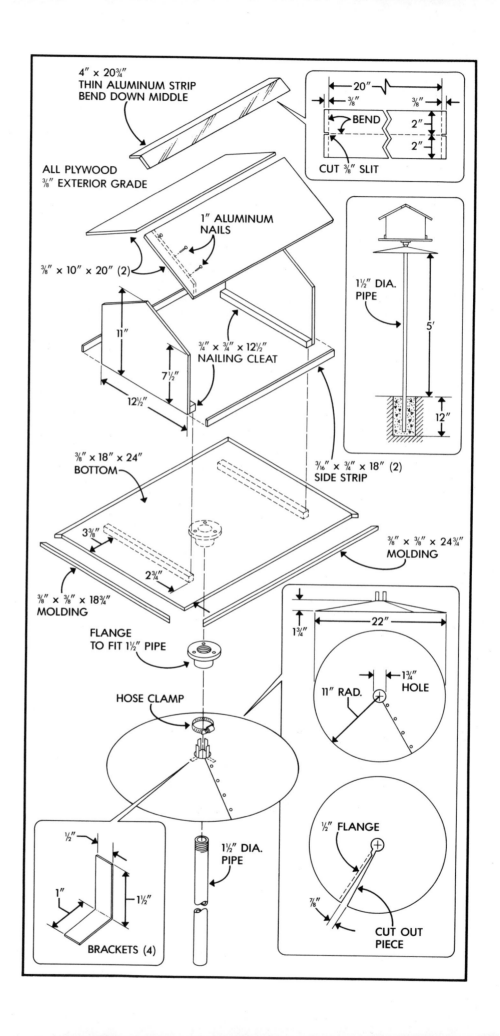

4" × 20¾"
THIN ALUMINUM STRIP
BEND DOWN MIDDLE

ALL PLYWOOD
⅜" EXTERIOR GRADE

20"
⅜"   ⅜"
BEND   2"
2"
CUT ⅜" SLIT

1" ALUMINUM
NAILS

⅜" × 10" × 20" (2)

11"

7½"

12½"

¾" × ¾" × 12½"
NAILING CLEAT

1½" DIA.
PIPE

5'

12"

⅜" × 18" × 24"
BOTTOM

3⅜"

2¾"

3/16" × ¾" × 18" (2)
SIDE STRIP

⅜" × ⅜" × 24¾"
MOLDING

⅜" × ⅜" × 18¾"
MOLDING

FLANGE
TO FIT 1½" PIPE

HOSE CLAMP

22"

1¾"

11" RAD.

1¾"
HOLE

½" FLANGE

7/8"

CUT OUT
PIECE

½"

1"

1½"

BRACKETS (4)

1½" DIA.
PIPE

PATTERN FOR SIDES

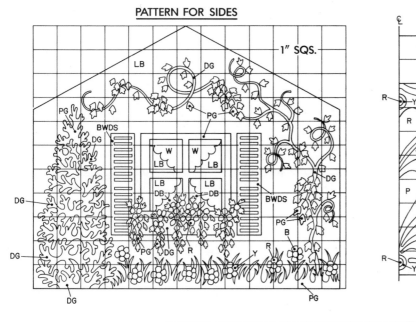

1" SQS.

HALF PATTERN FOR ROOF

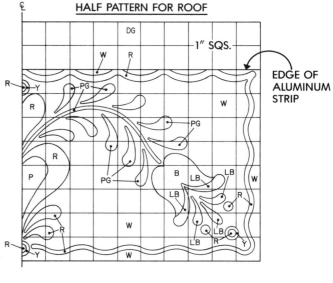

1" SQS.

EDGE OF ALUMINUM STRIP

COLOR KEY

R = RED	B = BLUE	PG = PALE GREEN
P = PINK	LB = LIGHT BLUE	DG = DARK GREEN
W = WHITE	DB = DARK BLUE	Y = YELLOW

BWDS = BROWN WITH DARK STRIPES

BACKGROUND IS WHITE OR LIGHT BLUE

Boot Jack

The boot jack is usually thought of as an antique, but it is just as useful today. Some early ones were made of wood, similar to the reproduction shown here. Others were cast from iron as illustrated.

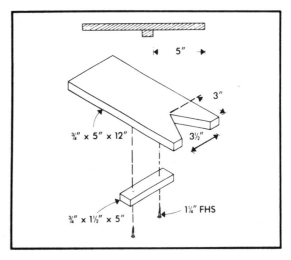

5"

3"

¾" × 5" × 12"

3½"

¾" × 1½" × 5"

1¼" FHS

Cedar Wren House

This wren with its seven parts can be built in a matter of hours, and no finishing is required if you use cedar, as I did, or redwood. Pressure-treated lumber is not recommended, as the preservatives could be dangerous to baby birds.

I used ⅝-in. rough cedar and the dimensions shown are for that stock. If you use thinner or thicker material, adjust for the changes. The main thing is to have an adequate roof overhang. The local Audubon Society provided the ¾-in. diameter size of the entrance hole. A perch is an option, but the reasoning is that wrens don't need it, and it would help predators.

Cut the several pieces of wood to size, making the sides a bit higher than the 5 in. shown, to allow for cutting the angles on the upper and lower edges. The front and back of the house are identical, and each is cut from a piece of stock 6½ in. wide and 7⅝ in. high. Mark a center line, then measure 2½ in. on each side of the line at the bottom. Measure up 5 5/16 in. and draw a line at right angles to the center line. Draw lines from the base to the ends of this line and from the ends of the line to the center of the top of the board.

MATERIALS LIST
(All ⅝-in. stock)
Back, front, 6½″ × 7⅝″ (2)
Side, 5″ × 5″ plus (to allow
    cutting angles) (2)
Bottom, 5″ × 5″ (1)
Roof, 5⅜″ × 6¾″ (1)
   6″ × 6¾″ (1)

Cut on the lines and you will create the two ends for the house. You might want to tack nail the pieces together and cut them both at once to ensure that they are identical. Bore the ¾-in. hole, then nail both ends to the bottom of the house. Cut the two sides, which are identical, with the proper angles at top and bottom. Nail them to the bottom, then nail through the ends into the edges of the sides. Because the stock is somewhat thin and you are nailing near the edges, I recommend drilling pilot holes for the nails to prevent splitting. To permit easy removal of the front of the house so it can be cleaned at the end of the season, I used roundhead wood screws to hold it. Cut the two pieces for the roof, noting that one piece is shorter up and down to allow for the thickness of the stock. A medium-size screweye can be driven into the center of the roof to allow suspending the house from a light chain.

When the house is finished, locate a secluded spot for it next spring. Male wrens usually come into an area first and choose several nesting sites, leaving the final selection to the female. If you do attract wrens to your house, you quite likely will find the same pair returning each year as long as you keep the house clean.

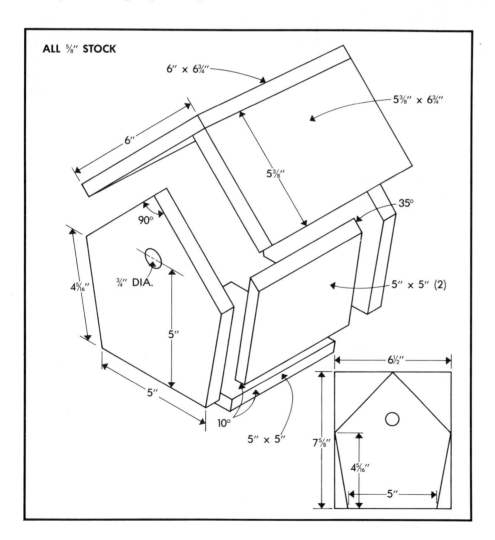

Ram and Lion Planters

The planter boxes are both the same, with differences created by adding the heads of your choice.

Each box is composed of two ends, two sides and a bottom. The ends are identical, except that the "back" end has a hole bored in it to accept a length of rope to simulate a tail for the animal.

The first step is to make patterns by enlarging the squared drawings. The lion head is cut to shape and notched to fit over the end of the planter, then the separate mane is joined to the head with a half-lap notch. Note that the ears are common to both animals.

The heads can be preassembled and painted. Just be sure that the notch in the head portion allows the flat section of the mane, etc. to be joined firmly to the end of the planter.

The sides and bottom of the planter can be ripped for 1 × 8 shelf lumber, or from plywood. In the latter case, it should be the exterior grade to allow for water spilled from plants. Whether solid stock or plywood is used, you may want to cut equally spaced kerfs as on the original to create a "slat" appearance. Or, you might have slat stock on hand that could be used in place of the solid material. The bottom also could be made of slats.

The planter ends also require enlarging a squared drawing to make a pattern.

The originals were stained a light walnut color, then varnish was applied. For outdoor use, you might want to consider paint. The eyes, nose and ears are subject to your own interpretation.

If the planters are to be used outdoors and moved inside when the weather gets cool, you might want to install some heavy-duty casters that would make the units more mobile. Scrap blocks of 2 × 4 should be attached to each leg to hold casters.

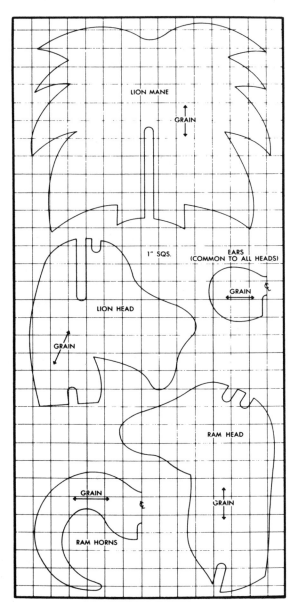

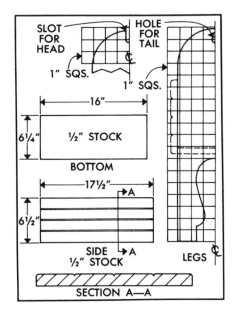

Wall Planter

This wall planter is a charming addition to any room or patio.

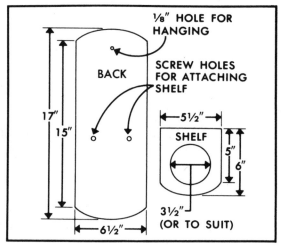

Plant Stand

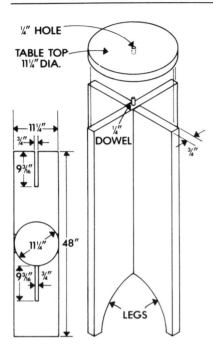

¼" HOLE

TABLE TOP
11¼" DIA.

11¼"

¾"

9³⁄₁₆"

DOWEL

¼"

¾"

11¼"

48"

9³⁄₁₆" ¾"

LEGS

With the rotating top, you can change light angles without touching the plant.

Hanging Planter

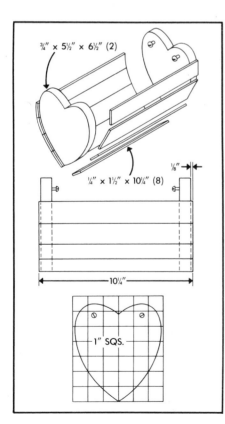

¾" × 5½" × 6½" (2)

¼" × 1½" × 10¼" (8)

⅛"

10¼"

1" SQS.

An attractive alternative to the usual hanging planter or pot, this heart-shape unit can be made from a couple of pieces of 1 × 6 and some lattice stock or strips of wood ripped for ¼-in. material such as exterior-grade plywood.

Enlarge the squared drawing to make a pattern for the ends. Make the pattern of heavy cardboard or ⅛-in. hardboard so you can have it handy for making more than one of the planters.

Cut the two ends to shape, then join them with 10¼-in. lengths of the ¼-in. stock. You might want to make them shorter or longer.

Hang the planter with plastic clothesline or light chain. To ensure water tightness, line the planter with thin sheet metal or heavy plastic sheeting.

Flowerpot Tree

The tree is most easily made by cutting and prefitting the pieces, then disassembling and finishing the pieces prior to final assembly. The shelves swivel so weight can be distributed and plants shown to best advantage.

Start by making the base as shown in the drawing. Butt joint the frame pieces using glue and finishing nails, then round all corners when dry. Plywood or solid stock can be used for the top of the base, and it is attached to the frame with glue and finishing nails. Decide where you want the post located, then drill a 1-in. hole at that spot.

Now, cut the post pieces to length and drill the 1-in. holes where necessary. Use a drill press to ensure the holes are plumb. However, a portable drill will work if you mark and drill carefully.

The shelves can be plywood or solid stock. Before cutting and rasping to shape, stack the shelves and drill the 1-in. hole through all pieces. If you have a band saw, all the pieces can be cut at the same time.

Preassemble the pieces by attaching the bottom post assembly to the base with lag screws. This post will not have to be removed again, so use glue in the assembly. Place the next piece of tubing in the hole of the first post and secure it with sheet metal screws as shown. Add a washer, shelf, then another washer. Now, place the second post piece in position and repeat the procedure. You don't have to drive in the sheet metal screws, but make sure all pilot holes are drilled through the tubing.

When you have the tree assembled, disassemble it in reverse order. Apply finish and, when the pieces are dry, start the reassembly. Be sure to include the plastic laminate washers in the final assembly. The washers will make the shelves fit tight when you drive the sheet metal screws into position.

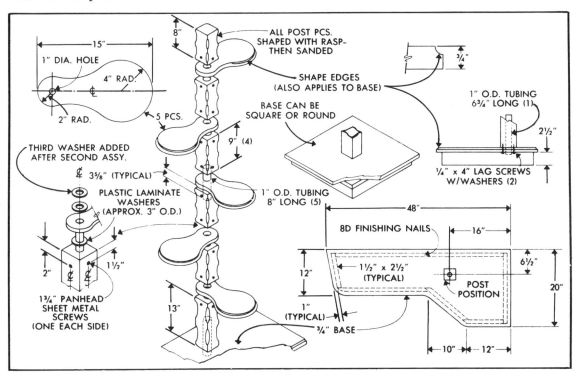

Birdhouse Planter

Begin by cutting five pieces of ½ × 1½-in. stock to the required 18 in. Now glue and brad these pieces to the horizontal strips that measure ½ × 1½ × 10½ in. Make sure you have spaced the pieces the required ¾ in.

The pot shelves are made by cutting the stock to size. Then locate the center of each hole to be cut. Adjust your circle cutter to a 1½-in. radius and make the holes for the pots. When you have made both shelves, glue and screw them in the positions shown.

Make the front of the birdhouse following the dimensions given and drill the 1-in. diameter hole. The two roof pieces are each 5 in. long and have a 25-degree angle cut on each piece where they meet at the peak of the house.

Glue the roof pieces to the top of the house, then attach the assembly to the planter with glue and brads.

Planter Bookends

Cut the five pieces of stock to the dimensions given. Now, mark the top pieces for drilling the 3-in. holes for the flowerpots. With a circle cutter set at a 1½-in. radius, cut the holes for the flowerpots. Finally, glue and brad the pieces together as shown in the drawing and sand all joints and surfaces smooth.

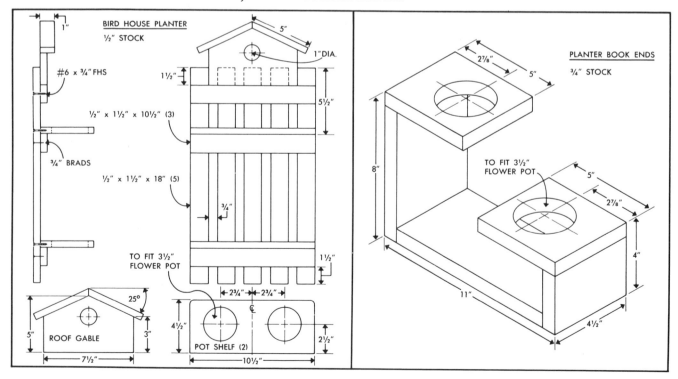

Keep in mind that if you use real flowers with the bookends, you might have to set the bookends in a sunny spot. You may want to opt for artificial flowers or a variety that requires little light.

Antique Plant Stand

Using plywood eliminates the need for edge gluing the stock and, as indicated in the cutting diagram, one 4 × 8-ft. sheet of ¾-in. plywood could provide pieces for three of the plant stands.

The first step is to enlarge the squared drawing to make a pattern for the three legs.

The three shelves are cut to the shapes indicated. If solid stock is used, sand the edges smooth; if plywood is used, cover the edges with veneer tape.

Note that the forward projecting leg is dowled between the two legs that are at right angles to it. You might want to make a "dry assembly" to be sure the notches for the shelves are horizontal. Even better, make two or three patterns and check the assembly for level shelf notches.

Make any adjustments necessary, then dowel and glue the three legs together. Casters were installed in the bottoms of the legs on the original, and should be on any reproduction to make it easy to move around. Be very careful in drilling for the shanks of the casters, as the stock of the legs is relatively thin.

The shelves can be glued and doweled to the legs to create a rigid assembly, or can simply be set in place for easy removal when the stand is cleaned.

The design of the plant stand has interesting possibilities in variations on the original assembly: hinging the two side legs to the center, and having the shelves fitted on dowels that project from the legs, would permit the stand to be disassembled and folded for storage.

Only six pieces are required for assembly of the plant stand: three legs, three semicircular shelves.

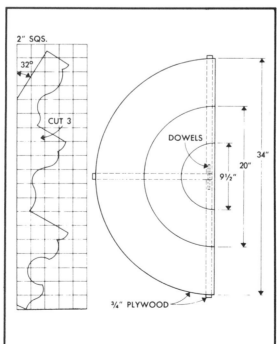

2" SQS.

32°

CUT 3

DOWELS

34"

20"

9½"

¾" PLYWOOD

Plant Shelf

This sturdy shelf unit is designed to fit in front of the fixed half of a sliding glass door, making it ideal for a collection of houseplants. The framing members are narrow enough so they don't overwhelm the plants, and the design adds visual interest.

The vertical supports, and the crosspieces, are stock 2 × 2 material, while the shelves are standard 1 × 10 shelving lumber. The actual dimensions of the 2 × 2s are 1½ × 1½ in., and the 1 × 10s are 9½ in. wide.

All joints are glued and screwed, but some craftsmen might want to notch the uprights and slightly lengthen the crosspieces to allow for the change. Note that the bottom crosspieces are flush with the lower ends of the uprights, while the upper crosspieces are positioned so the top shelves are flush with the tops of the uprights.

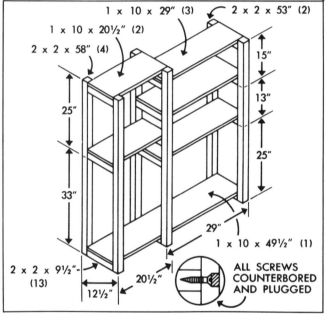

Garden Kneeler

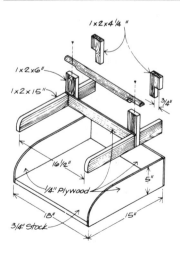

Dimensions can be varied to suit. Foam rubber or scrap-carpet kneeling pad should be large enough to provide comfort to user, and tray section large enough to hold tools you use often. Handle is broomstick or dowel with ends flattened to allow screwing or nailing to uprights.

Garden Basket

Scraps of hardwood or softwood are used for handle, ends and bottom of basket, while ¼-in. dowels are used to create curved portion of two sides.

Start construction by making two patterns from squared drawings, making sure to mark on patterns locations of holes for dowels along a line parallel to edge of each end.

Cut the ends, clamping them together so they will be identical. Keep pieces clamped together and drill dowel holes.

Cut base to size, then cut rabbet in each end.

Use pattern to mark out shape of curved handle. Before cutting curved shape, saw out notches that fit over ends. "Dry assemble" ends and bottom and match handle notches to ends. If any variation, you can adjust for it now.

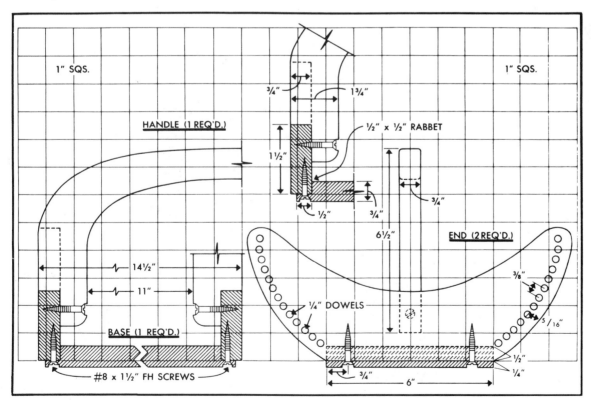

Glue and screw ends to bottom, then measure for lengths of dowels. This dimension will vary according to individual assembly.

If white glue is used, be sure to wipe away any excess with a damp cloth. An even better system is to stain all pieces before assembly. This will ensure that all surfaces will be stained uniformly, and there will be no unseen smears of glue to prevent stain from penetrating wood. If there are any hidden glue stains, they make it impossible for the stain to penetrate and a "blotchy" look is produced.

Holes for the 26 dowels are slightly oversize, to permit sliding dowels through the sides. Dipping the ends in varnish used for finish is as good as applying glue. Also, the varnish blends with the final finish.

Covered-bridge Bird Feeder

Modeled after the covered bridges of New England, this bird feeder has the same quiet charm and look of ageless serenity.

Start construction by making rectangular frames for the sides from ¾ × ¾-in. strips cut from 1-in. stock, which is ¾-in. net. A 15-in. length is nailed to the tops of two 8-in. posts. The lower part of each frame is joined by a panel of ¼-in. exterior plywood.

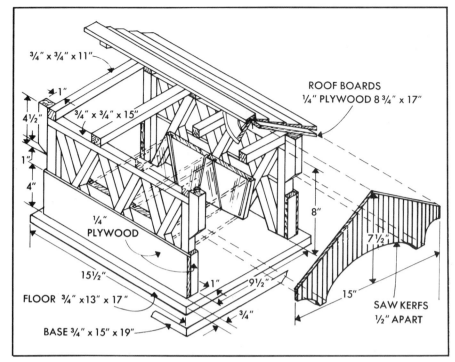

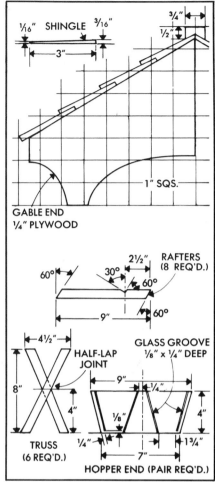

The six X-frames (trusses) are cut and assembled next, from the same ¾ × ¾-in. stock. The half-lap joints are held by waterproof glue and are clamped firmly while the glue sets.

With the trusses set aside temporarily, cut and assemble the two-piece floor/base, using waterproof glue. The two side frames are attached to the floor/base by driving nails up through the base into the posts, and also using waterproof glue. Double check to make sure the side frames are square, then install the trusses, using glue and finishing nails driven up through the base, and down through the top plate of the frames.

Four joists now are cut to length and glued and nailed to the tops of the plates. Space them as shown, one being located on the ends above the posts, the other two located above the joints between the trusses.

Hopper ends are cut next; note that the inner glass of each hopper touches the floor, the two outer glasses are ⅛ in. above the floor. Attach the hopper ends inside the trusses. Cut single-strength glass to fit.

Eight rafters are cut and installed, then wood "shingles" are ripped to the profile shown, cut the full length of the roof and nailed in place. A V-groove is cut in a strip of ¾-in. stock and nailed to the ridge of the roof.

Finish on the original was white paint on the floor and side panels; stain was used on the trusses and the roof.

Smorgasbord Bird Feeder

This oversize feeder holds plenty of food of various kinds for many types of birds.

The glass dadoes on the hopper take a bit of skill using hand tools, but a saw cut and a ⅛-in. chisel will do the job well enough.

Any kind of wood scraps can be assembled for the project and a penetrating sealer will protect it from the weather.

Cut the bottom and end pieces to size and nail them together. Then cut the four hopper pieces to shape; they're all the same size. Chisel out the glass slots in the feed hopper and drill the holes in the suet holder to accept the ⅜-in. dowels. Drill the holes about halfway through the end pieces.

Nail the hopper end pieces to the uprights, and cut dowels to fit between the suet hopper pieces. Cut the dowels long enough to slip in

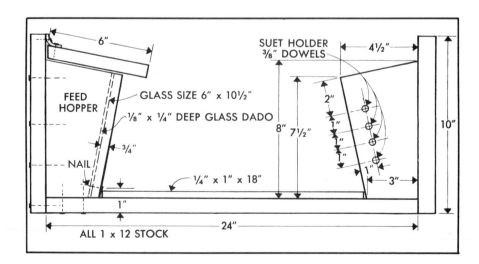

the holes when you slightly bend out the hopper ends. With all the dowels in place, nail the hopper bottom ends in position.

Nail the grain hopper sides in place. About 1 in. from the bottom of the grain hopper, drive a small nail in from the front edges to provide a stop that keeps the glass from sliding all the way down. Cut the grain hopper top and hinge it to the feeder.

Slip the glass down in the slot and tack ¼ × 1-in. strips to each side to prevent birds from scratching so much grain off the sides.

Basic Bird Feeder

A simple bird feeder such as this can be completed using a few hand tools and some ¾-in. wood scraps. First, cut the two end panels to the correct shape and then cut the bottom and two top pieces. Next, rip enough ¼-in. thick strips from a ¾-in. board to rim the perimeter of the top of the feeder's base and fasten them with brads. Mark the center of the base's ends and the center of the end panels. Place each end in a vise, line up the marks and nail from the bottom using galvanized nails. Set the feeder upright, nail on the roof (note one roof half is ¾ in. wider than the other) and fasten a screweye in the middle to hang it.

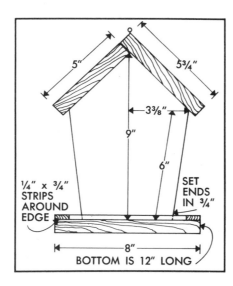

Pagoda Bird Feeders

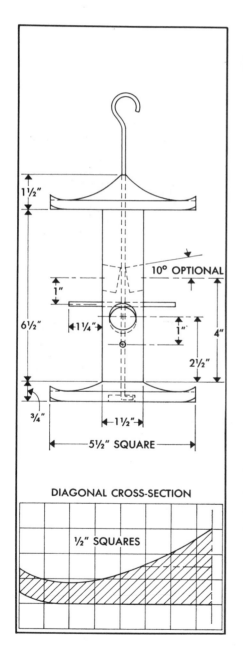

DIAGONAL CROSS-SECTION

½" SQUARES

These feeders require no fasteners other than a length of wire, and can be made in any size. The dimensions given are based on standard lumber sizes, but use whatever you have. Tools required are a saw, lathe and drill press or portable electric drill.

Start by squaring the top and bottom and locating their centers. Mount the squares on a faceplate and turn at slow speed, taking light cuts to avoid splitting corners. Move your toolrest to the faceplate side to turn up the corners. A contour gauge or template is a good idea, especially if you plan to make several of the feeders. The base is turned the same as the top, except the center of the block is left flat for the feeder section to rest on.

Cut the center section to size. The length may be changed to provide for more feeder holes if you wish. Drill the 1-in. holes for the feeders and ¼-in. holes for the perches. The feeder holes may be drilled at a 10-degree angle. Glue 2-in. lengths of ¼-in dowel in the holes for perches, using waterproof glue, then drill the longitudinal hole

Drill feeder holes and holes for the perches on drill press. Size and depth can vary as you wish.

Drill the longitudinal hole in the feeder section from both ends. Make sure they are on center so they meet.

through the center section. Also drill holes in the center of the top and bottom.

Assemble the feeder by threading a corrosion-resistant wire through the three sections after drilling a recess in the bottom piece. Make a 90-degree bend in the wire to retain the three parts on the wire. Bend the other end to form a hook so the feeder may be hung from trees and in other locations.

The feeder may be painted, stained, oiled, varnished or left to weather as desired. Fill the holes with suet, melted suet and seed, peanut butter, soybean meal paste or any other semisolid food, and hang it out for the birds. Since the center section is free, the feeder can easily be filled by laying it on its side and turning it. If you drilled the feeder holes at an angle, it's possible to fill it with dry food, too.

When laid on its side the center of the feeder turns freely for filling the feeder holes with a variety of food.

Squirrel Feeder/Wood Duck Nest

This weatherproof squirrel feeder also makes an ideal nesting box for wood ducks. For these water birds, a small "porch" is added, about 4 in. high. In both cases the opening of 4 in. seems to be about right.

Standard 1-in. stock (¾ in. net) is used for the feeder. Redwood or cedar is good, as both withstand weather well and do not require a finish. Wild animals generally are shy of structures that are finished.

Feed squirrels sunflower seed and shelled raw peanuts.

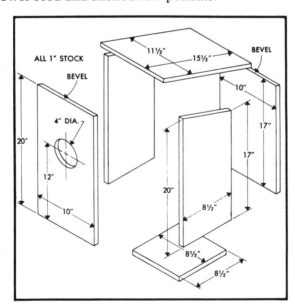

Jumbo Bird Feeder

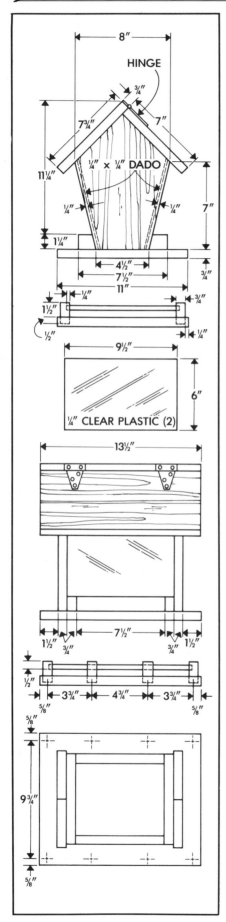

This feeder's generous capacity minimizes the number of trips required to refill it.

Stock 1-in. lumber is used for the feeder, and only the two ends require any special layout; all the other pieces are simple rectangles. The ends and base can be cut from 1 × 10 lumber, while the roof requires 1 × 8 stock.

Cut the two ends to shape, then saw a ¼ × ¼-in. dado ¼ in. in from each edge as detailed, to accept the clear plastic.

Join all pieces with nails or screws, except for the short side of the roof which is hinged to permit filling the feeder.

Fence rails are ¼-in. dowels, the posts are ¾-in. dowels. Each of the four corner posts has blind holes drilled at right angles, centered ½ in. below the top. The four center posts are drilled through with a bit a fraction larger than ¼ in. to allow easy insertion of the rails.

When the rails are attached to all four sides, fasten the 1¼ × 7½-in. cleats to each end, then drive screws up through the base into the cleats to hold the ends. Insert the plastic in the slots to properly space the ends when attaching them to the base.

Make sure the plastic pieces fit snugly but do not bind, then attach the fixed half of the roof and hinge the other half to it with butt or T-hinges.

To make the joint between the roof halves watertight, glue a strip of weatherstripping to the edge of the fixed roof half.

Squirrel-proof Bird Feeder

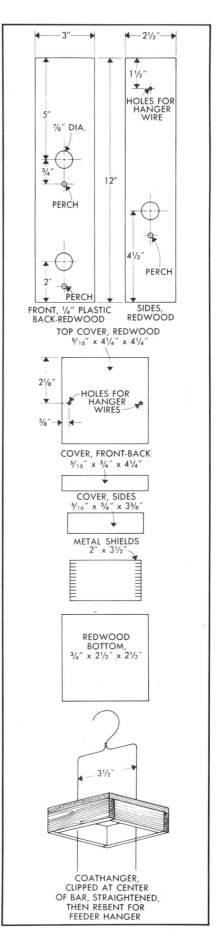

The plastic front plainly shows when it's time to refill, and this is a simple job since the top cover slides up the hanger, allowing you to pour in the seed.

To create ⅜-in. stock, ¾-in. garden-grade redwood is split in half for the sides, back and top cover. The full thickness of the board is used for the bottom, and ¼-in. clear plastic for the front. Perches are ¼-in. dowels 6 in. long, and the metal shields that keep the seeds from spilling out of the feeder holes are made of soft aluminum. An aluminum beverage can works fine.

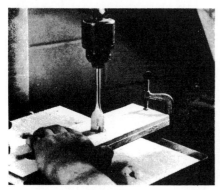

1. Clamp matching sides together and drill holes for feeder tubes and dowel perches. Sides are identical.

2. Attach the plastic front by passing the escutcheon pins through the predrilled holes in the plastic.

The feeder is assembled with waterproof glue and brass escutcheon pins. The hanger for the feeder is made from a coat hanger.

3. Shape the feeder hole shields by bending the aluminum around a 3/4 in. dowel after notching ends.

4. Push the tubes through the matching holes in the sides, front and back. Ends should protrude 1/4 in.

5. Spread the clipped ends and press flat against sides with wood block. "Slot" in tube faces down.

6. Slip the perches in place and secure each one with a bead of waterproof glue.

7. Assemble the removable top cover with waterproof glue and clamp until dry. Round all edges.

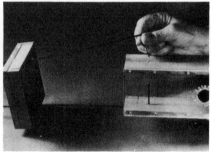

8. Bend hanger wire ends at right angles to each other and fit into holes in sides of feeder.

Barn Birdhouse

The barn birdhouse can be mounted on a post or hung from a beam—either way, it will bring a bit of "country" anywhere.

Material for the barn sides and roof is ¼-in. exterior plywood throughout; ¾-in. exterior plywood is used for the base. The "battens" on the sides are ordinary wooden coffee stirrers, cut to length and butted together where necessary. The shingles shown were cut from regular full-size shakes. Waterproof glue should be used for all joints.

Begin by making full-size cutting patterns for the front, back and sides. Mark the stock and cut pieces to exact size. Mark the front and back for doors and windows, then cut the required entrance hole through the front door area. Trim the doors and windows with stirrer sticks, then add the battens.

Cut ¾ × ¾ × ¾-in. triangular corner braces (glue blocks) from solid scrap, then assemble the barn walls. Use glue and brads, and be sure to keep the walls square. Note that the side walls butt against the front and back walls.

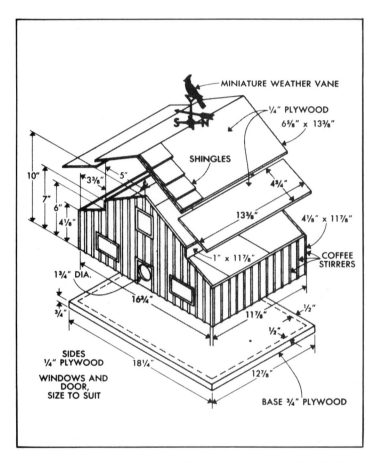

Next, cut all roof and other top pieces. Check the fit, modify as necessary, then glue and clamp in place.

Cut the rectangular base to size, then mount the barn on it. A removable base is recommended. Drill holes through the base at the corners into the bottoms of the triangular braces, then epoxy threaded rod into the triangular braces, using wingnuts with washers to attach the base.

Paint the barn and base the traditional red, windows and door trim white. If you prefer the appearance of an aged barn, you can simulate it with one of the antiquing paints that renders a weathered gray look.

If shake shingles aren't readily available, or if you'd rather make your own shingles scaled to size, rip several lengths of thin, wedge section stock. Cut the strips to small random lengths (all within ¼ in. of each other).

Attach the shingles with brads and glue, and the birdhouse is ready for the final touch—the miniature weathervane (widely available through hobby shops and dollhouse suppliers, or fashion your own).

Jig-sawn Wren House

The height is well within the 6 to 8 in. that wrens like best. The entrance hole is best located about 4 or 5 in. above the floor and the size of the entrance for a house wren need be but ⅞ in. high by 2½ in. wide. Where Bewick's wrens are to be attracted, the entrance hole should be 1 in. high, and for the Carolina wrens it should be 1½ in. high. Wrens can easily enter the home without a perch, but they can make use of the support when building their nests.

Start construction by making patterns by enlarging the squared drawings.

Paint the cutout birds light blue, the flowers yellow and the roof brick red. The house is coated with spar varnish to weatherproof it.

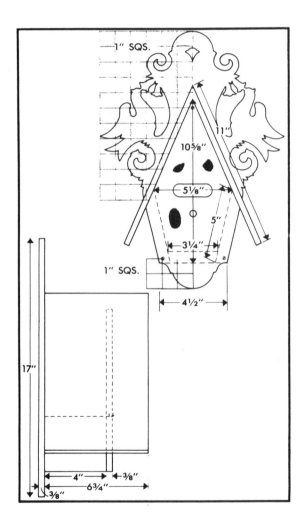

Swedish Wren House

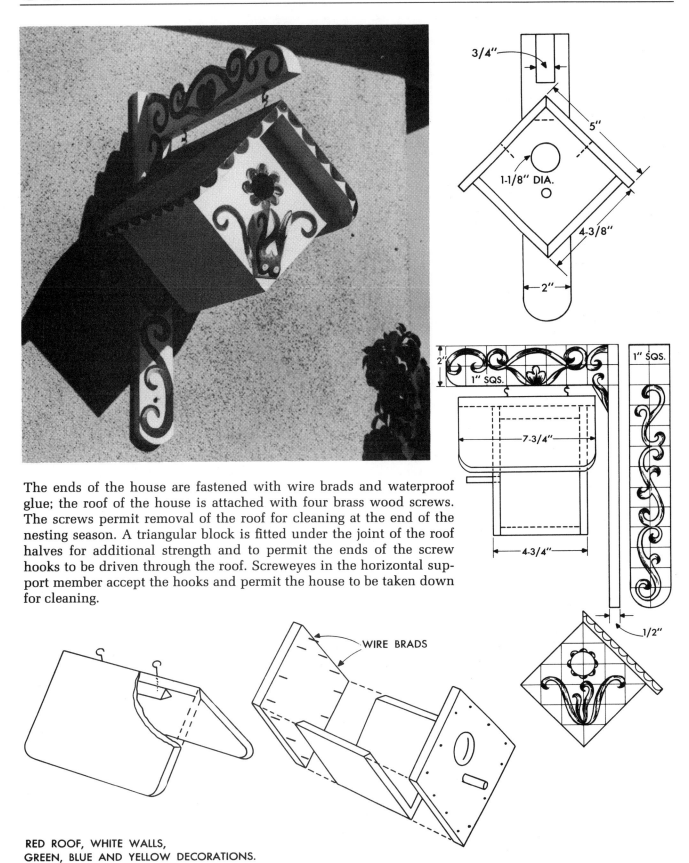

The ends of the house are fastened with wire brads and waterproof glue; the roof of the house is attached with four brass wood screws. The screws permit removal of the roof for cleaning at the end of the nesting season. A triangular block is fitted under the joint of the roof halves for additional strength and to permit the ends of the screw hooks to be driven through the roof. Screweyes in the horizontal support member accept the hooks and permit the house to be taken down for cleaning.

RED ROOF, WHITE WALLS,
GREEN, BLUE AND YELLOW DECORATIONS.

Round Birdhouse

Looking for a new and unique birdhouse design? Try this 12-sided house, using a table saw and joining the pieces with waterproof glue and corrugated fasteners at the top and bottom of the angled strips. The birds will love it, and you'll use up those wood scraps.

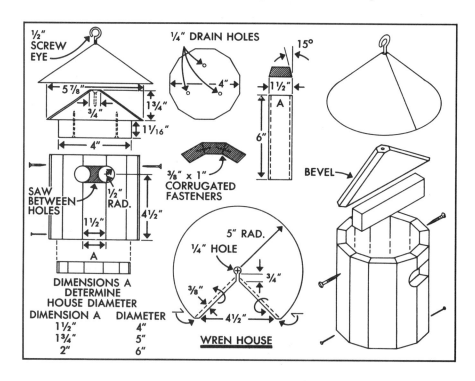

Insulated Doghouse

Hunting dogs should not be kept in the house most of the year, then expected to handle bitter cold weather during the hunting season. Rather, they should live outdoors year-round, but in a well-insulated doghouse. The well-built house is the answer.

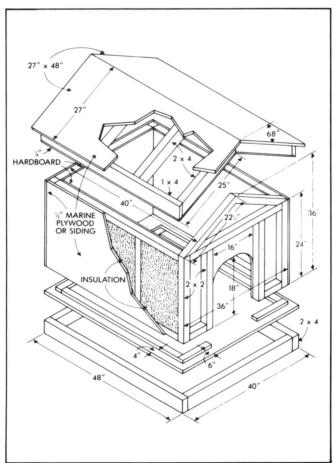

If the house is properly built and insulated, the dog's body heat will keep him warm even during the coldest weather. The insulation also will help keep the house cooler in hot weather.

The doghouse shown is about right for one large dog. A smaller dog will require a scaled-down version.

Build this house from the inside out. The framing is constructed, then the inside is covered with hardboard. Build the base first from 2 × 4s and cover it with ½-in. or thicker marine plywood. Fill it with 3 in. of insulation. The cleats on the top of the base position the house so that it can be swung back on hinges fitted at the rear wall for cleaning.

Wall framing is 2 × 2s, with hardboard applied on the inside. Rigid or batt-type insulation can be used. This is the kind of insulation used between floor joists and applied by stapling to the undersides of the joists. Place the vapor barrier on the "warm" side of the wall, as in a regular house.

There should be a small, screen-covered vent near the peak of the back gable. Cover the outside of the doghouse with siding to match your house.

Frame the roof and cover the underside with hardboard after installing insulation, and cover the roof with shingles to match your home.

Before painting the outside, caulk all joints. Place the doghouse on blocks or a concrete slab. The use of pressure-treated lumber for the base will ensure long life for the house.

Attach a canvas or insulated curtain over the door, with the bottom end weighted to keep it in place.

Grow-pup Doghouse

Building a doghouse for a puppy can be frustrating. If you make the door a size that lets the little rascal walk in and out easily, yet keeps out the weather, very shortly you'll find that he's grown too big to fit through the door.

This doghouse, besides being simple to construct, has an adjustable door that "grows up" with your pet. The center panel is removable, being held at the top by a single screw, and on each side near the bottom by wooden cleats inside and outside.

As the dog grows taller, you remove the screw and the cleats and saw off the top edge of the center panel. When you replace the panel you'll have to move up the cleats.

Construction of the doghouse is straightforward, using ⅝-in. exterior-grade plywood or particleboard. Nail the floor to the 4 × 4 skids, then nail the floor cleats ⅝ in. in from the edges and ends of the floor.

Cleats now are nailed to the upper edges of the sides, front and back. Note that the front can be cut from one piece; it may be necessary to fit strips behind the joints to cover the saw kerfs.

Nail on the back and two sections of the front, then fit on the roof and nail it in place. Attach the adjustable panel, then cover the roof with tarpaper or shingles to match those on your house.

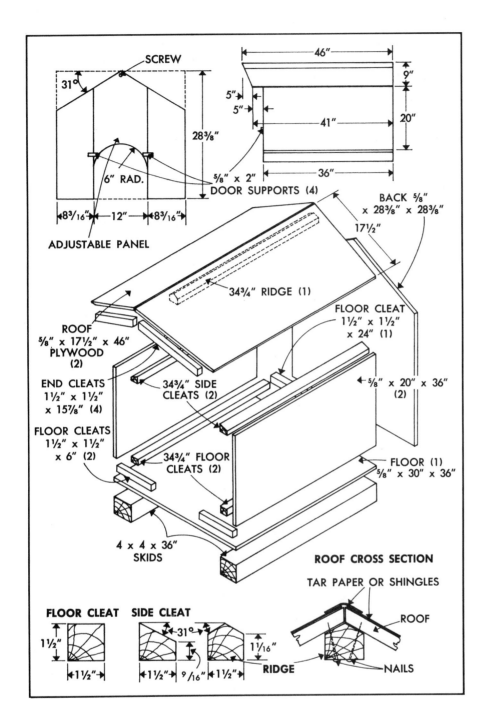

SCREW

31°

28⅜"

6" RAD.

8³⁄₁₆" — 12" — 8³⁄₁₆"

ADJUSTABLE PANEL

46"

9"

5"
5"

41"

20"

36"

⅝" × 2"
DOOR SUPPORTS (4)

BACK ⅝"
× 28⅜" × 28⅜"

17½"

34¾" RIDGE (1)

FLOOR CLEAT
1½" × 1½"
× 24" (1)

ROOF
⅝" × 17½" × 46"
PLYWOOD
(2)

END CLEATS
1½" × 1½"
× 15⅞" (4)

34¾" SIDE
CLEATS (2)

⅝" × 20" × 36"
(2)

FLOOR CLEATS
1½" × 1½"
× 6" (2)

34¾" FLOOR
CLEATS (2)

FLOOR (1)
⅝" × 30" × 36"

4 × 4 × 36"
SKIDS

ROOF CROSS SECTION

TAR PAPER OR SHINGLES

FLOOR CLEAT

SIDE CLEAT

1½"

1½"

31°

1½" 9⁄16" 1½"

1¹⁄₁₆"

ROOF

RIDGE

NAILS

Three Sawhorses

The kind of sawhorse you build for yourself depends on how you will use it.

If you need a multi-purpose sawhorse, one that can be used for a step stool anywhere in the house, as well as for supporting lumber to be cut and worked, then the step stool unit is for you. It can be made of standard 1 × 12 white pine shelving, if you'd like to stain or paint it for appearance, or you can use ¾-in. plywood.

The first step is to cut the ends and top to size. Bore ⅜-in. holes in the ends as indicated, then saw out the V-shape notches. Cut the hand hole in the top by boring two 1-in. holes and sawing between them. Round and smooth the cut edges. Notch the upper edges to accept the side braces, then assemble the horse with glue and nails or screws.

Very strong in relation to its weight, this "standard" sawhorse has 2 x 6 for top, legs cut from 1 x 6 stock.

Multipurpose stepstool sawhorse is favorite among many homeowners because of its versatility.

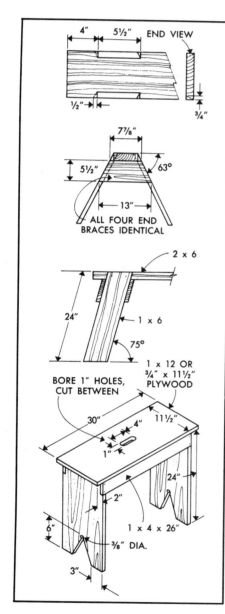

Legs are attached to top at an angle, which requires chiseling bevels in four places on top 2 x 6.

Quick and easy is sawhorse assembled from 2 x 4s and brackets from the hardware store. It readily disassembles.

If you use a sawhorse frequently, and both inside and out, the "standard" would be your choice. It is very strong for its weight, and a pair of them can handle anything from a hollow core door to a roof truss.

The 2 × 6 top is notched and angled so the four legs are splayed to provide a maximum of support. Four braces are used, one inside and one outside each pair of legs.

For occasional use, you can't beat sawhorses assembled from lengths of 2 × 4 and metal brackets. They are easily taken apart for storage, or to toss in the trunk of the car. The brackets are available from hardware stores, lumber dealers and do-it-yourself centers.

Tool Caddy/Step Stool

All the parts, except the saw scabbard, are cut from ¾-in. exterior-grade fir plywood and are assembled with waterproof glue and 6-penny nails. The best bet is to shape the two sides first, then add the bottom and the two dividers.

Adding the top, the step and the front ledge completes the main project. To make the saw scabbard, make an outline of the handsaw you wish to carry with you, then cut ½ × ½-in. strips to match the outline. Cut the cover of ¼-in. plywood to fit the scabbard frame you have designed. Attach the strips with waterproof glue and 6-penny nails, and do the same for the plywood.

To finish the tool caddy/step stool, apply two coats of sealer, with a light sanding between applications. A final touch you might want to add is to cover the step and top with indoor-outdoor carpeting.

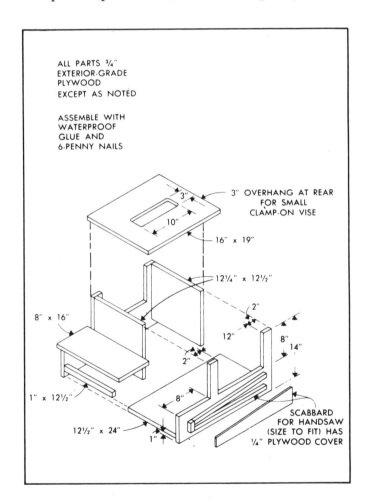

ALL PARTS ¾"
EXTERIOR-GRADE
PLYWOOD
EXCEPT AS NOTED

ASSEMBLE WITH
WATERPROOF
GLUE AND
6-PENNY NAILS

3" OVERHANG AT REAR
FOR SMALL
CLAMP-ON VISE

3"

10"

16" × 19"

12¼" × 12½"

8" × 16"

2"

12"

8"
14"

2"

1" × 12½"

8"

12½" × 24"

1"

SCABBARD
FOR HANDSAW
(SIZE TO FIT) HAS
¼" PLYWOOD COVER

Log Basket

The dimensions given need not be considered ideal; they can be increased or decreased to suit the kinds of logs you burn in your fireplace. We would caution against making the basket too large or you'll end up needing wheels to move it.

Begin the assembly by making the two ends that consist of 2 × 4s with half-lapped joints at the bottom corners. Use glue and screws from inside the corner joints—the screws you see in the photo are the two that are driven into the bottom spacers on each side.

Mark out and cut the curved shapes on the inside of each U-shape assembly of 2 × 4s, then sand smooth.

When assembling the various components, start at the bottom on each side and attach the two 2 × 4 spacers with glue and screws driven through from outside. Next, shape the two top crosspieces with

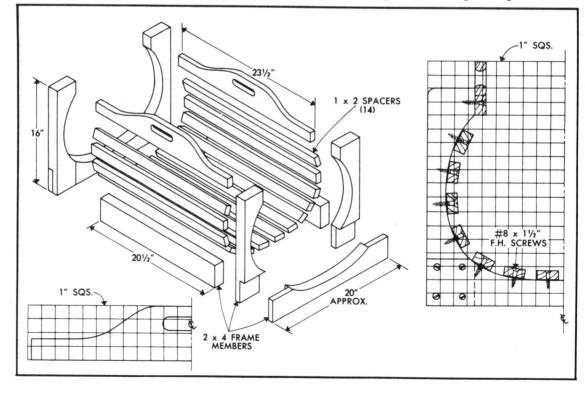

their handholds. Attach them to the tops of the end assemblies with glue and one no. 8 × 2-in. screw at each end.

Finally, cut fourteen intermediate spreaders and attach them around the insides of the ends, spacing them equally. Start at the top and work down, so that if there is any minor misspacing of the spreaders it will be at the bottom.

One screw, plus glue, is used in each end of each of the spreaders. The spacing between the two top spreaders and the crosspieces with the handholds is a bit more than the spacing between the individual spreaders. If you want this space to be less, add two more spreaders and space them a little closer together.

Log Bin

There are no dimensions given on the drawing as the log bin should be made to suit the size of logs you use. This bin was made with 1 × 12 pine, but you may want to use plywood or another stock of your choice.

The easiest method of construction is to first glue and screw the legs to the bottom. The legs can be "ready made" or you can turn your own on a lathe. Now, cut the sides to length and round the front edges. Or, you may want to create your own design to complement the decor in your home. Attach the sides to the back using glue and no. 10 × 1¼-in. wood screws. Finally, glue and screw the bottom assembly to the sides. Wipe away any excess glue that seeps from the joints, as it will not accept stain when dry. The bin shown was stained a dark walnut color, then given several coats of clear lacquer for protection.

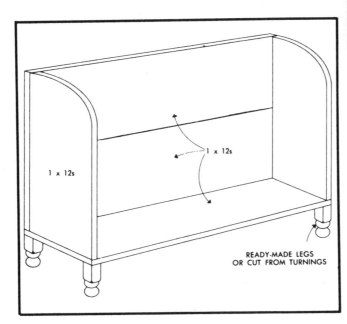

1 x 12s

1 x 12s

READY-MADE LEGS
OR CUT FROM TURNINGS

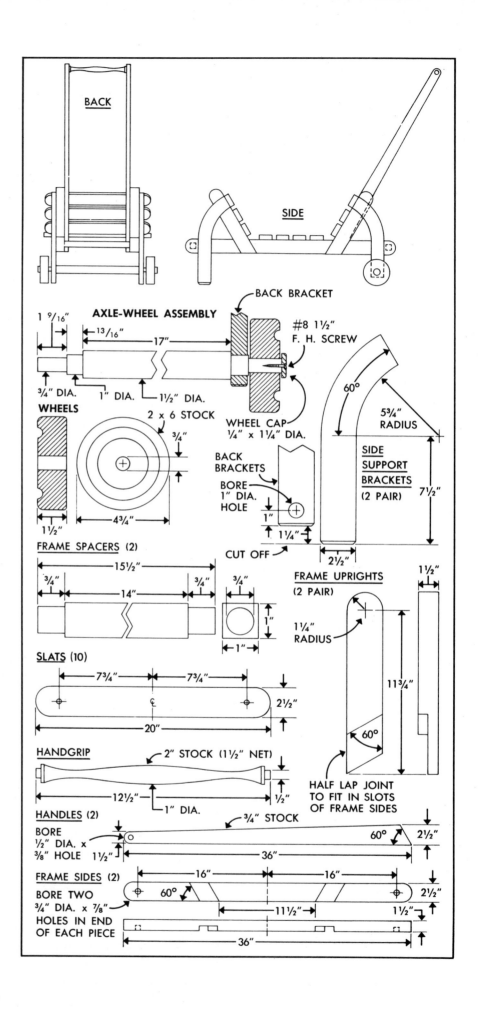

BACK

SIDE

BACK BRACKET

AXLE-WHEEL ASSEMBLY

1 9/16"
13/16"
17"
#8 1½" F. H. SCREW
¾" DIA.
1" DIA.
1½" DIA.
2 x 6 STOCK
WHEEL CAP ¼" x 1¼" DIA.

WHEELS

¾"
4¾"
1½"

BACK BRACKETS
BORE 1" DIA. HOLE
1"
1¼"

CUT OFF

60°
5¾" RADIUS
SIDE SUPPORT BRACKETS (2 PAIR)
7½"
2½"

FRAME SPACERS (2)

15½"
¾"
14"
¾"
¾"
1"
1"

FRAME UPRIGHTS (2 PAIR)

1½"
1¼" RADIUS
11¾"
60°
HALF LAP JOINT TO FIT IN SLOTS OF FRAME SIDES

SLATS (10)

7¾"
7¾"
C
2½"
20"

HANDGRIP

2" STOCK (1½" NET)
½"
12½"
1" DIA.

HANDLES (2)

BORE ½" DIA. x ⅜" HOLE 1½"
¾" STOCK
60°
2½"
36"

FRAME SIDES (2)

BORE TWO ¾" DIA. x ⅞" HOLES IN END OF EACH PIECE
16"
16"
60°
2½"
11½"
1½"
36"

Log Cart

Start by cutting two frame sides and making half-lap joints in each piece (drawing at left). Each is drilled to accept frame spacers. Next, make frame uprights and cut half-lap joint in each so it fits snugly with frame side. Glue and screw together.

The frame spacers are a full 1 × 1-in. stock, ends turned to ¾ in. in diameter. Attach spacers between frame sides with glue and no. 8 × 2-in. screws driven up through bottom of sides and into ends of spacers.

Wheels are rough cut from 2 × 6 stock, chucked in a lathe and turned to required diameter. Outside face of each wheel is dished for appearance. The wheel axle is a 2 × 2 turned to 1½-in. diameter; then to 1-in. diameter where it rests in side support brackets and ¾-in. diameter to support wheels.

To make side support brackets identical, saw all four at once by stacking them. Back supports are cut slightly shorter and drilled to accept axle. Glue and screw supports to frame assembly, installing axle between rear supports. Fit wheels on axle; screw wheel cap to each axle end.

Handle is simple turning. Attach handle and bed slats. Finish as desired.

Boot and Mitten Dryer

Assembled without fasteners, this handy rack can be taken apart at the end of the snow season and stored in a small space. In use, it can be hung on a wall or door, or set on the floor. Ideally it should be located near a radiator or heat register.

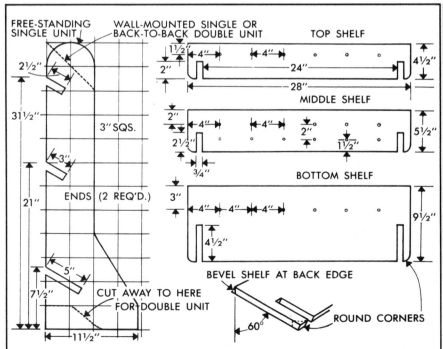

The rack can be extended for greater capacity, allowing about 8 in. for each pair of boots. A large, freestanding rack can be made by building two identical units and joining them back to back with flat mending plates on the end. A plastic mat on the floor under the rack, topped with a cotton rug or towel, catches melted snow.

Cut the pieces for the rack from 1-in. solid stock or ¾-in. plywood. The slots should be cut to fit loosely so the shelf ends will not split off or break. The back edges of each shelf can be beveled to 60 degrees for a neater fit against the wall, but this is not necessary if the unit is freestanding. The weight of the shelves will hold them in place in the rack.

Cut pegs from ½-in. dowel as follows: top shelf (hats, scarves, shoes) six pieces 6 in. long; middle shelf (mittens) twelve pieces 9 in. long; bottom shelf (boots) six pieces 12 in. long. Drill ½-in. holes almost through the shelves and sand the ends of the pegs round.

Paint or stain and varnish the pieces before final assembly so they are waterproofed. If plywood is used, fill the edges with wood putty or use veneer-tape. Do not paint or varnish the portion of each peg that fits in the holes in the shelves.

Four Sundials

Designing and making sundials, called "dialing," is an ancient craft that can be practiced with modern tools and materials. If you accurately lay out and assemble the dials, these "solar clocks" can be almost as accurate as an electric timepiece.

There are four basic types of sundials, and each can be adapted to your particular home setting and artistic tastes. All sundials consist of two basic parts, the gnomon (NO-mun) that casts the shadow, plus a dial that indicates the hours. For all sundials it is necessary that the gnomons point as accurately as possible toward the celestial pole, which is the North Star.

To make any of the sundials, you will need a protractor, and one that has half-degree increments will permit a more accurate layout. You will need a good straightedge and an atlas in which you can find your latitude and longitude.

Draw the dial on paper first so you can see how large you want the finished product to be. The larger the dial, generally the easier it is to make it accurate. If you make a full-size drawing, you also can determine how the various parts fit together.

Because sundials are subject to sun and weather, use a weather-resistant wood such as cedar or redwood, and use waterproof glue and brass fasteners when assembling them. Coat all surfaces of the finished project with an exterior-grade urethane varnish.

Horizontal sundials are probably the most familiar, and these traditional styles consist of a circular dial to which is fastened a triangular gnomon that projects at right angles to the surface of the dial. The angle of the upper edge of the dial is equal to the degrees of your latitude. The more accurately this angle is cut, the more accurate your sundial will be.

Cut the circular dial, then mark a baseline across the center of the dial. A noon line is marked at right angles to the baseline, at the center

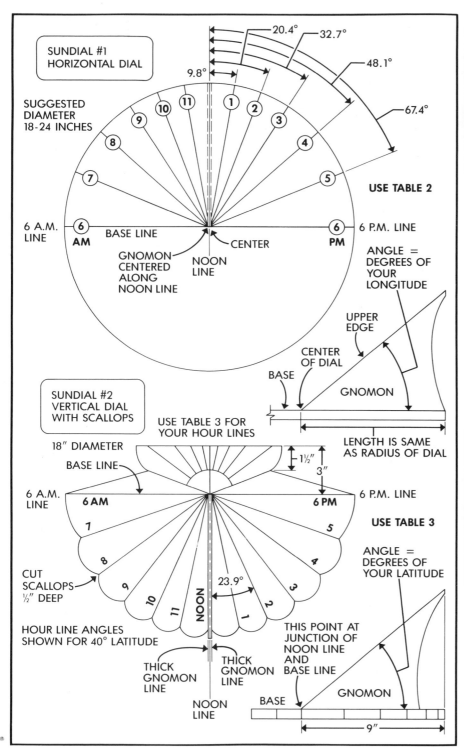

SUNDIAL #1 HORIZONTAL DIAL

SUGGESTED DIAMETER 18-24 INCHES

20.4°
32.7°
9.8°
48.1°
67.4°

USE TABLE 2

6 A.M. LINE

BASE LINE

GNOMON CENTERED ALONG NOON LINE

CENTER

NOON LINE

6 P.M. LINE

ANGLE = DEGREES OF YOUR LONGITUDE

UPPER EDGE

CENTER OF DIAL

BASE

GNOMON

LENGTH IS SAME AS RADIUS OF DIAL

SUNDIAL #2 VERTICAL DIAL WITH SCALLOPS

USE TABLE 3 FOR YOUR HOUR LINES

18" DIAMETER

BASE LINE

1½"
3"

6 A.M. LINE

6 AM

6 PM

6 P.M. LINE

USE TABLE 3

23.9°

ANGLE = DEGREES OF YOUR LATITUDE

CUT SCALLOPS ½" DEEP

HOUR LINE ANGLES SHOWN FOR 40° LATITUDE

THICK GNOMON LINE

THICK GNOMON LINE

NOON LINE

NOON

THIS POINT AT JUNCTION OF NOON LINE AND BASE LINE

BASE

GNOMON

9"

Horizontal sundial is "traditional," gnomon pointing generally north, then gnomon shadow is set to correct time.

Vertical sundial is faced due south, should be shimmed so that it does if wall is not truly facing south.

of the baseline. The noon line locates the gnomon. From the noon line/baseline intersection, mark the appropriate hour, half-hour and even quarter-hour lines, using the angles listed in Table 2 on page 186.

If you want to accurately draw in quarter-hour lines, you will have to plug in the appropriate hour-angle degrees from Table 1 into the formula: A = arc tan [(sin L) × (tan H)] where A is the angle you want to draw from the noon line, L is the degrees of your latitude, H is the hour angle from Table 1 and arc tan is the inverse of a tangent.

TABLE 1

Part of Hour	Hour Angle Degrees
One hour	15
Half hour	7.5
Quarter hour	3.75
Five minutes	1.25
One minute	.25
30 seconds	.125

This table shows the angular amount of the sky that the sun traverses in a given amount of time.

TABLE 2. HORIZONTAL DIAL

Hour Line

Latitude	5:30 6:30	5:00 7:00	4:30 7:30	4:00 8:00	3:30 8:30	3:00 9:00	2:30 9:30	2:00 10:00	1:30 10:30	1:00 11:00	12:30 11:30
					Angles from Noon "Zero Line"						
30	75.2	61.8	50.4	40.9	33.1	26.6	21.0	16.1	11.7	7.6	3.8
31	75.7	62.5	51.2	41.7	33.9	27.3	21.6	16.6	12.0	7.9	3.9
32	76.0	63.2	52.0	42.5	34.6	27.9	22.1	17.0	12.4	8.1	4.0
33	76.4	63.8	52.7	43.3	35.4	28.6	22.7	17.5	12.7	8.3	4.1
34	76.8	64.4	53.5	44.1	36.1	29.2	23.2	17.9	13.0	8.5	4.2
35	77.1	65.0	54.2	44.8	36.8	29.8	23.8	18.3	13.4	8.7	4.3
36	77.4	65.5	54.8	45.5	37.5	30.4	24.3	18.7	13.7	9.0	4.4
37	77.7	66.0	55.5	46.2	38.1	31.0	24.8	19.2	14.0	9.2	4.5
38	77.9	66.5	56.1	46.8	38.7	31.6	25.3	19.6	14.3	9.4	4.6
39	78.2	66.9	56.6	47.5	39.4	32.2	25.8	20.0	14.6	9.6	4.7
40	78.4	67.4	57.2	48.1	40.0	32.7	26.3	20.4	14.9	9.8	4.8
41	78.7	67.8	57.7	48.8	40.5	33.3	26.7	20.7	15.2	10.0	4.9
42	78.9	68.2	58.2	49.2	41.1	33.8	27.2	21.1	15.5	10.2	5.0
43	79.1	68.6	58.7	49.8	41.6	34.3	27.6	21.5	15.8	10.4	5.1
44	79.3	68.9	59.2	50.3	42.2	34.8	28.1	21.9	16.1	10.5	5.2
45	79.5	69.2	59.6	50.8	42.7	35.3	28.5	22.2	16.3	10.7	5.3

Find your latitude to nearest degree in left hand column, and the hour line which you wish to draw across the top. Read the angle to draw by cross matching latitude and hour.

(*Editor's Note: Those of us who have forgotten our geometric equations will have to settle for half-hour increments and guess at the time between.*)

The ends of the baseline are the 6 AM and 6 PM hour lines. Mount the gnomon exactly on the noon line and perpendicular to the dial. If the gnomon is more than ⅛ in. thick, make two noon lines separated by the thickness of the gnomon and mark the hour lines from each side of the gnomon.

Vertical sundials essentially are horizontal sundials that have been rotated 90 degrees. The gnomon makes an angle to the face of the dial 90 degrees minus the number of degrees in your latitude. For example, if you are in the middle of the United States at 40 degrees latitude, the upper edge of the gnomon would be 50 degrees in relation to the dial. Like the horizontal dial, start with a baseline and a noon line, but use the hour angles from Table 3. The vertical dial is mounted to face due south. If the wall is not facing due south, shim one edge of the dial until it does face true south.

TABLE 3. VERTICAL DIAL

Hour Line

Latitude	5:30 6:30	5:00 7:00	4:30 7:30	4:00 8:00	3:30 8:30	3:00 9:00	2:30 9:30	2:00 10:00	1:30 10:30	1:00 11:00	12:30 11:30
					Angles from Noon "Zero Line"						
30	81.4	72.8	64.4	56.3	48.8	40.9	33.6	26.6	19.7	13.1	6.5
31	81.3	72.6	64.2	56.0	48.5	40.6	33.3	26.3	19.5	12.9	6.4
32	81.2	72.5	64.0	55.6	47.9	40.3	33.1	26.1	19.4	12.7	6.4
33	81.2	72.5	64.0	55.8	47.9	40.0	32.8	25.8	19.2	12.7	6.3
34	81.1	72.3	63.7	55.5	47.5	40.0	32.8	25.8	19.2	12.6	6.3
35	80.9	71.9	63.2	54.8	46.9	39.3	32.2	25.3	18.7	12.4	6.2
36	80.8	71.7	62.9	54.5	46.5	39.0	31.8	25.0	18.5	12.2	6.1
37	80.6	71.5	62.6	54.1	46.2	38.6	31.5	24.8	18.3	12.1	6.0
38	80.5	71.2	62.3	53.8	45.8	38.2	31.2	24.5	18.1	11.9	5.9
39	80.4	71.0	61.9	53.4	45.4	37.9	30.8	24.2	17.8	11.8	5.8
40	80.2	70.7	61.6	53.0	45.0	37.5	30.4	23.9	17.6	11.6	5.8
41	80.1	70.5	61.2	52.6	44.5	37.0	30.1	23.5	17.4	11.4	5.7
42	80.0	70.2	60.9	52.2	44.1	36.6	29.7	23.2	17.1	11.3	5.6
43	79.8	70.0	60.5	51.7	43.6	32.2	29.3	22.9	16.9	11.1	5.5
44	79.6	69.6	60.1	51.2	43.2	35.7	28.9	22.6	16.6	10.9	5.4
45	79.5	69.3	59.6	50.8	42.7	35.3	28.5	22.2	16.3	10.7	5.3

Find your latitude to nearest degree in left hand column, and the hour line which you wish to draw across the top. Read the angle to draw by cross matching latitude and hour.

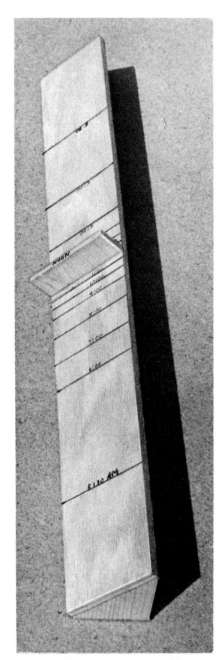

Polar sundial is placed so upper edge of face is to the north. Adjust position until it reads correctly.

For smaller time divisions on a vertical sundial, use the formula: A = arc tan [(cos L) × (tan H)] where the letters mean the same as in the formula for horizontal dials.

Polar sundials essentially are inclined planes. Cut the supporting wedges so the surface of the dial is inclined toward the celestial pole. The angle of the face is the same as your latitude. The gnomon is perpendicular to the dial, and its upper edge must be parallel to the surface of the dial.

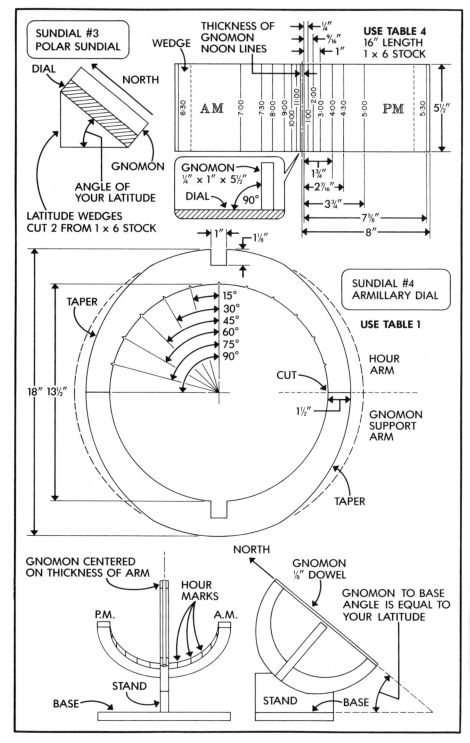

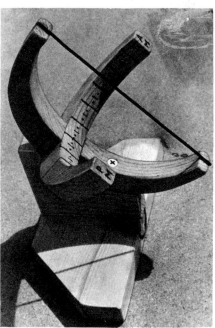

On this armillary sundial the upper end of gnomon points to celestial pole. Set shadow to clock time, position as necessary.

TABLE 4. POLAR DIAL
Hour Line

5:30	5:00	4:30	4:00	3:30	3:00	2:30	2:00	1:30	1:00	12:30
6:30	7:00	7:30	8:00	8:30	9:00	9:30	10:00	10:30	11:00	11:30

Distances in Inches from Each Edge of Gnomon

7.59	3.73	2.41	1.73	1.30	1.0	.77	.58	.41	.27	.13

These distances are based on a dial with a gnomon 1 in. tall, and a dial slightly over 15 in. long. To make a dial proportionally larger or smaller, multiply the distances and the height of the gnomon by the factor you choose.

TABLE 5
Standard Time Meridian:
Eastern = 75° longitude
Central = 90° longitude
Mountain = 105° longitude
Pacific = 120° longitude

Table 4 gives the distances from the gnomon for the hour angles when the gnomon is 1 in. high. For other sizes and fractions of an hour, use the formula: $D = T \times \tan H$ where D is the distance of the line from the gnomon, T is the height of the gnomon above the dial and H is the hour angle, Table 1.

When a polar dial is bent into a semicircle, you create an armillary dial. The gnomon still points to the celestial pole, but is a thin wire suspended by two arms across the center of the semicircle. The hour-angle divisions are equally spaced and measured from the center of the semicircle. Use the hour angles from Table 1. This type of sundial is the most difficult to construct, but also is the most ornamental.

Three correction factors can be applied to make your sundial more accurate: First, mark each hour line with a double set of numbers to indicate both daylight savings and standard times. Sundials normally show only daylight savings time. Second, apply a longitude correction factor. Subtract your longitude from the longitude of your standard time meridian (Table 5). If you live east of the meridian, subtract four minutes for each degree of difference. If you live west of the meridian, add four minutes per degree of difference.

The most difficult correction is to try to account for the vagaries of the earth's orbit around the sun. The simplest way is to purchase an almanac in which you will find for each day of the year a "sun fast" or "sun slow" time to add or subtract from your dial time.

Whorlwinds

 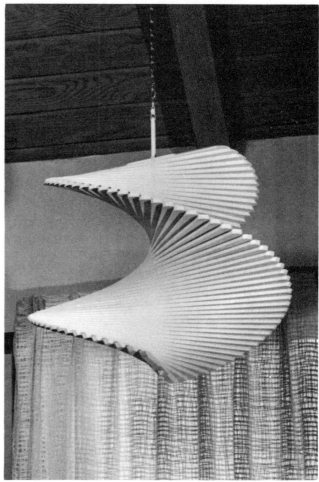

Part of home workshop time should be set aside for fun projects, an evening or weekend when it's therapeutic to get away from projects that *have* to be done.

These spiral-shape figures are great therapy, because they not only are fun to make, they are delightful as contemporary decorative accents indoors and out. When properly suspended, the shapes spin in the lightest movement of air, indoors or out, creating constant changes of movement and light.

There is no such thing as a specific design for the "whorlwinds," even though the construction procedure is the same no matter what the final shape. If the finished shape does not please you, you can redo the project quickly and with no waste in material.

The whorlwinds are a collection of similar strips of wood mounted on a threaded rod and secured with nuts. Whatever material you use, and there are many options, the strips should be dry, smooth and flat so they bear solidly against each other when assembled. Most of the projects shown are strips ripped from wide pieces of maple or birch, but you also can work with ready-made material such as lattice strips that are readily available in lumberyards.

Other possibilities are a good exterior-grade plywood, tempered hardboard, even ice cream sticks and tongue depressors. One of our

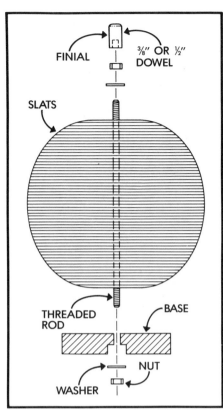

FINIAL

³⁄₈″ OR ½″ DOWEL

SLATS

THREADED ROD

BASE

NUT

WASHER

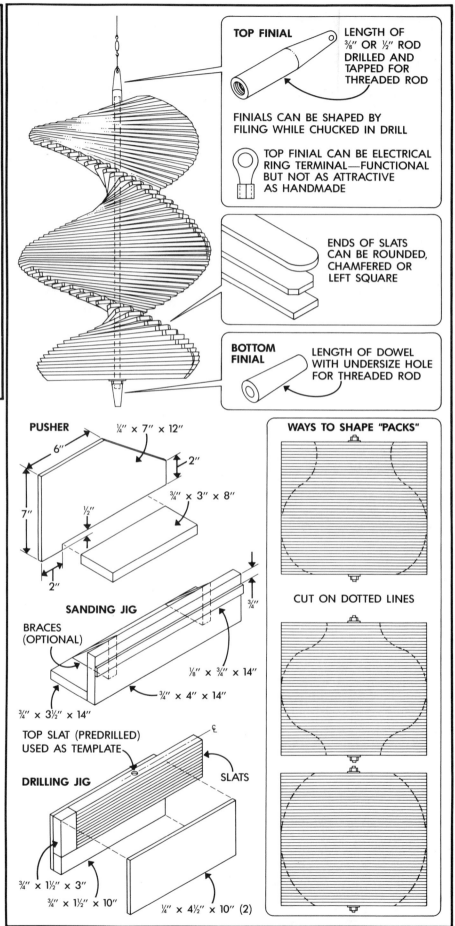

TOP FINIAL LENGTH OF ³⁄₈″ OR ½″ ROD DRILLED AND TAPPED FOR THREADED ROD

FINIALS CAN BE SHAPED BY FILING WHILE CHUCKED IN DRILL

TOP FINIAL CAN BE ELECTRICAL RING TERMINAL—FUNCTIONAL BUT NOT AS ATTRACTIVE AS HANDMADE

ENDS OF SLATS CAN BE ROUNDED, CHAMFERED OR LEFT SQUARE

BOTTOM FINIAL LENGTH OF DOWEL WITH UNDERSIZE HOLE FOR THREADED ROD

PUSHER

¼″ × 7″ × 12″

6″

2″

7″

½″

¾″ × 3″ × 8″

2″

SANDING JIG

¾″

BRACES (OPTIONAL)

⅛″ × ¾″ × 14″

¾″ × 4″ × 14″

¾″ × 3½″ × 14″

TOP SLAT (PREDRILLED) USED AS TEMPLATE

DRILLING JIG

SLATS

¾″ × 1½″ × 3″

¾″ × 1½″ × 10″

¼″ × 4½″ × 10″ (2)

WAYS TO SHAPE "PACKS"

CUT ON DOTTED LINES

Strips for whorlwinds can be cut on table saw, but use push stick to keep hands clear; blade should be carbide or hollow ground.

projects was assembled from strips of plastic laminate counter-top material.

If you rip the strips, or if the material you use is not smooth, sand the surfaces by using the jig shown that utilizes a drum sander in a drill press. Keep in mind that this is a sanding operation only. If you must remove a lot of material, make repeated light passes or run the stock through a thickness planer.

The next step after ripping the strips to width and cutting them to length, is to drill the mounting holes. This can be done accurately with the drilling jig shown. Use one strip as the drilling template, placing it on top of the stack of strips to be drilled. The same jig can be used for strips of various lengths. The jig shown is for strips ¾ in. wide; if you want to use narrower strips, make a jig to suit.

Strips are fitted on a length of threaded rod that is about 2 in. longer than the stack of strips. Use a nut and locknut on the bottom of the rod, with a single nut on top. Tighten the nut just enough to hold the strips firmly together with edges aligned, then place the "pad" on a flat surface and smooth the edges with a belt or pad sander.

Next, make the layout for the profile cuts, some examples of which are shown in the drawings and photos. There are many options for profiles, and once you've made one of the projects you'll see many possibilities for your own design. Cut the profile with a band, jig or saber saw or work with a hand coping saw.

The shape of the project will be more interesting if you do some shaping on the ends of the strips while the pad is still in flat form. Ends can be rounded, chamfered, even profiled a bit.

With the strips held firmly on the threaded rod, and after all have been sanded and shaped, grip the bottom end of the rod in a vise and turn each strip the same number of degrees. Once all strips are positioned, tighten the top nut. Do not tighten too much or the strips will bow.

The easiest way to hang the whorlwinds is to use an electrical lamp ring screwed onto the top of the rod. Another way is to drill and tap a length of steel bar that can be turned on the top of the rod. You can skip the drilling and tapping by using the center section of a small turnbuckle. These are available in steel or aluminum with a thread to match that of the rod.

These projects will spin in the lightest breeze if the hanger string is a length of fishing line with a swivel (also part of fishing tackle) at each end. The swivels are sold in various sizes and are fairly inexpensive.

The wood of the whorlwinds can be left natural, but it's a good idea to apply at least one or two coats of clear, exterior-type sealer. Seal the wood even if you decide to paint the projects. A glossy paint will cause light to travel from one strip to another as the project rotates, giving an unusual effect.

Hang a few of the whorlwinds in your yard, and a couple inside the house, and wait for enthusiastic reactions from friends. With a wide, solid base, the whorlwinds can be used as table decorations, although they will not spin. They make fine gifts, and novelty shops would be a good place to sell them.

Variation of whorlwind has two spiral sections separated by solid block of wood. Sizes and numbers of spacer blocks can be varied.

SERENDIPITY

Holiday Chandelier

One or more of these chandeliers provide a festive touch and can be used indoors or out. Scraps of plywood and solid stock provide the material.

Each chandelier requires two discs cut from plywood. Sand the edges smooth and break any sharp edges. Posts are ripped from 1-in. stock.

As an added touch, bevel the edges, either the full width of each post, or about halfway.

For quick assembly, glue and nail the 1 × 2 strips flat to the edges of the discs. The chandeliers shown have been left natural, with just a couple of coats of sealer.

Short lengths of metal or plastic chain can be used to suspend the chandelier, employing a screw hook driven into the center of the top disc.

A string of small lights can be entwined in the posts, or you might want to fit a socket or connector in the underside of the top, with an extension cord from the top to be plugged into a nearby receptacle.

If the chandelier is to be used outdoors, be sure to use lights designed for outdoor use, and all wiring and connectors should be of the weatherproof type.

Decorate the chandelier with evergreen branches slipped between the posts, and colored ribbons suspended from the bottom disc. The chandelier is especially attractive if you use strings of lights that "twinkle" so the light appears to be moving along the strings and through the evergreen branches.

Seal and finish the chandelier before doing the wiring, decorating and attaching the hooks and chains.

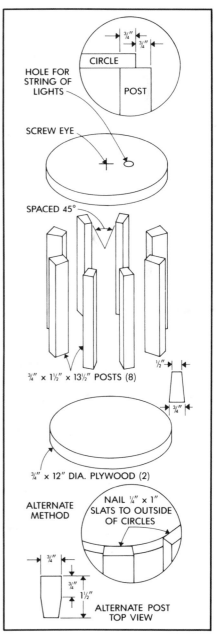

Single-loaf Breadbox

Letters were drawn on paper, then traced onto front piece of box by using carbon paper. Letters can be any style.

Small carving gouge or veining tool can be used for carving, even pocket knife if it is sharp and you take your time.

This decorative breadbox was made from ¼-in. oak and is sized to accept just one loaf of bread, plus a roll or two.

You may prefer to use other woods, but in this example the choice was ¼ × 2-in. oak strips cut into 12-in. lengths. These then are edge glued to make the several larger pieces required, as shown in the drawing. When the glue has set, sand all pieces to remove any dried glue. Cut one piece in half to create the two end pieces rounding one corner of each piece.

Using the pattern, draw the word "Bread" on paper, by enlarging the square as explained in the introduction. Trace the word onto the front piece of the breadbox, then carve the word into the front as shown. Keep the carving shallow on such thin stock.

Glue and clamp the box. When the glue has set, hinge the lid to the back. Stain and finish to complement any other wooden accessories in your kitchen. The box also could be painted, if you prefer.

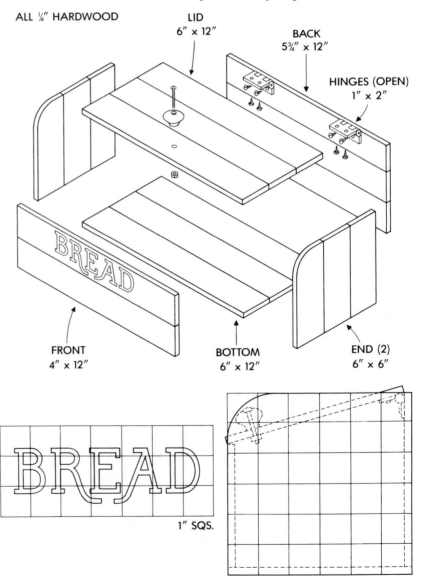

ALL ¼" HARDWOOD

LID
6" × 12"

BACK
5¾" × 12"

HINGES (OPEN)
1" × 2"

FRONT
4" × 12"

BOTTOM
6" × 12"

END (2)
6" × 6"

1" SQS.

Front, with carving, plus the ends and lid are shown here. Back and lid are same size, 6 x 12 in.

This breadbox would make a nice gift, or an item to sell. For variation, the carving could be changed, or left off. Many people would like to have a box this size for odds and ends, so it doesn't necessarily need to be just for bread. Some craftsmen may want to enlarge the box, or use heavier stock, or a different choice of wood.

Kitchen Utensils

As kitchen tools can be fairly expensive to buy, making your own involves very little time and money.

All these utensils should be made with a tight-grained hardwood and finished with salad oil or a salad bowl finish. As an added touch, a hole can be drilled in the end of each handle, perhaps with a leather thong or colorful ribbon inserted for hanging up.

The first step is to make patterns from the squared drawings, then some of the utensils are carved or turned to rough shape on a lathe, while the rest are rough cut using a band saw, scroll saw or coping saw.

SPOON. Carve or turn to rough shape on a lathe. Note that the large end is a turned oval, then shaped after it is removed from the lathe. Turn handle and large oval on the end, and sand as smooth as possible while still in the lathe. Using a band saw or hand saw with the spoon clamped in a vise, cut off the portion of the oval where the spoon will be. Using small gouges, or a small hand grinder, shape and smooth the bowl of the spoon. Round all edges and sand smooth.

FORK. The fork is roughed in exactly the same way as the spoon, then it is cut to shape using a band saw, scroll saw or coping saw. The first cut should be on the side pattern, followed by the top pattern. Then round all edges with a rasp and sand smooth.

STRAINER SPOON. This is made basically the same way as the spoon, except slots are cut in the bottom of the bowl by boring a line of overlapping ⅛-in. holes; use a small file followed by sandpaper to smooth out openings left by boring.

POTATO MASHER. This is strictly a carving or turning project. While turning to correct shape be careful at the top where the neck narrows not to force the chisel too much, or it will break the thin neck. Sand while it is still on the lathe.

FRENCH-STYLE ROLLING PIN. This one-piece project can be lengthened or shortened as fits your needs. However, the thickness should remain the same. Turn, sand and smooth before removing from lathe. Incidentally, when turning hardwoods, the last finishing cuts should be made with the lathe running at a fairly high speed, and if you use sharp tools, there will be little need for sanding.

SPAGHETTI LIFTER. Rough cut to shape. The large end will look like a "bulb" after turning. Finish sand the handle before removing from the lathe. Cut the paddle to correct shape shown in side view using a band saw or a stiff-backed hand saw while the handle is clamped in a vise. Pad vise jaws to prevent marring the finish on the handle. Sand the head end of the paddle, then bore the stopped holes

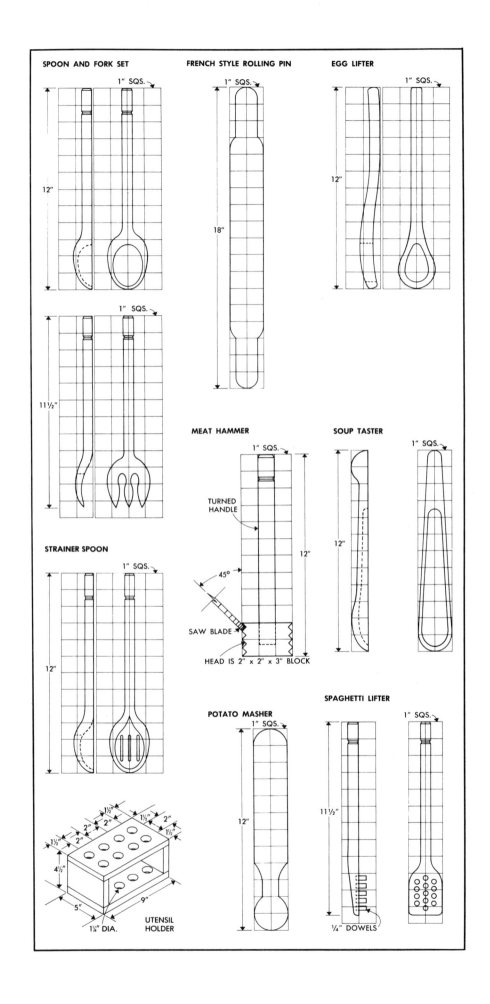

and glue in place pegs cut from ¼-in. hardwood dowels. Use a waterproof glue and sand smooth.

EGG LIFTER. This handy little tool is used for lifting eggs out of boiling water. Cut top outline first, then side outline; then bore overlapping holes around the edges of the inside circle. Use a sharp knife to break out the center hole; smooth with a rasp and sandpaper.

MEAT HAMMER. This easy-to-make meat tenderizer is both attractive and useful. To make the hammer head portion, cut a block of wood 2 × 2 × 3 in. as shown. The faces on the head have diamond facets cut in them. To make these facets, use a saw set at a 45-degree angle, cutting first in one direction, then turning the block 180 degrees to cut the opposite side of the V-shaped grooves. Turn the block 90 degrees and make the cross cuts. Turn it around 180 degrees for the last cut; this provides the diamond-shaped facets.

Carve or turn the handle on a lathe. Bore a stopped hole in the head and glue the handle in place using waterproof glue.

A V-groove cutter in a router can be used to make the diamond facets, or you can use a shaper, or even hand carve the groove if you prefer. Sand entire project as smooth as possible.

SOUP TASTER. The long hollowed-out bowl allows the soup to cool down faster, and the bump on the end permits the spoon to be set down while the soup cools for tasting. Rough cut the taster, cutting top outline first, then cutting side outline. Note the underside should be left fairly flat so that it won't roll over when it is set down. Use sharp wood-carving gouges or small hand grinder to carve out inside of spoon. Smooth and round edges and sand smooth.

UTENSIL HOLDER. Just four scraps of wood, either plywood or solid stock, are required for this handy counter-top utensil holder. Top and bottom of the holder are 5 × 9 in., while the ends are 4½ × 5 in.

Lay out the top to locate the holes, then clamp top and bottom together. Drill completely through the top, but only halfway through the bottom. If you have a Forstner bit, it will do the best job as this kind of bit produces a flat-bottom blind hole.

Cut the end pieces to size, then sand all surfaces smooth. You can stain and finish the four pieces before assembly, but leave the strips that are to be joined free of finish so the glue will adhere.

When the finish is dry, assemble the top and bottom to the ends with screws or nails and glue. Set the nails or countersink the screws and cover the heads with wood putty.

For an added design touch, counterbore holes for the screws and fill the holes with wooden plugs.

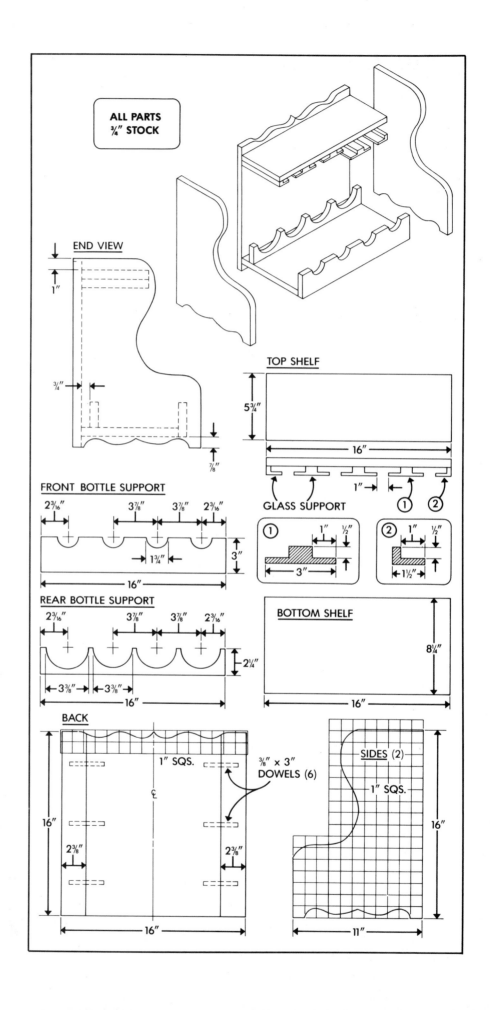

ALL PARTS ¾″ STOCK

END VIEW

1″

¾″

⅞″

TOP SHELF

5¾″

16″

1″

GLASS SUPPORT

① ②

① 1″ ½″ 3″

② 1″ ½″ 1½″

FRONT BOTTLE SUPPORT

2³⁄₁₆″ 3⅞″ 3⅞″ 2³⁄₁₆″

1¾″

3″

16″

REAR BOTTLE SUPPORT

2³⁄₁₆″ 3⅞″ 3⅞″ 2³⁄₁₆″

2¼″

3⅜″ 3⅜″

16″

BOTTOM SHELF

8¼″

16″

BACK

1″ SQS.

⅜″ × 3″ DOWELS (6)

SIDES (2)

1″ SQS.

16″

2⅜″ 2⅜″

16″

16″

16″

11″

Counter Wine Rack

Stock used for this attractive wine glass/bottle rack is standard 1 × 12 pine shelving.

Start by enlarging the squared drawings at left to make patterns for the two sides and the upper edge of the back. For the back pattern, you can make a half pattern, then fold the paper and cut the two halves of the pattern at the same time so they will be identical.

The sides, top and bottom shelf, and bottle supports are cut from single pieces of 1 × 12, but the back will require edge gluing and doweling a strip 2⅜ in. wide to each edge of a 16-in. length of the shelving.

Lay out the front and rear bottle supports. The layout shown was suitable for some bottles, but it would be a good idea to check the sizes of the bottles you regularly purchase, as the sizes and even the lengths may vary. Also, if you have a selection of more than four kinds, the rack can be made longer to accommodate the additional bottles.

Make the glass supports by cutting 3 × 5¾-in. strips from the stock, then cutting a ½ × 1-in. rabbet in each long edge. One of the strips is ripped in half lengthwise to create the two end supports that are L-shape.

Use glue and countersunk finishing nails or wood screws for the assembly of the rack. Cover the heads with wood putty, or counterbore and use wood plugs.

Wall Wine Rack

The 16½ × 29-in. back of this rack requires edge-gluing narrower strips of stock. Birch was used for the original, but any close-grained hardwood is suitable. You could even make an "early American" version by using pine or other softwood. It is very important to select straight-grained softwood for the notched bottle bracket, as this narrow cross-grained section will be weak.

Make patterns by enlarging the squared drawings on next page. Check to be sure the bottles and the stems of the glasses you use will fit the holes and grooves. If not, modify your pattern as needed.

Cut the various pieces to size and shape, then taper or profile the edges of the back and the shelf.

Use glue and screws driven through the back into the various pieces to assemble the rack. Stain and finish to suit, then drive two screweyes into the upper edge of the back to provide a means for hanging it on the wall. Or, drive a couple of screws through the back into wall studs, or use screw anchors in a plaster or plasterboard wall.

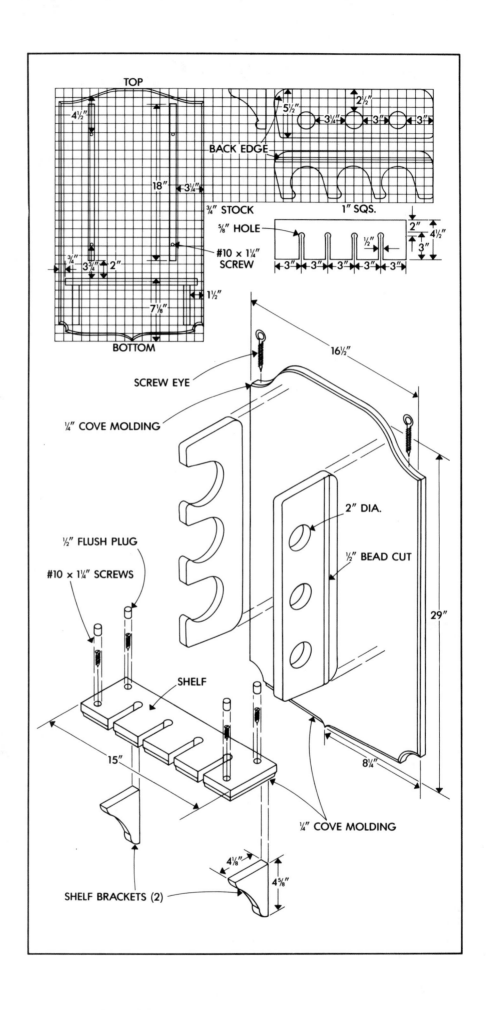

TOP

4½"

18" 3¼"

¾" STOCK

5/8" HOLE

#10 × 1¼" SCREW

¾" 3¾" 2"

7⅛"

1½"

BOTTOM

5½"

2½"

3¼" 3" 3"

BACK EDGE

1" SQS.

2" 4½" 3"

½"

3" 3" 3" 3" 3"

SCREW EYE

¼" COVE MOLDING

16½"

½" FLUSH PLUG

#10 × 1¼" SCREWS

2" DIA.

½" BEAD CUT

29"

SHELF

15"

¼" COVE MOLDING

8¼"

4⅛"

4⅝"

SHELF BRACKETS (2)

Animal Napkin Rings

Napkin rings are an excellent project for using leftover odds and ends of hardwood.

For this project, walnut was used, but any hardwood that will sand to a smooth finish is equally suitable. Often the designs can be fitted onto odd-shaped pieces of wood. Here 1¼-in.-thick stock was used.

First, lay out the outline on the piece of wood. Locate the center of the 1⅜-in. napkin cavity, and drill the hole with a spade bit or hole saw. Saw out the figure outline and then cut away as much of the waste wood as possible to rough shape the figure.

Rounding off the figures is easily done with a sander; it takes a little longer by hand. In either case, start with a coarse grit, to cut down the wood quickly, then use progressively finer grits to get a smooth finish.

When sanding is complete, use a nail set to "punch in" the eyes. Hold the nail set firmly against the wood in the location of the eye, apply pressure and rotate. The napkin rings may be left natural or stained.

Drill the napkin cavity hole through the wood with a spade bit before sawing out the figure.

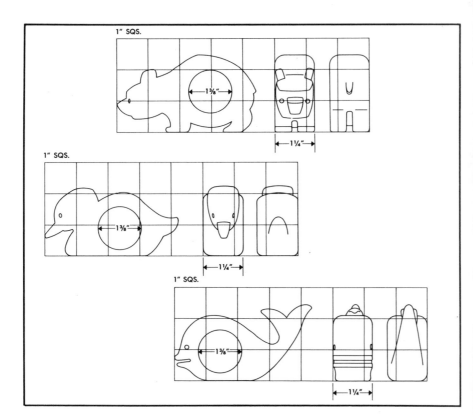

Finish shaping the figures with a knife. A little extra effort here will save much sanding.

After the figure has been sawed to shape, trim off as much of the waste wood as possible.

Perpetual Calendar

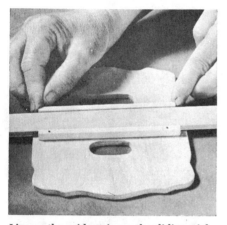

Line up the guide strips so the sliding sticks have about 1/16 in. clearance, then glue and nail them.

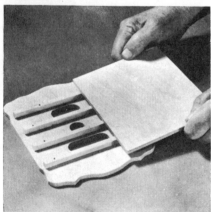

After the guide strips are in position, fit the back in place and glue and nail it to the strips.

This perpetual calendar will never become outdated. The day and date sticks are set each day, and the month changed as needed.

Front, back and the three sliding sticks are cut from ½-in. plywood, although solid stock could be used. The four divider strips that make the channels for the sliding strips are pine or other softwood ¼ in. wide, 5/16 in. thick and 5 in. long. They are spaced to provide 1/16-in. clearance for the strips, to ensure easy sliding.

Cut all pieces to size. Shape and sand thoroughly. Turn the front piece face down and locate the positions of the divider strips and mark these locations. Begin with the strips that hold the center sliding stick. Glue and nail the lower strip in place, then place a sliding strip against it. Position the next guide strip. Move the sliding strip back and forth to ensure free movement. Glue and nail the next guide strip to the front piece. It's better to have too much spacing between the guide strips than not enough. Guide strips later may swell slightly because of an increase in humidity.

Repeat the operation for the other guide strips. When the glue has set, countersink the nails slightly. Remove the sliding strips and glue and nail the back to the guide strips. Drill the mounting holes at the top and bottom, boring through from the front.

The calendar shown has an antiqued finish created by applying a white base coat glazed with light brown. The design on the front is in bright "folk colors." Numbers and letters are dark brown.

For a more formal look, you might want to use self-adhering letters and numbers. Apply antiquing over the characters after they are in place.

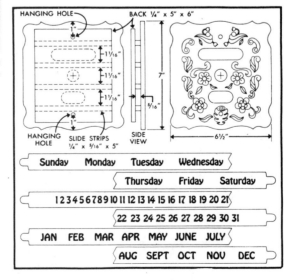

Cup Tree

An easy way to make the base is to clamp the two pieces together and cut the dadoes required for the half-lap joint. Cut the post and drill the holes for the hangers. A guide for drilling the holes is shown. Cut the guide to length, center drill it, then cut off the end at 10 degrees. Counterbore one part of the base for the screw, then assemble base to post with glue and the screw. Glue the dowels in the holes.

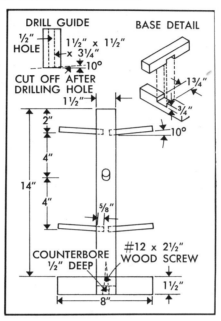

Two Knife Racks

Hardwood blocks, which you might have left over from a larger project, are the stock used for these two attractive knife racks.

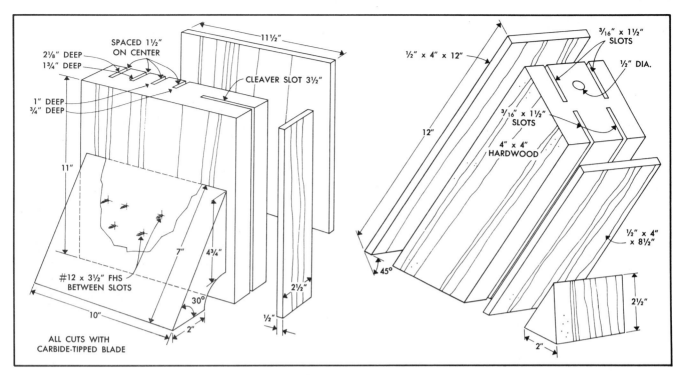

One rack is "personalized" with a carving of your choice on the support block, while the other is plain.

The rack with the decorated support block sits vertically and has a slot for a meat cleaver, while the other, angled unit has provision for knives only.

Start construction of the upright unit by gluing together two blocks measuring ½ × 6 × 10 in. Glue and clamp the pieces together overnight.

Saw a piece ½ in. thick from one long end and save it, as it will be glued back on. Cut the knife slots as indicated. A carbide-tipped saw blade is best, but with care a regular blade can be used. A 10-inch blade is the minimum size that can be used to cut the cleaver slot. Cut the slot and glue back and clamp the piece that was removed.

Make the slots for the knives, checking the ones you have to get the proper spacing and depth. Cut and glue on the back piece. Cut out the support block. Attach with 3½-in. screws as indicated.

The other rack is made from a block of wood 4 in. square. Cut the slots to fit your knife set, then glue on the two ½-in. pieces at the front and back to close in the slots.

Cut the support bracket as indicated, or make up your own design. If you cut the bracket from a square piece of stock, use the scrap piece to help clamp the bracket while the glue sets.

Utensil Caddy

Whether for a picnic or a patio party, this caddy will hold the silverware, napkins and condiments so they can be carried in one hand. Scraps of 1-in. stock (¾ in. net) were used for the original, but thinner material for the partitions would provide more space between them.

Dado the long partition to accept the two dividers that form the three spaces for knives, forks and spoons. If you use thinner stock, change the dimensions of the dadoes accordingly.

Enlarge the squared drawing to make a pattern for the two ends, mark the wood and cut out the ends. Mark and drill the blind hole on the inner surface of each end to accept the ⅝-in. dowel handle.

Assemble the various pieces with glue and 4-penny finishing nails, except for the ends, which should be joined to the sides and bottom with 6-penny finishing nails. As an alternative assembly method, use glue and dowels.

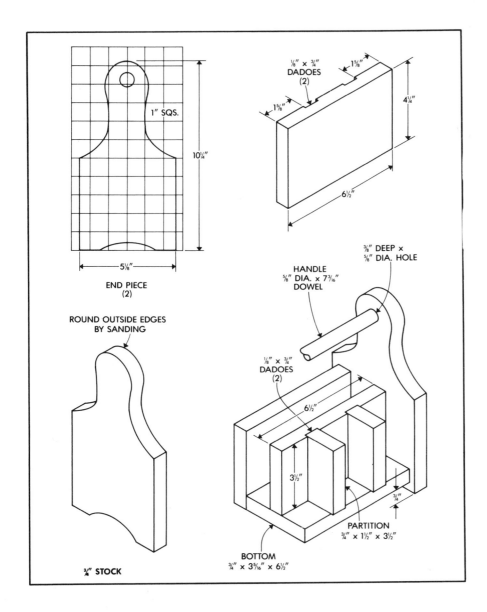

Fenced Cutting Board

Wipe the end of the ¼-in. dowels with glue and tap them into the holes. When glue has set, apply two coats of boiled linseed oil.

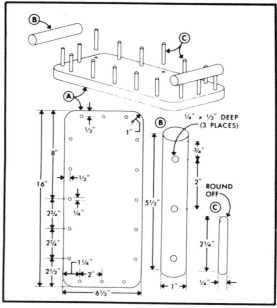

Cooling Rack

Miter the ends of two pieces of stock 11¾ in. long to 45 degrees. Clamp pieces together and drill both at the same time. Glue dowels into place and finish.

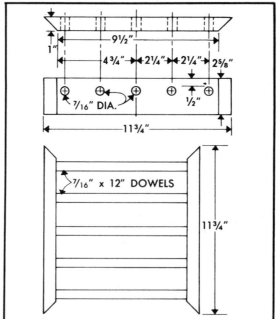

Multi-purpose Tote Box

The design of this project is simple enough so that it could be adapted to various uses. For example, during the barbecue season it's handy when it comes time to haul utensils, napkins, relishes and other goodies from the kitchen to the patio. The tote would also make a nice garden tool caddy. One side could be used for tools while the other side could hold bulbs, seeds and other supplies.

The tote shown was made out of fir plywood, but an even more attractive version could be made out of solid stock which could be painted or finished naturally.

The project calls for cutting dadoes, but if you don't have the tools available, use butt joints throughout. However, if butt joints are used, minor changes in some of the dimensions will be required.

Start construction by shaping the ends and center divider. Assemble these parts with glue and ¾-in. brads. Next, cut the sides and bottom to the dimensions given and attach these to the assembly, again using glue and brads. Finally, shape the partitions and handle, then glue and brad into position. Countersink all the brads and fill the holes with wood putty. Sand the tote until all surfaces and edges are smooth. Finish as desired.

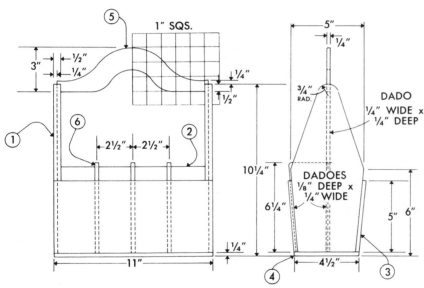

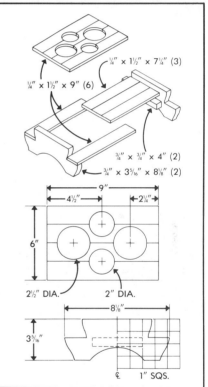

Condiment Rack

All that's required is some scrap lumber and about seven feet of lattice stock.

Make a pattern for the ends by enlarging the squared drawing. Cut out the ends and glue and brad the supports for the sub-top to the ends. Cut six pieces of lattice stock 9 in. long and attach two to the ends to serve as benches. Edge glue the other four pieces together. After the glue has set, bore two 2-in. holes and two 2½-in. holes.

Cut three 7¼-in. lengths of the lattice for the sub-top and attach these to the supports on the ends, then glue and brad the top to the ends. Finish as desired.

Towel Ladder

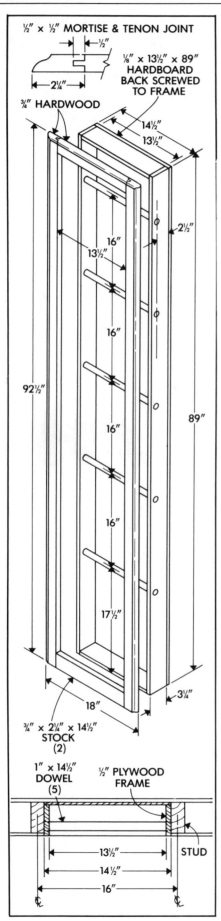

This decorative towel holder provides racks for several towels, yet need not project into the room. The ladder can be recessed into the wall between two studs.

Select a location for the holder that is free of pipes, electrical wiring or outlets, or heating vents. Cut an opening in the wall to the size you desire. The dimensions shown in the drawing are for a wall with studs 16 in. on center, but yours may vary. If you want it wider, you will have to move a stud, unless your stud spacing is 24-in. Once you have determined the size, cut the frame pieces, locate and drill the holes for the dowels, then assemble the frame.

Next, make the molding for the facing. A mortise-and-tenon joint is shown, but doweled or splined joints would work equally well. Attach the facing to the frame with glue and finishing nails. Add finish to the facing, frame and dowels.

Cut ⅛-in. hardboard to size and paint or wallpaper it as desired. Attach it to the frame with screws, but use no glue. Fit the towel ladder into the opening in the wall and shim it as necessary to level it. Fasten it to the studs with four wood screws, one on each side at top and bottom.

Toothbrush Holder

This charming little bear will hold your child's toothbrush, which should make brushing fun instead of a chore.

First enlarge the squared drawings and, using the stock indicated, cut out the pieces. Assemble with a waterproof glue. Paint. The face can be either painted on or drawn with a marking pen.

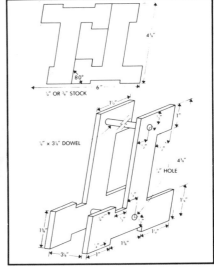

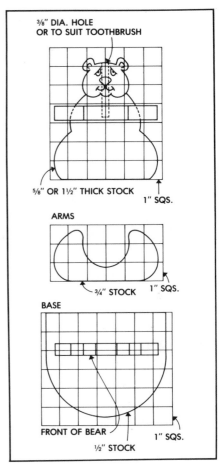

Plate Stand

The drawing shows how side pieces can be cut out of a small piece of stock to minimize waste. Overall size and angle of tilt may need to be changed to fit plate.

Bathroom TP/Magazine Rack

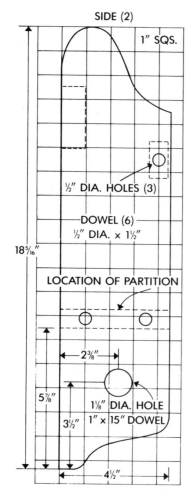

SIDE (2)

1" SQS.

½" DIA. HOLES (3)

DOWEL (6)
½" DIA. x 1½"

18⁵⁄₁₆"

LOCATION OF PARTITION

2³⁄₈"

5⁷⁄₈"

1¹⁄₈" DIA. HOLE

3½"

1" x 15" DOWEL

4½"

Standard 1-in. (¾ in. net) lumber is used throughout except for the ½-in. dowels for the rack and the 1-in. dowel to hold the tissue.

Enlarge the squared drawing to make a pattern for the sides, trace the patterns on the stock and cut the two sides together to ensure they are identical. Also drill the several holes with the sides still clamped or tack nailed together.

Round the front edges of the sides and sand all surfaces smooth. Cut out the front and back rails and the shelf, and drill the holes as indicated on the drawing. All blind holes are ½ in. deep in the back and front rails and the shelf (partition). Use a spur or Forstner bit, if you have one, to make the holes flat bottomed. If you use a regular bit, it may be necessary to drill slightly deeper than ½ in. to allow the dowels to fit between the shelf and rails.

Glue the ½-in. dowels, the shelf and the two rails together, then slip the assembly between the sides and glue and nail the back rail with finishing nails that are set and covered with wood putty. The front rail and shelf are held by dowels glued in the sides.

To ensure alignment of the dowel holes, you can clamp the assembly of sides, rails and shelf together, then drill through the sides into the rails and shelf. Unclamp the assembly, sand as necessary, apply glue and clamp the assembly.

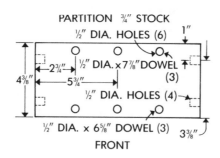

FRONT RAIL ¾" STOCK

11½"

1½"

½" DIA. HOLES (2)

2¾"

5¾"

¾"

½" DIA. HOLES (3)

BACK RAIL 1" STOCK

11½"

2½"

ALL HOLES ⅝" DEEP

2¾"

5¾"

½" DIA. HOLES (3)

PARTITION ¾" STOCK

½" DIA. HOLES (6)

1"

2¾"

½" DIA. x 7⅞" DOWEL (3)

4⅜"

5¾"

½" DIA. HOLES (4)

½" DIA. x 6⅝" DOWEL (3)

3⅜"

FRONT

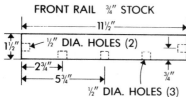
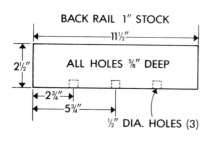

Turned Candlesticks

This walnut candlestick trio should pose no problems, even for the novice. Start by chucking stock between lathe centers and "roughing" to approximate length and shape. Increase speed of lathe and use skew chisel to make a smooth contour. Turn interior of top using parting chisel, but leave "stem" in which lathe center chucked. Use parting chisel to free base; leave about ½ in. attached to waste stock so you can sand while still in lathe. Sand until smooth. Remove from lathe and saw base free. Align ¾-in. drill bit with mark left by tailstock center and drill hole for candle. Top is shaped with sharp knife. Sand interior and bottom and finish as desired.

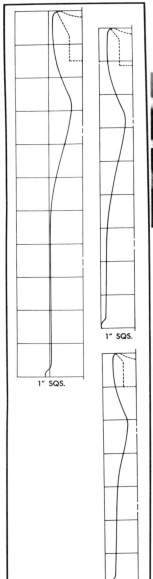

1" SQS.

1" SQS.

After profile of candlestick is turned, stock from interior is removed using parting chisel.

Hole to accept candle is bored using 3/4 in. drill bit. Align bit with mark created by tailstock center.

Before final sanding, waste at base of candlestick is turned to about 1/2 in. thickness. Use parting chisel.

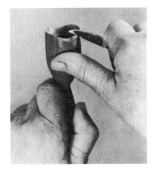

Final step is to shape candle cup with a sharp knife followed by light sanding and application of finish.

Carved Wall Plaque

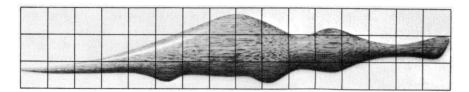

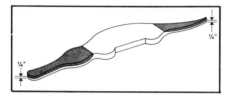

Clamp the work piece vertically if a hand scroll saw is used, horizontally if portable electric jig saw is the tool.

An ideal project for the weekend woodcarver, this crocodile can be shaped quickly with the aid of a hand scroll saw and a round and flat rasp.

The first step is to enlarge the squared drawing to full size and make a pattern of light cardboard. If you think you'd like to make more than one, make the pattern from ⅛-in. hardboard.

Trace the pattern on a piece of 1-in. stock (¾ in. net) that measures 3 × 16 in. Saw out the shape. If you are making more than one, stack the pieces to a thickness that the saw will handle.

Smooth the edges of the cutout shape with a round rasp to remove saw marks, and shape the pattern down to the saw marks (saw just outside the pencil line).

Next reduce the end thirds of the shape down to ¼ in., tapering down from the center one-third of the pattern. Use a flat rasp to round the upper and lower edges as indicated to give the crocodile its shape, but leave ⅛ in. at the top and bottom flat; do not round over the back edges.

The wood can be left natural with a clear sealer, or stained or painted. Hang the crocodiles by drilling shallow blind holes at the back, and fitting them over small nails tapped into the wall.

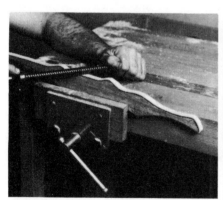

Rasp the cut out shape to remove saw marks, smooth up the edges down to the pencil line of the pattern.

Two end sections are thinned by removing 1/2 in. of stock, so remaining portion is just 1/4 in. taper down from center.

Final step is to round edges of both ends with flat rasp, keeping edge 1/8 in. wide at the top and the bottom.

Photo Statuettes

Use white glue to attach photo of your choice to ¾-in. wood block. Cut out at slight angle. Smooth and finish block. Practice with an old photo first.

Candelabra

The base of this unique candelabra is turned on the faceplate from dressed 1-in. stock. Walnut or mahogany is suggested, but any good hardwood can be used. If you are an early American enthusiast, and have sharp turning chisels, you can even use pine or another softwood.

Turn the column from a length of clear, straight-grained stock. This is especially important with softwood, because any knot or weak spot will cause the column to break when you are turning between centers.

To locate the six holes for the dowels that hold the candle cups, mark off the bottom of the base in 60-degree segments. Glue the base to the column, then set the column in a V-block and align the marks on the bottom of the base with a mark you make on the V-block. This locates the holes, which will be at the upper surface of the column so you can bore them with a drill press or portable electric drill.

The candle cups are turned with the aid of the screw center in the head stock. After you have turned all six of them, bore a hole in a scrap block of wood to create a drilling "vise." The block should be a bit higher than the cups, and the hole for the cups should be a bit larger in diameter than the largest diameter of the cups.

Set the cups in the "vise" and bore the holes for the candles with the aid of the drill press or portable drill. Size the candle holes to fit the candles you will use.

The base, column and cups can be stained and finished while they are still in the lathe. The advantage, for those who have not tried "lathe finishing," is that the stain and finish can be burnished into the wood with a cloth, and the surface is dry and ready the moment the piece is removed from the lathe.

You can readily change the style of the candelabra by using different shapes for the cups. Shown are the profiles of the cups used on the original, plus two alternatives.

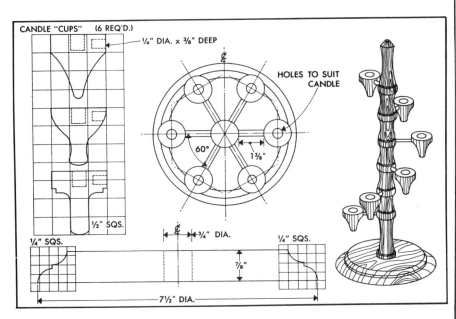

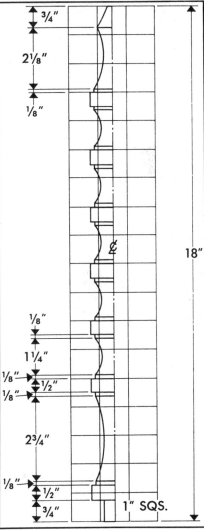

Spool Rack

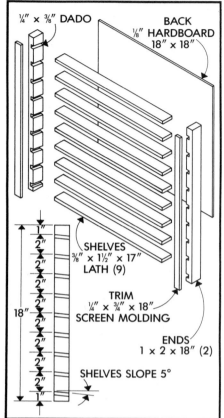

What better way to please a seamstress than by providing her with this colorful and handy way to display her spools of thread?

Begin by cutting the pieces to size. Dado the ends to receive the shelves, being sure to maintain a 5-degree slope towards the back. The slope prevents the spools from rolling off the shelves. Lightly sand each piece.

Glue the shelves into the ends and attach the back with glue and brads. Fasten the front trim to the ends with glue. Clamp until the glue dries.

Sand the unit and finish to match the decor of the sewing area. Mount the rack on a wall over or near the sewing machine.

Folding Book Rack

When placed on a kitchen counter, this handy rack holds a cookbook for easy reading, on a desk it will position a reference volume or papers for reading, typing or entering on a word processor. When folded, the rack is only 1⅛ in. thick so it will fit easily in a drawer.

Cut all the pieces to size, using the Materials List, then refer to the drawing for making the notches and rabbets. Also drill ³⁄₁₆-in. holes on the center line 3½ in. above the bottom of both the long and short legs. Note that the book support rail starts as a strip 1 × 1½ × 10⅛ in., then is rabbeted ¼ × 1¼ in. and, finally, notches ¾ × ¾ in. are cut at

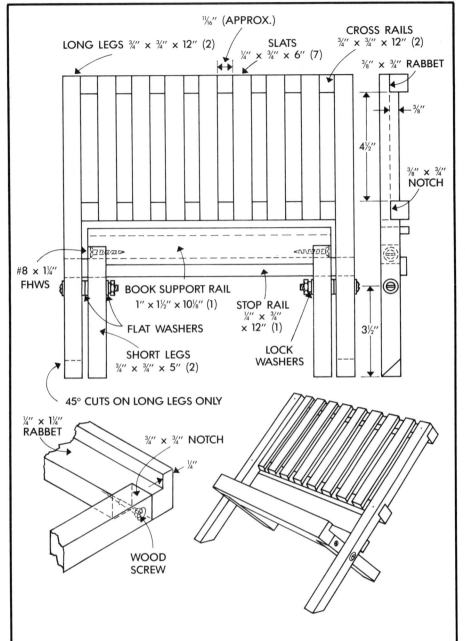

LONG LEGS ¾″ × ¾″ × 12″ (2)

¹¹⁄₁₆″ (APPROX.)

SLATS
¼″ × ¾″ × 6″ (7)

CROSS RAILS
¾″ × ¾″ × 12″ (2)

⅜″ × ¾″ RABBET

⅜″

4½″

⅜″ × ¾″
NOTCH

#8 × 1¼″
FHWS

BOOK SUPPORT RAIL
1″ × 1½″ × 10⅛″ (1)

STOP RAIL
¼″ × ¾″
× 12″ (1)

FLAT WASHERS

SHORT LEGS
¾″ × ¾″ × 5″ (2)

LOCK
WASHERS

3½″

45° CUTS ON LONG LEGS ONLY

¼″ × 1¼″
RABBET

¾″ × ¾″ NOTCH

¼″

WOOD
SCREW

MATERIALS LIST

All ¾″ stock except as noted
Legs, long, ¾″ × 12″ (2)
Legs, short, ¾″ × 5″ (2)
Cross rail, ¾″ × 12″ (2)
Slats, ¼″ × 6″ (7)
Book support rail,
    1″ × 1½″ × 10⅛″ (1)
Stop rail, ¼″ × 12″ (1)
Hardware #8 × 1¼″ FHWS (2)
8-32 × 2″ RH machine screws (2)
8-32 hex nuts (2)
³⁄₁₆″ ID flat washers (8)
³⁄₁₆″ ID lock washers (2)

each end of the strip to accept the short legs. Join the short legs and book support rail with screws and glue.

Next, glue and nail the cross rails in the notches in the long legs, making sure the assembly is square. Glue and brad (or use small finishing nails) to attach the seven slats to the cross rails.

When the glue has set, join the support rail/short leg assembly to the long legs with 8-32 roundhead screws, fitting ³⁄₁₆-in. ID washers between the short and long legs to center the book support rail between the long legs.

Position the pivoting assemblies at right angles to each other and clamp them, then glue and brad the stop rail to the backs of the two long legs so the short legs bear against it. The angle between the back and the book support rail could be varied, of course, so the book or papers are tilted back a bit more if that is your preference.

Sand all surfaces, and round all edges slightly, then stain or paint and finish to suit the location where the rack will be used.

Student's Portable Book Rack

This handy, take-apart book rack requires only four pieces of ¾-in. (net) stock and a minimum of time and tools. Actually, the only tools you need are a radial-arm or table saw that is equipped with a dado blade and a chisel to square up the slots and dadoes in the stock. Soft or hardwood can be used for construction, although using hardwood is recommended if the rack will be taken apart quite often, or if you plan on making the rack extra long. You'll note in the drawing that there is no overall length given, as the rack can be made to suit one's particular needs.

To begin, you need two 8 × 9-in. boards for the ends. Mark the 20- and 70-degree angles on each board and pencil in the lines for the slots and dadoes. Draw a heavy line where the slots end and dadoes begin so you don't accidentally remove more stock than necessary. Mark both sides of each board, then set your saw to make the cuts. Make the ¼-in.-deep dadoes first, then make the slots by adjusting your dado blade to cut completely through the stock. After these steps are completed, square up the cuts in the pieces with a chisel. Now, clamp both end pieces together and make the remaining cuts. The curved portion is done freehand so you may want to change the design to suit yourself.

Next, make the back and shelf by first slotting each piece, then rabbeting and dadoing where necessary. Be sure to square the ends of the slots after the parts are completed. Lastly, stain and finish the pieces and allow to dry. Assemble by fitting the ends on the shelf, then attaching the back to the ends, fitting the rabbet into the dado of the shelf.

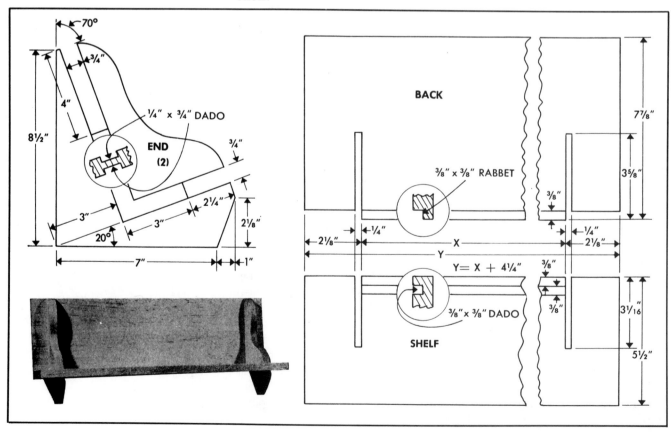

Butcher-block Cutting Board

We needed a butcher-block-type cutting board to use on the top of an apartment-size freezer. While it would add welcome work space in the small kitchen, it could be only ½ in. thick to be level with the top of the adjacent counter. Additionally, it had to be "portable," in that it occasionally must be removed from the freezer top. This feature makes it ideal for almost any kitchen, as it can be located where it is needed.

With the restriction of the ½ in. thickness, it was obvious that the "standard" method of butcher-block construction using thick blocks of wood was impractical. Our solution was to use ¼-in. plywood for a base, to which ¼-in. thick strips of three contrasting woods were glued. We used birch, walnut and cherry for the strips, and walnut for the trim strips on the edges. Other kinds of hardwood could be used, but should be of contrasting colors.

The cutting board can be made any reasonable size required, using the technique described. Check the Materials List on the next page to determine the sizes and numbers of the strips required. After cutting the required strips, lay out the diagram for the center vertical strips on a piece of ¼-in plywood 23 in. square, as per the drawing.

Cover the plywood base with waxed paper; the diagram guidelines will show through. Place the center birch strip directly over the center strip position and clamp the ends to the plywood. Make sure this strip is exactly at right angles to the edge. Edge glue the various strips to the center strip and each other, then clamp the assembly with boards on top to keep it flat while the glue sets.

When the glue has set, remove all clamps except those holding the center birch strip. Mark the four corners of the square on the glued-up assembly, matching them to the corners of the plywood. Draw the

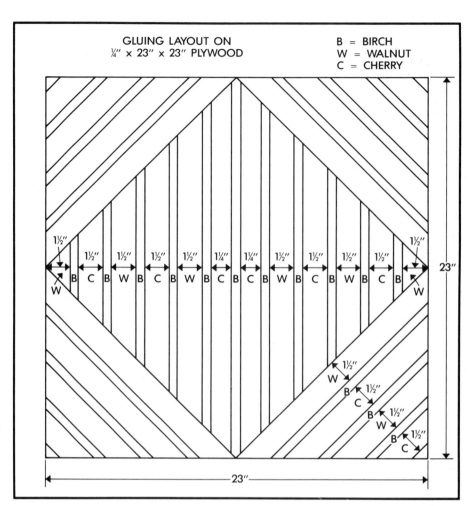

GLUING LAYOUT ON
¼″ × 23″ × 23″ PLYWOOD

B = BIRCH
W = WALNUT
C = CHERRY

MATERIALS LIST

Base, ¼″ × 23″ × 23″ plywood
(1) Center, vertical strip section
    (All stock ¼″ thick)

Walnut
    1½″ × 3¼″ (2)
    1½″ × 11¼″ (2)
    1½″ × 19½″ (2)

Cherry
    1½″ × 7½″ (2)
    1½″ × 15¼″ (2)
    1¼″ × 23″ (2)

Birch
    ½″ × 4½″ (2)
    ½″ × 8½″ (2)
    ½″ × 12½″ (2)
    ½″ × 16½″ (2)
    ½″ × 20½″ (2)
    ½″ × 23½″ (1)

Diagonal corner strips

Walnut
    1½″ × 17½″ (4)
    1½″ × 9″ (4)

Cherry
    1½″ × 13″ (4)
    1½″ × 5″ (4)

Birch
    ½″ × 14″ (4)
    ½″ × 10″ (4)
    ½″ × 6½″ (4)

Edge, trim, walnut
    ⅜ × ½″ × 21½″ (2)
    ⅜″ × ½″ × 22″ (2)

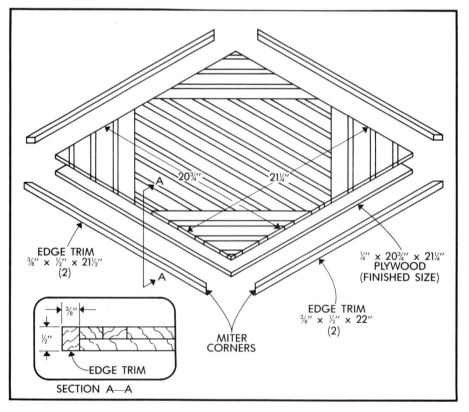

EDGE TRIM
⅜″ × ½″ × 21½″
(2)

¼″ × 20¾″ × 21¼″
PLYWOOD
(FINISHED SIZE)

EDGE TRIM
⅜″ × ½″ × 22″
(2)

MITER
CORNERS

EDGE TRIM

SECTION A—A

square on the glued-up strips, then unclamp the assembly and cut it to shape. Glue and clamp the trimmed square to the plywood base. Sand it smooth after the glue has set.

Glue on the diagonal strips at each corner of the base. Again, clamp the assembly with boards on top to keep it flat. After the glue has set completely, cut the board to the size required for its intended use.

Glue the diagonal strips to oversize plywood base and each other, at corners. Clamp solidly, let glue set completely; overnight is best.

Walnut edging is cut to size, corners mitered, then glued and clamped to assembly. Use waxed paper so work is not glued to bench.

Walnut trim strips are cut next to fit with mitered corners and glued to the edges of the assembled board and base. After fitting all four strips, glue and clamp opposite pairs, fitting waxed paper under the board so it will not be glued to the work surface.

When the glue has set completely, a finish sander is used for the final sanding. The edges and underside of the board are finished with polyurethane varnish. The surface of the blocks is treated by rubbing in several coats of salad oil. More oil should be applied every few months, since it gradually is removed when the board is cleaned.

Letter Organizer

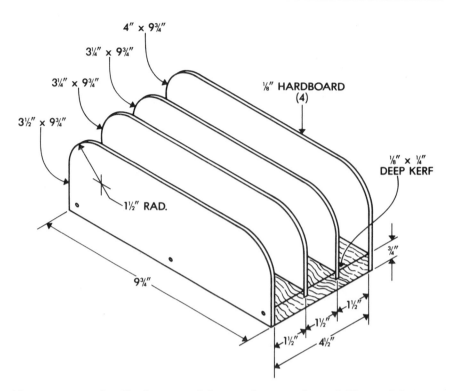

4″ × 9¾″

3¼″ × 9¾″

3¼″ × 9¾″

3½″ × 9¾″

⅛″ HARDBOARD (4)

⅛″ × ¼″ DEEP KERF

1½″ RAD.

9¾″

¾″

1½″

1½″

1½″

4½″

Almost every family has need for a place to keep bills and letters handy for various members, and this simple device can be placed on a hall table or perhaps the kitchen desk.

Because it is easy to make, you can assemble it in one evening. Material required is a piece of 1-in. (¾ in. net) stock 4½ × 9¾ in. and some scraps of ⅛-in. material to the sizes given, then round the two upper corners. Dado the piece of 1-in. stock, spacing the dadoes as indicated in the drawing and cutting them ¼ in. deep. Two passes with a regular saw blade should create a dado that makes a snug fit for the ⅛-in. stock.

We made the "front" piece ½ in. shorter than the back, but you might want to make these two pieces the same height. Glue the dividers in the slots and glue and screw the front and back pieces to the base piece.

Stain or paint to suit.

Two Desk Organizers

To build these convenient organizers, use ¼-in. hardboard or plywood. Glue and brad the various pieces together. With a little care, you can cut ⅛-in. dadoes in some of the partitions into which the shelves can be glued.

Before you start the project, determine what the various compartments will hold, and size them to suit. The dimensions given are for a particular desk with definite requirements, and may not necessarily suit your needs.

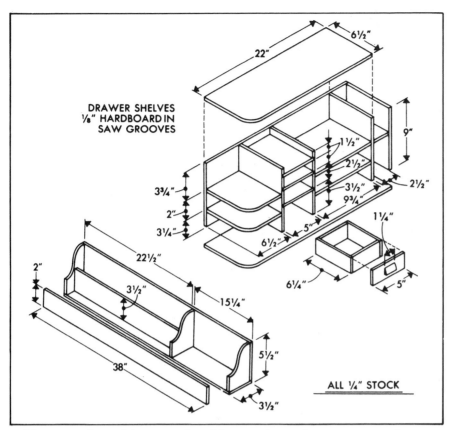

The curved partitions can be either an inward or an outward curve. Or just make the partitions square with rounded corners.

If you use hardboard, it's best to bore pilot holes for the finishing nails.

If the two assemblies are to be moved from the desk occasionally, make the bottoms of slightly heavier stock. If the units are to sit on a desk with a finished surface, glue pieces or spots of felt on the undersides.

Size each drawer to fit its opening. Note that a 5-in. drawer is shown for a 5-in. opening. This should be reduced by at least 1/16 in. to ensure the drawer will slide in and out easily.

Coin Counter

Drill holes through solid stock, then slice block in half to create grooves. Cut block to correct height after stacking coins in groove. Block shown is for 50 pennies to a groove. Bore holes slightly larger than coins.

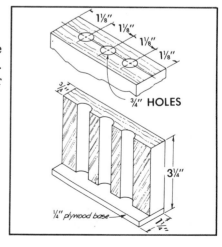

Elegant Wall Shelf

While basically a simple project to build, this colonial wall shelf has a few challenges to the woodworker that should be kept in mind. Note

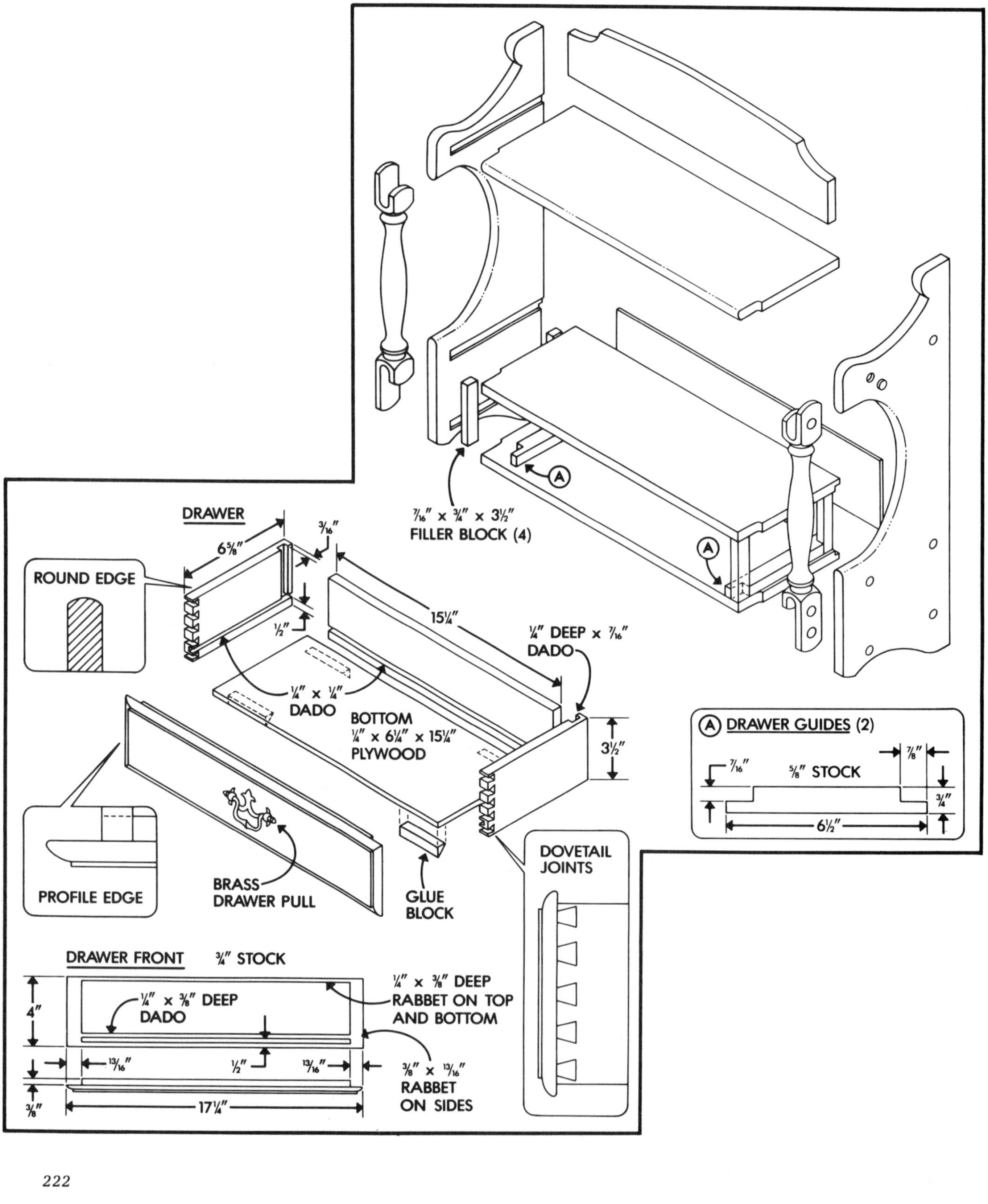

7/16" x 3/4" x 3 1/2"
FILLER BLOCK (4)
A
DRAWER
6 5/8"
3/16"
ROUND EDGE
1/2"
15 1/4"
1/4" DEEP x 7/16"
DADO
1/4" x 1/4"
DADO
BOTTOM
1/4" x 6 1/4" x 15 1/4"
PLYWOOD
3 1/2"
A DRAWER GUIDES (2)
7/16"
5/8" STOCK
7/8"
3/4"
6 1/2"
PROFILE EDGE
BRASS
DRAWER PULL
GLUE
BLOCK
DOVETAIL
JOINTS
DRAWER FRONT
3/4" STOCK
1/4" x 3/8" DEEP
DADO
1/4" x 3/8" DEEP
RABBET ON TOP
AND BOTTOM
4"
13/16"
1/2"
13/16"
3/8" x 13/16"
RABBET
ON SIDES
3/8"
17 1/4"

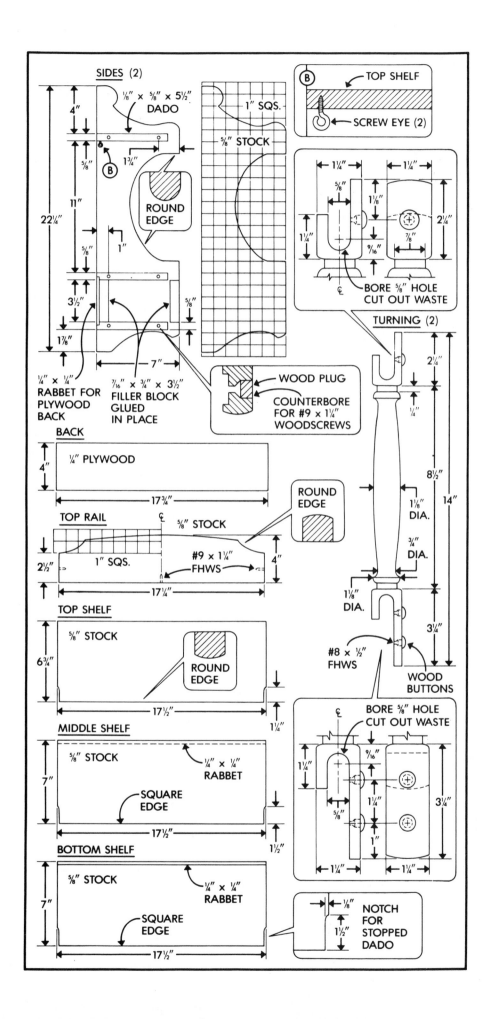

SIDES (2)

$\frac{1}{8}'' \times \frac{5}{8}'' \times 5\frac{1}{2}''$ DADO

1" SQS.

$\frac{5}{8}''$ STOCK

ROUND EDGE

4"

$\frac{5}{8}''$

B

$1\frac{3}{4}''$

11"

22$\frac{1}{4}''$

$\frac{5}{8}''$

1"

$3\frac{1}{2}''$

$\frac{5}{8}''$

$1\frac{7}{8}''$

7"

$\frac{1}{4}'' \times \frac{1}{4}''$ RABBET FOR PLYWOOD BACK

$\frac{7}{16}'' \times \frac{3}{4}'' \times 3\frac{1}{2}''$ FILLER BLOCK GLUED IN PLACE

WOOD PLUG

COUNTERBORE FOR #9 × 1$\frac{1}{4}''$ WOODSCREWS

BACK

$\frac{1}{4}''$ PLYWOOD

4"

17$\frac{3}{4}''$

TOP RAIL

$\frac{5}{8}''$ STOCK

1" SQS.

$\frac{5}{8}''$ STOCK

ROUND EDGE

#9 × 1$\frac{1}{4}''$ FHWS

$2\frac{1}{2}''$

4"

17$\frac{1}{4}''$

TOP SHELF

$\frac{5}{8}''$ STOCK

ROUND EDGE

$6\frac{3}{4}''$

17$\frac{1}{2}''$

$1\frac{1}{4}''$

MIDDLE SHELF

$\frac{5}{8}''$ STOCK

$\frac{1}{4}'' \times \frac{1}{4}''$ RABBET

SQUARE EDGE

7"

17$\frac{1}{2}''$

$1\frac{1}{2}''$

BOTTOM SHELF

$\frac{5}{8}''$ STOCK

$\frac{1}{4}'' \times \frac{1}{4}''$ RABBET

SQUARE EDGE

7"

17$\frac{1}{2}''$

B

TOP SHELF

SCREW EYE (2)

$1\frac{1}{4}''$ $1\frac{1}{4}''$

$\frac{5}{8}''$

$1\frac{1}{8}''$

$2\frac{1}{4}''$

$1\frac{1}{4}''$

$\frac{7}{8}''$

$\frac{9}{16}''$

BORE $\frac{5}{8}''$ HOLE CUT OUT WASTE

TURNING (2)

$2\frac{1}{4}''$

$\frac{1}{4}''$

$8\frac{1}{2}''$

14"

$1\frac{1}{8}''$ DIA.

$\frac{3}{4}''$ DIA.

$1\frac{1}{8}''$ DIA.

#8 × $\frac{1}{2}''$ FHWS

WOOD BUTTONS

$3\frac{1}{4}''$

BORE $\frac{5}{8}''$ HOLE CUT OUT WASTE

$1\frac{1}{4}''$

$\frac{9}{16}''$

$\frac{5}{8}''$

$1\frac{1}{4}''$

1"

$3\frac{1}{4}''$

$1\frac{1}{4}''$ $1\frac{1}{4}''$

$\frac{1}{8}''$

NOTCH FOR STOPPED DADO

$1\frac{1}{2}''$

that the turnings are slotted at top and bottom, with the inner half of the ends cut short to fit under the top shelf and above the lower one.

Enlarge the squared drawing (page 223) to make a pattern for the two sides. Draw the pattern on the stock, but cut the three dadoes in each piece (on the inner surface) before cutting the sides to shape. All three dadoes are stopped short of the front, as detailed. The shelves are notched to accommodate the stopped dadoes.

Round the front edges of the two sides, using a router or shaper, or simply rasp, file and sandpaper. Drill the counterbored holes for the screws that hold the shelves in the dadoes. Wood plugs then are glued in the counterbores after assembly.

Cut the shelves to size, notch them and assemble sides and shelves with glue and screws. Enlarge the squared drawing, make a pattern and cut the top rail to size and shape. Install it with glue and screws driven through the sides.

Cut the back to size and brad it into the rabbets in the lower portion of each side and those in the middle and bottom shelf. Some craftsmen might prefer to shorten the middle shelf ¼ in. and make the back large enough to run up to the top shelf. The top shelf would have to be rabbeted to accept the enlarged back as would the inner, back edges of the center portion of the sides.

Turn the two spindles and notch the ends as detailed. This is done by drilling a ⅝-in. hole, then cutting to the hole. One side then is cut short so the spindles fit between the shelves. Screws are driven through the ends of the spindles in counterbored holes that then are plugged with wooden buttons. Note that the filler blocks keep the drawer inside the spindles.

The drawer assembly is pretty straightforward with back and sides dadoed to accept the bottom, while the front is rabbeted all around and dovetailed to the sides. If you can't handle the dovetails, simply glue and nail the front ends of the sides into the edges of the rabbets in the front.

Birch was used for the original shelf, and it was stained and varnished. It is a good idea to finish sand the various parts before you assemble them. It is a lot easier than after assembly. The drawer pull is installed last, and can be any colonial style you wish.

Multi-purpose Wall Shelves

Wall shelves can display all manner of objects to give your home a special look. Vases, figurines, candlesticks, models, clocks—you name it.

The proper size for a wall shelf is determined by the wall space available and the item to be displayed. A clock or some books will require a wide shelf, while a collection of china plates can be placed on a narrow shelf.

Fig. 1 (next page) gives the general dimensions for a medium-size shelf, as illustrated in the photo. One photograph shows the shelf "in the white" with the edges profiled and a plate groove cut in it. The groove can be made with a saw or router.

The support brackets are shown in the photo, with the clamp released. Two L-shape components are mitered and joined with glue, with two diagonally opposite miters not glued, Fig. 2. When the glue

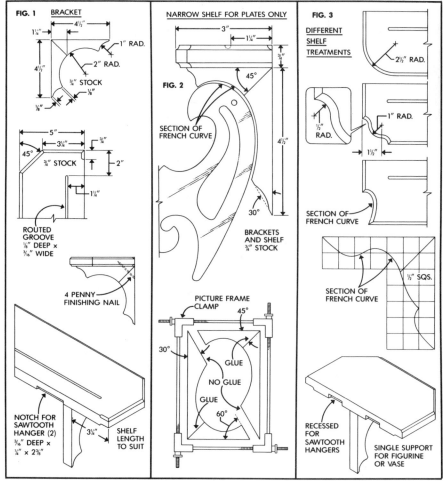

Plate display shelf and its two brackets. Brackets are mitered and clamped, then cut to suitable shape.

Brackets are positioned flush with back edge of shelf; sawtooth picture frame hangers are screwed into notches cut in back edge.

has set on the miters, the brackets are cut to shape; the curves may be drawn with the aid of a French curve.

The lower back edges of the shelves are notched to accept sawtoothed picture frame hangers, as in Fig. 3 and the photograph showing the two-bracket shelf inverted. Cut the notches just a bit longer than the hangers and just deep enough so the hangers are slightly below the surface of the back edge of the shelf, Fig. 1.

Longer shelves require two or more brackets; short shelves need only one.

Shelves used for displaying plates can be quite narrow, Fig. 2, with the plate groove cut along the center of the shelf. The lower projection of the bracket should be longer than the horizontal portion, Fig. 2, for appearance and better support.

The overall design of a display shelf can be varied. Fig. 3 illustrates just a few ideas. Also, the upper and lower edges of a shelf can be profiled in any of a dozen ways, as can the brackets.

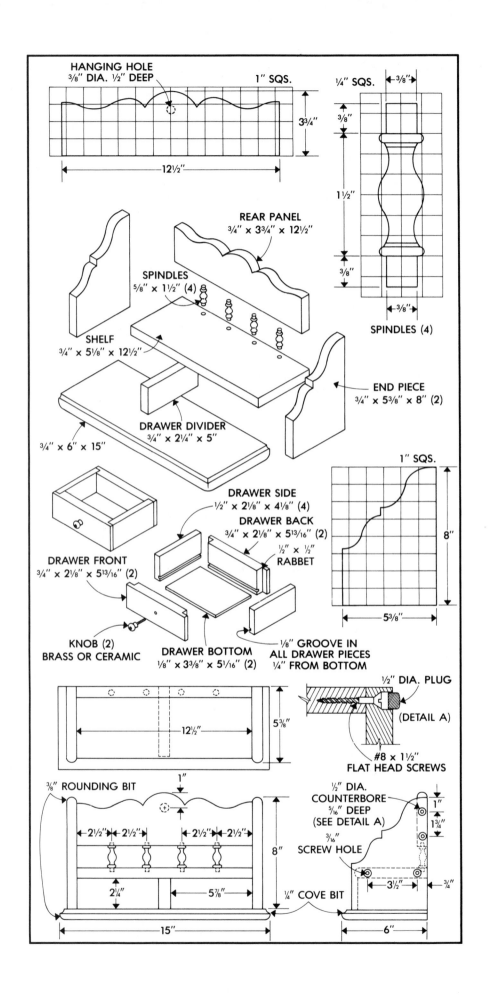

HANGING HOLE
3/8" DIA. 1/2" DEEP

1" SQS.

3 3/4"

12 1/2"

1/4" SQS.

3/8"

3/8"

1 1/2"

3/8"

3/8"

3/8"

SPINDLES (4)

REAR PANEL
3/4" × 3 3/4" × 12 1/2"

SPINDLES
5/8" × 1 1/2" (4)

SHELF
3/4" × 5 1/8" × 12 1/2"

END PIECE
3/4" × 5 3/8" × 8" (2)

DRAWER DIVIDER
3/4" × 2 1/4" × 5"

3/4" × 6" × 15"

1" SQS.

8"

5 3/8"

DRAWER SIDE
1/2" × 2 1/8" × 4 1/8" (4)

DRAWER BACK
3/4" × 2 1/8" × 5 13/16" (2)

1/2" × 1/2"
RABBET

DRAWER FRONT
3/4" × 2 1/8" × 5 13/16" (2)

KNOB (2)
BRASS OR CERAMIC

DRAWER BOTTOM
1/8" × 3 3/8" × 5 1/16" (2)

1/8" GROOVE IN
ALL DRAWER PIECES
1/4" FROM BOTTOM

12 1/2"

5 3/8"

1/2" DIA. PLUG

(DETAIL A)

#8 × 1 1/2"
FLAT HEAD SCREWS

3/8" ROUNDING BIT

1"

2 1/2" 2 1/2" 2 1/2" 2 1/2"

8"

2 1/4"

5 7/8"

1/4" COVE BIT

15"

1/2" DIA.
COUNTERBORE
5/16" DEEP
(SEE DETAIL A)

3/16"
SCREW HOLE

1"

1 3/4"

3 1/2"

3/4"

6"

Two-drawer Shelf

When the rear panel is cut to size and shape, bore the blind hole for hanging as indicated (drawing at left). Next, mark the locations of the spindles and drill ⅜ × ⅜-in. blind holes as detailed. Mark and drill the spindle holes on the shelf to match those on the real panel.

Use the pattern to mark and cut out the two end pieces. Drill counterbored holes for screws as dimensioned. Because the ends are a pair, be sure the holes are on the outside surface of each one.

Join the shelf and rear panels with spindles, using a drop of glue in each hole. Fasten the drawer divider to the underside of the shelf with glue and 1½-in. finishing nails. Attach the bottom to the ends by driving 1½-in. flathead screws up through counterbored holes.

Glue plugs or buttons into all counterbored holes. Drive a couple of finishing nails up through the bottom into the drawer divider, making sure it is square with the bottom. Glue should be applied to the divider before attaching the ends and bottom.

Drawers are assembled as shown. The backs and fronts are the same, but the ends of the fronts are rounded over. Bottoms are fitted in the grooves in the front, back and sides as they are assembled with glue and brads.

Recess nail heads with a nailset, cover with wood putty, sand flush. Finish as desired.

Curio Shelf

Miters are shown at the four corners, but can be eliminated and the two side pieces, A1, shortened by 1½ in. to maintain overall size (drawing on next page). Use a miter box to ensure right-angle cuts on all pieces.

Assemble shelf with white glue and 6- or 8-penny finishing nails. Wipe off excess glue immediately with a damp cloth, set all nails and cover them with wood putty.

Obtain tiles before you start, so you can make any required adjustments in dimensions. Finish as desired.

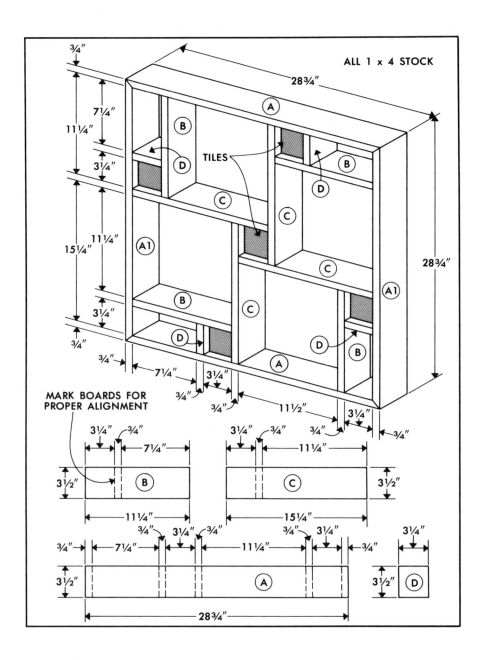

Contemporary Spice Shelf

This simple wooden shelf provides an attractive way to store spice jars or display small treasures, not only in the kitchen, but in other areas of the home as well. It can be easily completed in an afternoon or evening.

We used ½-in. mahogany for the sides and shelves, but ¾-in. stock would work as well. Be sure to adjust the dimensions if thicker stock is used.

Begin by ripping the stock for the sides and shelves. Cut the dadoes for the shelves, then rabbet the sides and top and bottom shelves to receive the mirror back. Make these rabbets ½-in. deep to allow for the ⅜-in. retainer strips that hold the mirror in place. The decorative top is cut to shape, rabbeted as shown, and the top edge shaped. The design can be changed, of course.

Assemble the shelf with glue and clamps. When dry, the front edges may be rounded if desired. Finish as desired then install the mirror. Tack the ⅜-in. retainer strips in place with wire brads. Attach shelf hangers or cut a key slot in the back.

The top is cut to shape, rabbeted to fit into side pieces. Shape top edge as desired.

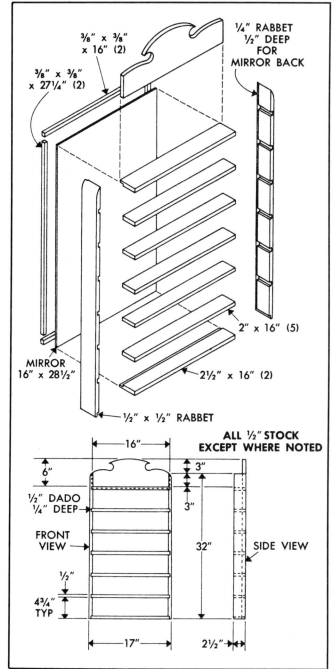

3/8" x 3/8" x 16" (2)

3/8" x 3/8" x 27¼" (2)

¼" RABBET ½" DEEP FOR MIRROR BACK

2" x 16" (5)

2½" x 16" (2)

MIRROR 16" x 28½"

½" x ½" RABBET

ALL ½" STOCK EXCEPT WHERE NOTED

16"

6"

½" DADO ¼" DEEP

FRONT VIEW

½"

4¾" TYP

3"

3"

32"

SIDE VIEW

17"

2½"

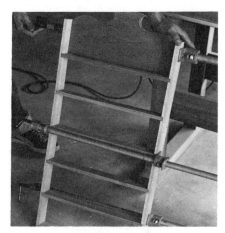

Shelf is assembled with glue and bar clamps. Be sure to keep unit square when clamping.

Edges of sides and shelves can be sanded smooth or rounded with a router as shown here, after the cabinet has been assembled. Use rounding-over router bit.

Silverware Chest

There are three storage areas in this silver chest: the chest proper, the lid and the drawer. Spoons and forks are fitted in the chest, the lid accepts up to eight knives and the drawer will accept serving utensils, candlesticks, salt and pepper shakers and the like.

The chest basically is a box to which molding is attached to create its character. I had some willow that I used for the chest, but ½-in. hardwood plywood also could be used, with molding shaped from hardwood.

Assemble the basic box as one unit, with top, bottom and four sides, then saw the top free. This will ensure an absolute match between the top and chest proper. Because of this, make the sides about ³⁄₁₆ in. higher than shown. The added height will allow for the width of the saw kerf and the light sanding required to remove the saw marks.

Note that the sides, back and front are rabbeted on the top and bottom edges to accept the top and bottom. Also, a dado is cut 3¾ in. from the bottom edges to accept the shelf (horizontal partition) that is positioned to create the drawer opening.

When you glue together the basic box, make sure there is no twist in the assembly. If there is, when you cut the box apart the stress will distort one or both parts so the lid does not close properly. You want a tight joint to keep out the air to minimize tarnish.

Start the embellishments by creating a ¾ × ¾-in. molding that is glued along the lower edges of the box. You can use the profile shown or create one of your own. Raised panels fit above the bottom molding, with a single panel at each end, and two at the back and front. The two front panels are applied to the drawer after it is fitted.

To make the raised panels on a table saw, first cut a ¹⁄₁₆ to ⅛-in. groove ⅞ in. from the four edges of each panel. Next, tilt the blade to 12 or 15 degrees and cut the bevel edge to meet the groove. This requires running the work pieces over the saw on the edges. Use hold-ins, hold-downs and push sticks to keep your fingers away from the blade. An auxiliary wooden fence clamped to the rip fence will aid in supporting the work piece.

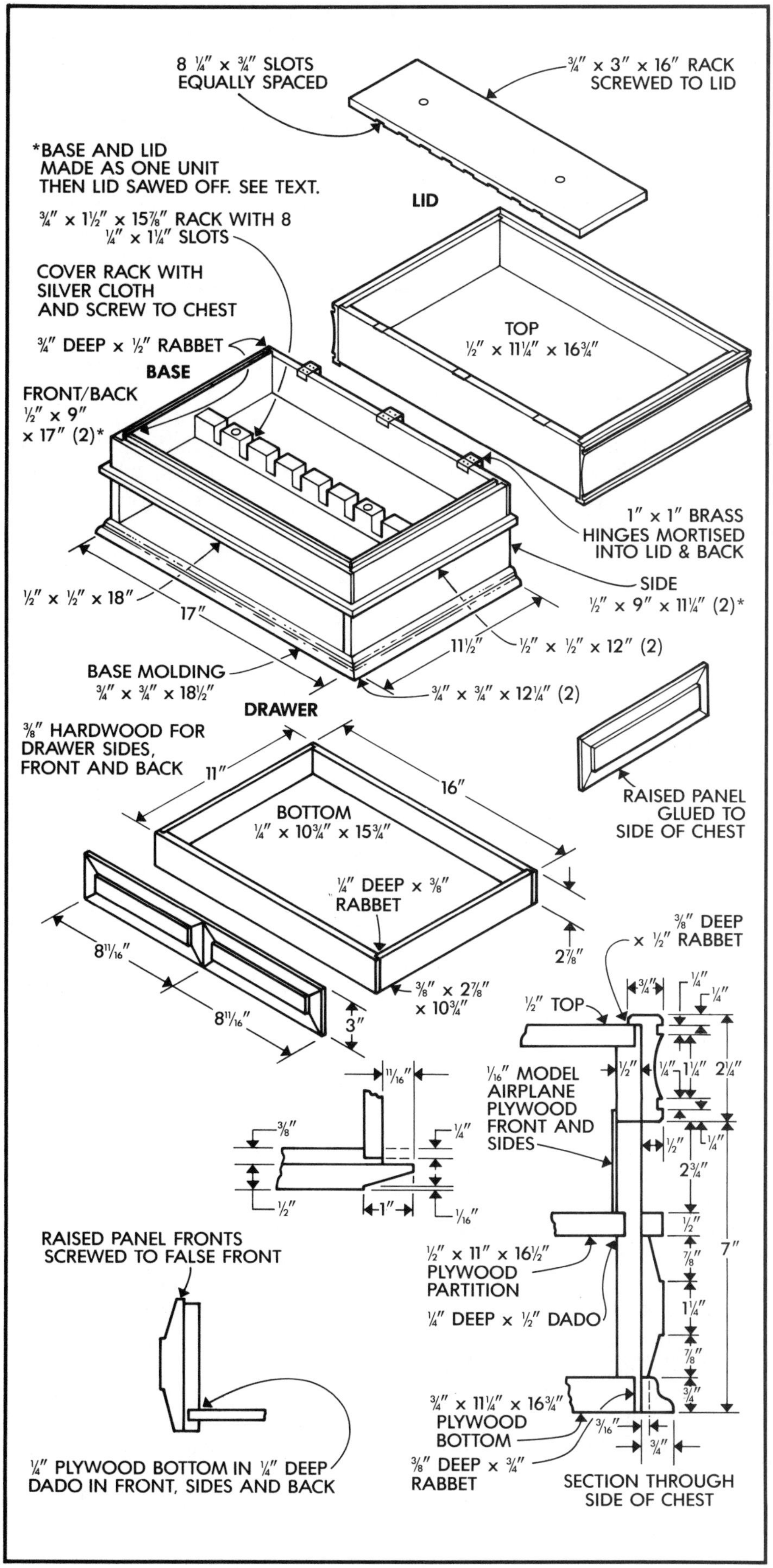

8 ¼″ x ¾″ SLOTS
EQUALLY SPACED
¾″ x 3″ x 16″ RACK
SCREWED TO LID
*BASE AND LID
MADE AS ONE UNIT
THEN LID SAWED OFF. SEE TEXT.
LID
¾″ x 1½″ x 15⅞″ RACK WITH 8
¼″ x 1¼″ SLOTS
COVER RACK WITH
SILVER CLOTH
AND SCREW TO CHEST
TOP
½″ x 11¼″ x 16¾″
¾″ DEEP x ½″ RABBET
BASE
FRONT/BACK
½″ x 9″
x 17″ (2)*
1″ x 1″ BRASS
HINGES MORTISED
INTO LID & BACK
SIDE
½″ x 9″ x 11¼″ (2)*
½″ x ½″ x 18″
17″
11½″
½″ x ½″ x 12″ (2)
BASE MOLDING
¾″ x ¾″ x 18½″
¾″ x ¾″ x 12¼″ (2)
DRAWER
⅜″ HARDWOOD FOR
DRAWER SIDES,
FRONT AND BACK
11″
16″
BOTTOM
¼″ x 10¾″ x 15¾″
RAISED PANEL
GLUED TO
SIDE OF CHEST
¼″ DEEP x ⅜″
RABBET
2⅞″
8¹¹⁄₁₆″
8¹¹⁄₁₆″
⅜″ x 2⅞″
x 10¾″
3″
⅜″ DEEP
x ½″ RABBET
½″ TOP
¾″
¼″
¼″
11⁄16″
⅜″
¼″
½″
1″
1⁄16″
1⁄16″ MODEL
AIRPLANE
PLYWOOD
FRONT AND
SIDES
½″
¼″
1¼″
2¼″
½″
¼″
2¾″
½″
7″
⅞″
1¼″
⅞″
¾″
RAISED PANEL FRONTS
SCREWED TO FALSE FRONT
½″ x 11″ x 16½″
PLYWOOD
PARTITION
¼″ DEEP x ½″ DADO
¾″ x 11¼″ x 16¾″
PLYWOOD
BOTTOM
3⁄16″
¾″
⅜″ DEEP x ¾″
RABBET
SECTION THROUGH
SIDE OF CHEST
¼″ PLYWOOD BOTTOM IN ¼″ DEEP
DADO IN FRONT, SIDES AND BACK

Make the drawer as detailed and fit it into the opening in the chest so it slides easily, then glue on the raised panels. All the raised panels can be additionally attached by driving flathead screws from the inside of the box.

Make the ½ × ½-in. strips next, fit them to the box, miter the ends and attach with glue. A couple of brads will aid in holding the strips. Set the nails and cover the heads with wood putty.

The upper molding is shaped as indicated, making shallow saw kerfs near the top and bottom after first coving the center portion. The cove can be created with the aid of a Safe-T-Planer, or by running the stock at an angle over the blade on a table saw. Make several passes, raising the blade a bit at a time for each pass until you reach the finished depth of the cove.

Before attaching the molding at the back, notch the molding for the three hinges.

I lined the chest with silver cloth (Pacific cloth), using one piece for the bottom and rear of the chest, and one piece for the back and top of the lid. The front and sides of the chest are lined with ⅟₁₆-in. model airplane plywood to create a flange to which the cloth is glued.

When gluing the cloth to the sides and front of the lid, lap it over onto the edges. Cloth is applied to all surfaces of the chest and lid.

Make the rack for the chest and the knife holder for the lid as detailed. Glue and screw the rack to the bottom of the chest, the knife holder to the lid. Force the cloth down over the two holders.

Alternately, start the screws to hold the two racks, wrap the cloth around them, then cut small slits to permit fitting a screwdriver into the screw slots to drive them home. If the cloth is wrapped around the bottoms of the racks, this last operation will ensure the cloth is held firmly in place.

If you have not already finished all surfaces before applying the cloth and installing the racks, finish the exposed wood to suit the location where the chest will be displayed. If the chest will be placed on a finished surface, glue felt to the bottom after the finish has completely dried.

Redwood Medicine Cabinet

Stopped mortises for shelf ends are cut from both sides to prevent wood splintering. Mark them accurately with square.

Because this project is designed as a medicine cabinet for a bathroom where high humidity is a problem, redwood was the lumber chosen for its construction.

At first glance the cabinet may seem a simple project, but it actually combines some challenging joinery and a considerable amount of hand work. Both through and half-blind dovetails are required, plus a through mortise-and-tenon joint for each shelf.

The sides, top, bottom and shelves of the cabinet, plus the drawer fronts and door insert are cut from ½-in. stock. The door frame, hinges and handles are from 2-in. lumber and the drawer sides and bottoms are ¼-in. materials.

Begin the project by cutting to size the sides, top and bottom of the cabinet. Cut the shelves the same length as the top and bottom, but make them ¼-in. narrower to allow for the ¼-in. back. Lay out and cut the through dovetails for the four corners of the cabinet. Cut tails on the side pieces, the pins on the top and bottoms.

Next, cut the rabbets on all four pieces to accept the back. Rabbets

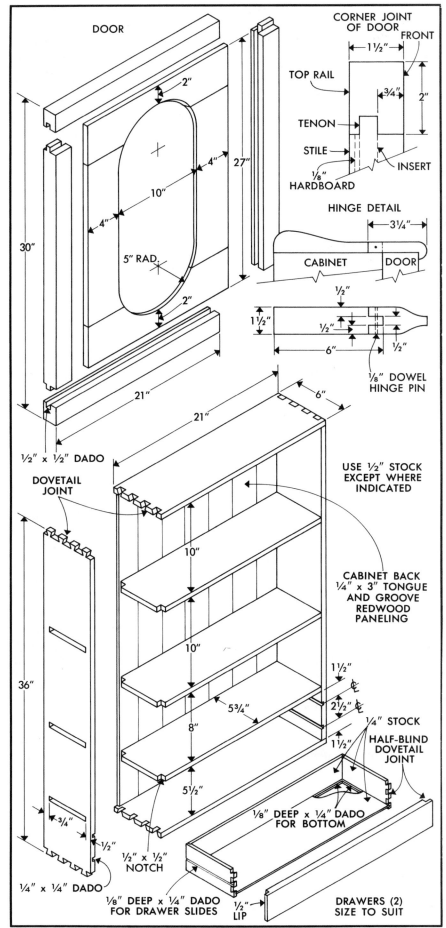

DOOR

2"

27"

30"

4"

4"

10"

4"

5" RAD.

2"

21"

½" × ½" DADO

DOVETAIL JOINT

36"

¾"

½"

¼" × ¼" DADO

⅛" DEEP × ¼" DADO FOR DRAWER SLIDES

½" × ½" NOTCH

⅛" DEEP × ¼" DADO FOR BOTTOM

½" LIP

DRAWERS (2) SIZE TO SUIT

10"

10"

8"

5½"

1½"

2½"

1½"

5¾"

21"

6"

USE ½" STOCK EXCEPT WHERE INDICATED

CABINET BACK ¼" × 3" TONGUE AND GROOVE REDWOOD PANELING

¼" STOCK

HALF-BLIND DOVETAIL JOINT

CORNER JOINT OF DOOR

FRONT

TOP RAIL

TENON

STILE

HARDBOARD

INSERT

1½"

¾"

2"

⅛"

HINGE DETAIL

CABINET

DOOR

3¼"

½"

1½"

½"

6"

½"

⅛" DOWEL HINGE PIN

Rabbet for cabinet back must be stopped on top and bottom pieces. Rabbets on side pieces are cut full length.

Edges of shelves were profiled with molding plane on the original, but router or shaper can be used.

Shelf ends are wiped with glue and tapped into stopped through mortises in the sides. Shelves should fit snugly.

Rabbet for mirror is routed around back of oval opening before the insert is fitted into the door frame. Frame is grooved.

Hinges are shaped from 2 x 2 stock, pins are ⅛-in. dowels that are cut flush after hinges are glued and assembled.

Back on original was made from ¼ x 3-in. redwood paneling glued and nailed to sides, top, bottom and the shelves.

on top and bottom pieces are stopped near the ends, while those on the sides run the full length.

Cut a ½ × ½-in. notch in each corner of each shelf to create a tenon. Next, lay out the mortises in the sides, marking both sides and cutting through halfway from both sides to prevent any surface splintering. Cut the dadoes for the drawer guides across the side pieces from front to back.

The cabinet now is assembled, using glue sparingly on the shelf tenons and the dovetails on the top, bottom and sides. Be sure the assembly is square. Set it aside for the glue to dry and work on the drawers and the door.

The door frame is made from 1½ × 2-in. stock. Measure the cabinet to determine the size of the door and cut the pieces to length, making the vertical stiles 1 in. longer than your measurement to allow material for the tenons. Shape the tenons, then dado the inside edges of the four pieces. The dadoes accept the insert and also the tenons on the stiles.

The door insert is assembled from four pieces. Place these so they form a rectangle and lay out the oval openings. Cut the curves on the separate pieces, then glue the four together. When the glue has set, rout the rabbet around the oval in which the mirror will be fitted. You will have to have this mirror cut to shape at a glass shop.

Round over the front edge of the oval, then assemble the door frame around the insert. Glue and clamp it together and set aside for the glue to harden.

The two small drawers are made with half-blind dovetails joining the sides to the front. Since the ends of the dovetails are hidden, you can cut the grooves for the drawer bottoms the full length of the pieces without concern that gaps will show. The drawer backs are dadoed into the sides. Be sure to make a ½-in. lip on each end and bottom of the lower drawer front. The lips cover the edges of the cabinet when the drawer is closed.

Before assembling the drawers, cut a ⅛ × ¼-in. dado in each drawer side for the guides. Assemble the drawers with glue and put them aside for the glue to set.

The back of the cabinet is made from ¼ × 3-in. tongue-and-groove redwood paneling, which also is the source for the stock used to make the drawers. Glue and nail the back to the rabbets of the cabinet, and also drive a few nails into each shelf. Set the mirror in the opening. Use a piece of ⅛-in. tempered hardboard as a backing for the door.

Cut the hinges to shape and assemble them, making sure the pins are glued to only one "leaf." One way to ensure the hinges are not glued solid is to move the leaves frequently while the glue sets. To prevent the pin moving in both leaves, drive small brads into the leaf in which you want the pin to be fixed.

Attach the hinges, and the handles, with glue and screws driven from the inside. Sand all surfaces of the completed cabinet and finish with a Danish oil sealer, followed by several coats of paste wax.

Magnetic Perpetual Calendar

This calendar is perpetual, but you do have to manually change the day, date and month as necessary. It is a rather unique workshop project and just might become an heirloom.

Start by cutting the main board 5¾ × 23 in. from stock that is re-sawed or thickness planed to ½ in. Enlarge the squared drawing to

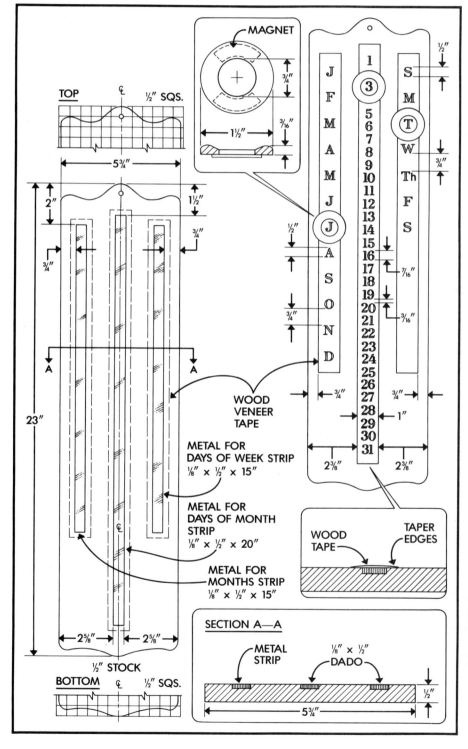

Dadoes are cut in board, ends squared, then metal strips are glued into the grooves, flush with the surface.

Veneer tape is glued over metal strips, using contact adhesive. Edges of strips are sanded to feather edge.

Numbers are drawn on the veneer tape strips with soft pencil. Simple template helps. Alternatively, use purchased numbers.

Burning pencil with small tip is used to further define the numbers and letters on the face of the calendar.

make a pattern that is cut at the top and bottom. Do this after first cutting the three dadoes, locating them as detailed on page 235.

Next, glue in steel strips, making sure they are flush with the surface of the board. If the dadoes are cut with a dado blade, it will be necessary to square up the ends with a wood chisel.

Epoxy glue is best for adhering the metal, and when the adhesive has set, apply hardwood veneer tape over the metal. Contact adhesive would be best for this. Feather the edges of the tape strips by sanding to remove the sharp edges.

Draw the numbers and letters as shown, or use purchased stick-on letters you can get at art supply and stationery outlets. If you draw the characters, burn them in with a fine tip in a burning pencil.

Turn the rings as indicated, or use wooden rings normally utilized in macrame or for hanging drapery. Sheet magnetic material that is available at hobby shops is cut into small segments and two are glued to the back of each ring, on opposite sides. The rings should be of a contrasting color, or stained to be so.

Seal the surface of the board and the rings after you stain them, then apply a coat of varnish.

Paper Towel Holders

If you are tired of the paper towel roll popping out of commercial-type holders, why not make a sure-lock holder? Here are two versions of a wooden paper towel holder; one to be fastened horizontally to the cabinet and one to carry vertically on a handy tote. Choose the holder that best suits your needs, then decide on a hardwood to use for the project, preferably a wood that will match your cabinets.

For the under-the-cabinet holder, use ¾-in. stock for the top board, cut to the dimension given. Cut rabbets across the ends ⅜ in. to accommodate the end pieces. Clamp a fence to the band saw to make a uniform cut, then split a piece of ¾-in. hardwood stock for the two ⅜-in. end pieces. Sand the cut faces thoroughly. Lay out the two end pieces on the split stock and drill a 1⅜-in. hole for the towel rod. A stop block clamped to the drill press table will keep the bit from twisting the stock.

Glue together two pieces of ¾-in. stock to make a turning block for the towel rod (or use a 1½-in. square turning block). Turn the rod to the dimensions given. Hold the rod on a V-block to drill the holes for the tapered lock pegs. Turn the pegs, slightly tapered, to fit the holes. Screw the ends to the top board. Push a lock peg through one of the holes till it is tight, pass the rod through the holes in the ends, then lock by pushing the second peg until it is tight. When the holder is mounted it is loaded in the same manner. The pegs are easily tapped out for replacing rolls.

The base and top of the vertical paper towel tote are of ¾-in. stock, the upright of ½-in. stock and the rod made from a 1-in. turning block. Saw out the circle for the top and mount on the screw center of the lathe for turning. Cut a waste stock circle, fit it against the spur of the tailstock and crank up the tailstock to bring the small circle against the large circle for support while turning. True up and sand the edges of the tote top.

Draw a line (chord) at the edge of the tote top circle 1½ in. long. Saw off this portion to create a flat edge for fastening the top to the upright. Drill a ⅞-in. hole through the top, using the lathe screw center hole as the location for drilling.

Turn the dowel rod to the dimensions given, shaping the top into a handle. Cut base and upright to the dimensions given. Assemble base, upright and top to locate the hole for the rod recess in the base; it will be slightly off-center from front to back because of the cut-off portion of the circle top. Pass the rod through the hole in the top. With the bottom of the rod resting on the base, use a square to line it up at right angles to the base and parallel to the back. Hold the rod down in this position and draw around the base to mark the location of the recess. Remove the base from the upright and drill the recess, ⅞ × ⅜ in. deep. Reassemble and finish the tote using your preferred method.

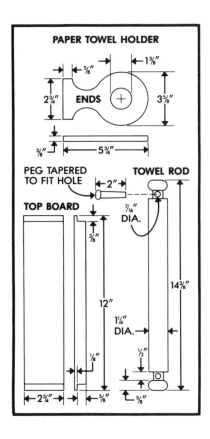

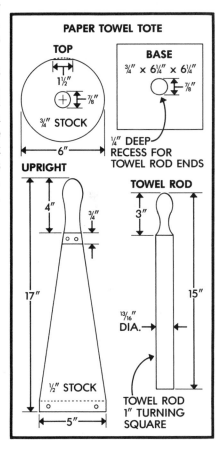

Compact Clock

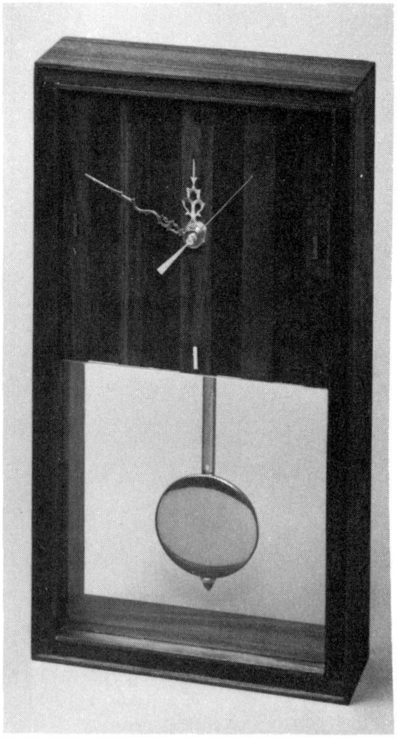

Designed to accept a quartz clock movement with a 10-in. pendulum, this clock with contemporary styling is a practical accessory that will grace any home.

The thin plywood and thin hardwood required will have to be purchased at a hobby shop, if local lumberyards and home centers do not carry it.

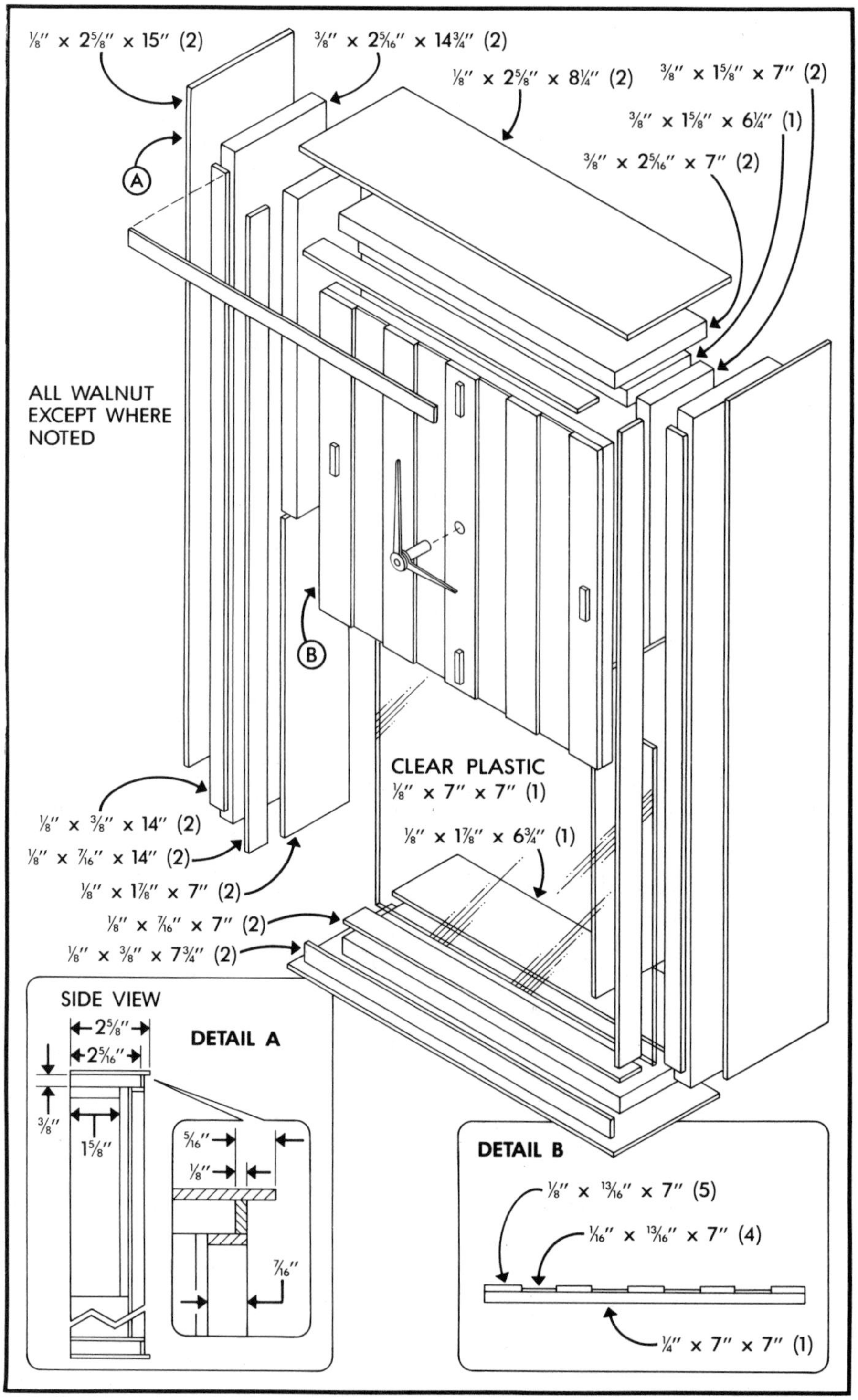
1/8" x 2 5/8" x 15" (2)
3/8" x 2 5/16" x 14 3/4" (2)
1/8" x 2 5/8" x 8 1/4" (2)
3/8" x 1 5/8" x 7" (2)
3/8" x 1 5/8" x 6 1/4" (1)
3/8" x 2 5/16" x 7" (2)
A
ALL WALNUT EXCEPT WHERE NOTED
B
CLEAR PLASTIC
1/8" x 7" x 7" (1)
1/8" x 1 7/8" x 6 3/4" (1)
1/8" x 3/8" x 14" (2)
1/8" x 7/16" x 14" (2)
1/8" x 1 7/8" x 7" (2)
1/8" x 7/16" x 7" (2)
1/8" x 3/8" x 7 3/4" (2)
SIDE VIEW
2 5/8"
2 5/16"
3/8"
1 5/8"
DETAIL A
5/16"
1/8"
7/16"
DETAIL B
1/8" x 13/16" x 7" (5)
1/16" x 13/16" x 7" (4)
1/4" x 7" x 7" (1)

Cut the four pieces of ⅜-in. plywood and make the basic case as detailed, using glue and nails. Next nail three strips of ⅜-in. plywood 1⅝ in. wide inside the top and sides, flush with one edge that will be the back of the clock case.

Cut a piece of ¼-in. plywood to 7 × 7 in., then glue alternating strips of 1/16 and ⅛-in. walnut to it, as detailed, to create the clock face. When the glue has set, glue the assembly inside the case to the ⅜-in. backing strips. The walnut strips are positioned vertically.

Next, glue the four strips of ⅛-in. walnut 7/16 in. wide inside the front edge of the clock frame, against the clock face. These strips that run the full length and width of the case will project about ⅛-in. Two strips of ⅛ × ⅜-in. walnut 14 in. long and two strips 7¾ in. now are glued to the front edges of the case. These strips conceal the edge grain of the ⅜-in. plywood used for the basic case frame. Two strips of ⅛-in. walnut are ripped to a width of 2⅝ in. and a length of 15 in. Glue these strips to the sides of the case with the edges flush with the back of the case. They will project about 3/16 in. at the front.

When the glue has set on these strips, trim and sand the ends flush with the top and bottom of the case. Next, glue on two 2⅝-in. strips 8¼ in. long to the top and bottom of the case. When the glue sets, trim and sand the ends so they are flush with the longer side strips.

Cut a piece of ⅛-in. clear acrylic plastic 7 × 7 in. and insert it from the back of the case against the 7/16-in. strips that serve as stops. Rip two pieces of ⅛-in. walnut to 1⅞-in. wide and 7 in. long. Glue these inside the case to hold the plastic in place. Clamp as necessary. A third strip of ⅛ × 1⅞-in. walnut is cut to a length of 6¾ in. and glued in the bottom of the case to also hold the plastic in place.

Drill a hole in the center of the clock face for the clock shaft. At this point, sand where necessary, then apply paste filler, stain and Danish oil or varnish as preferred.

When the finish is dried, install the clockworks.

Small Storage Shelves

Storing small screws, watch parts, snaps, rings and similar items so they are readily accessible is easy if you use the plastic containers in which 35-mm film is supplied.

Two storage devices are shown: a "ferris wheel" and a fixed shelf. To make the "ferris wheel," cut the six shelves to length and width, then

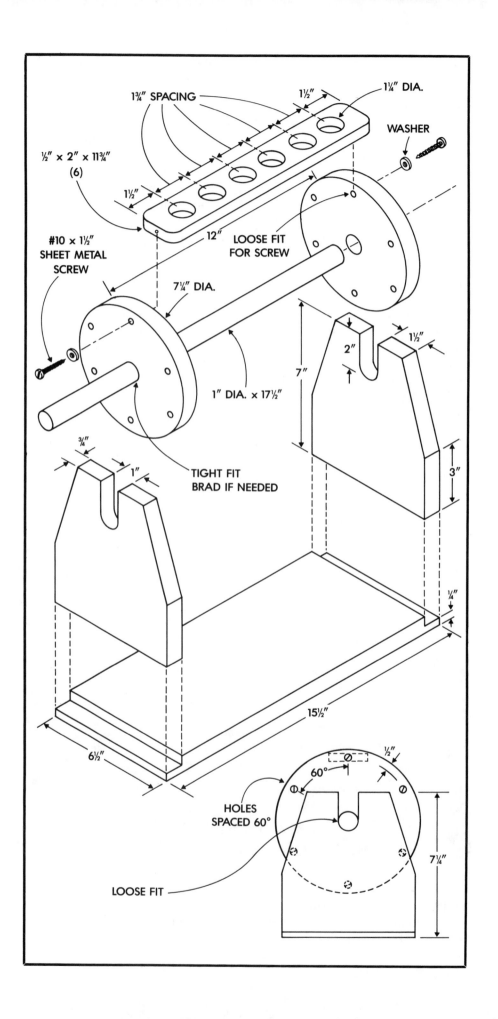

1¾" SPACING

1½"

1¼" DIA.

WASHER

½" × 2" × 11¾"
(6)

#10 × 1½"
SHEET METAL
SCREW

12"

LOOSE FIT
FOR SCREW

7¼" DIA.

1" DIA. × 17½"

7"

2"

1½"

3"

¾"

1"

TIGHT FIT
BRAD IF NEEDED

¼"

15½"

6½"

½"

60°

HOLES
SPACED 60°

7¼"

LOOSE FIT

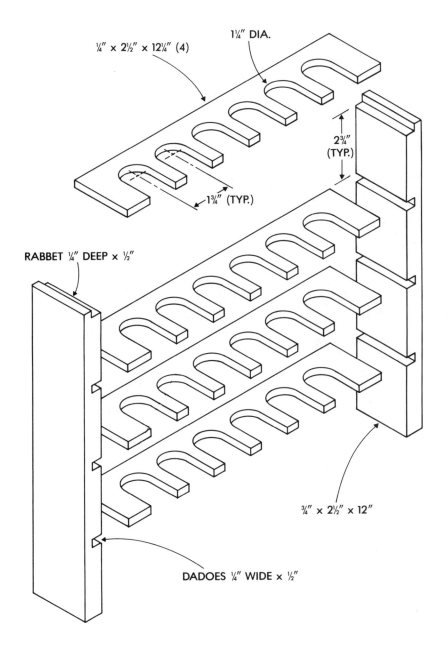

¼″ × 2½″ × 12¼″ (4)

1¼″ DIA.

2¾″ (TYP.)

1¾″ (TYP.)

RABBET ¼″ DEEP × ½″

¾″ × 2½″ × 12″

DADOES ¼″ WIDE × ½″

clamp them in a pad and bore the 1¼-in. holes with a spade bit or hole saw. The film containers fit easily in these holes.

Round the ends of the shelves as shown, then attach them to the end discs with pan head sheet-metal screws. Holes in the discs are slightly oversize so the screws turn easily, keeping the shelves level as the assembly is rotated.

The second method is a simple shelf assembly with the shelves glued into dadoes cut into the end pieces. Slots in the shelves are formed by first drilling 1¼-in. holes. Parallel, tangent lines then are cut to the circular cutouts to create the slots.

The simplest way of doing the machining is to cut the shelves to length and width from ¼-in. stock, then clamp them in a pad. Drill the holes and cut to form the slots while the shelves are still in the pad form.

The finished shelf will hold 24 of the film containers. Friends who use 35-mm film can supply you the containers, and professional film developers discard them by the hundreds.

Jewelry Box

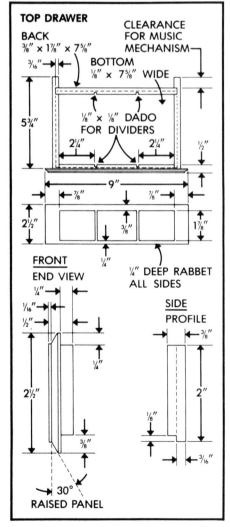

TOP DRAWER

BACK
3/8″ × 1 7/8″ × 7 5/8″

CLEARANCE FOR MUSIC MECHANISM

3/16″

BOTTOM
1/8″ × 7 5/8″ WIDE

5 3/4″

1/8″ × 1/8″ DADO FOR DIVIDERS

2 1/4″   2 1/4″   1/2″

9″

7/8″   7/8″

2 1/2″   3/8″   1 7/8″

FRONT
END VIEW

1/4″

1/4″ DEEP RABBET ALL SIDES

SIDE
PROFILE

1/4″
1/16″
1/2″

3/8″

1/4″

2 1/2″

2″

3/8″

1/8″

3/16″

30°
RAISED PANEL

This chest is beautiful as well as being practical and has several special features. The partitions in the drawers are removable and may be stored under the bottom drawer when not needed. As an added attraction, a musical movement is activated when the top drawer is opened.

Usually a straight-grained hardwood is recommended for a project such as this, but in this case, the irregular grain pattern is what makes the chest distinctive. Also, redwood is not the species of wood that normally would be used but it is easy to work and looks nice when finished. You can, of course, use whatever wood appeals most to you. And you will need some straight-grained wood—for the inside drawers and drawer slides/guides.

Begin by cutting the sides, top and bottom as shown in the drawing. Rabbets are cut on both ends to create tenons which fit in stopped dadoes in the top and bottom. Dadoes are cut in the sides, top and bottom to receive the 1/8-in. plywood back. Dadoes also are cut near the front of the sides for facings.

Make the eight drawer guides/slides. They can be formed from a single piece of stock 45 in. long and then cut into individual lengths. Note that a 3/8 × 1/2-in. strip is glued to the bottom outer edge of the two upper slides to act as guides for the top inside drawer. Attach the slides to the sides with glue and flathead wood screws.

Cut and assemble the stiles and rails for the facing. The top and bottom rails are joined to the stiles with dowels. The stiles are notched to receive the center rail and are reinforced with dowels as shown. Use glue and clamps to assemble the facing, paying particular attention to keep the assembly square and flat.

From ⅛-in. plywood or hardboard, cut the back, then dry assemble the cabinet case. Now is the time to check the inside measurements to determine any size adjustment of the drawers that may be necessary.

All the drawer components are made from ⅜-in.-thick redwood except for the front of the top drawer, which is ½ in. thick. Redwood

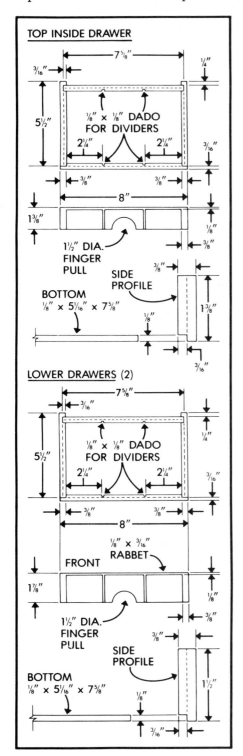

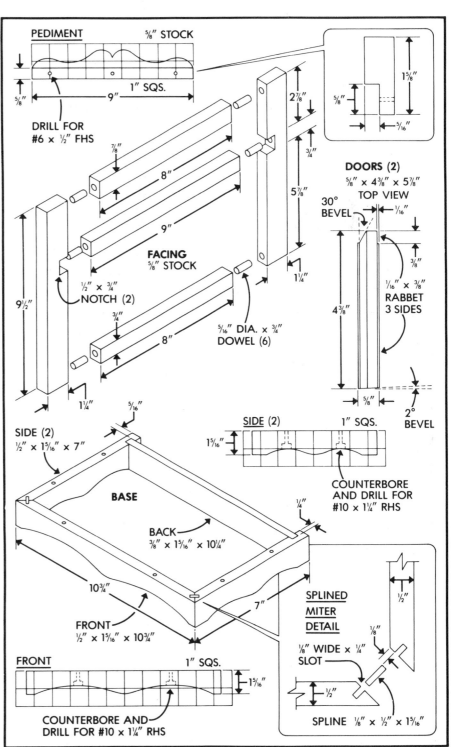

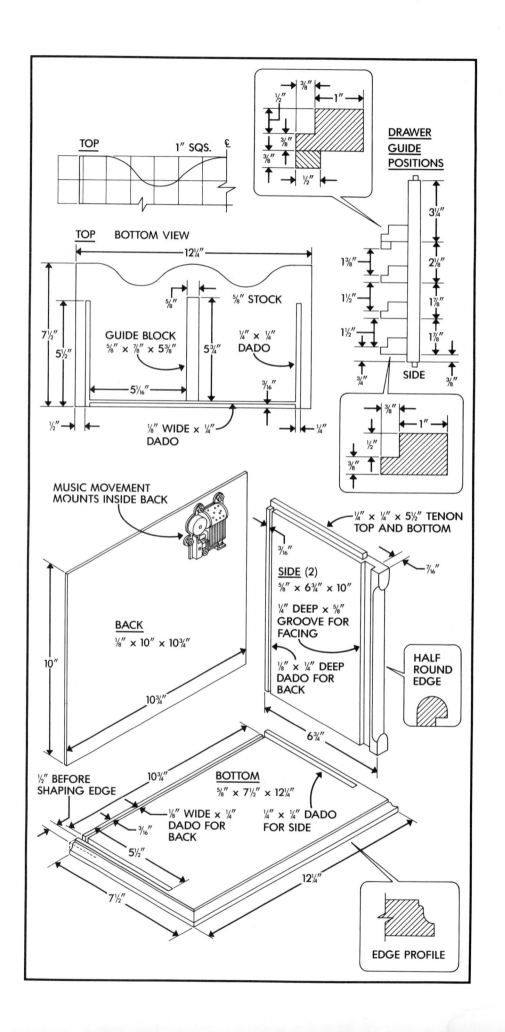

TOP   1" SQS.

TOP   BOTTOM VIEW

DRAWER
GUIDE
POSITIONS

12¼"

⅝"
⅝" STOCK

7½"
5½"

GUIDE BLOCK
⅝" × ⅞" × 5⅜"

¼" × ¼"
DADO

5¾"

3¼"

2⅛"

1⅞"

1⅞"

1⅜"

1½"

1½"

SIDE

¾"   ⅜"

5 1/16"

3/16"

½"

⅛" WIDE × ¼"
DADO

⅜"
1"
½"

⅜"
½"

MUSIC MOVEMENT
MOUNTS INSIDE BACK

¼" × ¼" × 5½" TENON
TOP AND BOTTOM

3/16"

7/16"

SIDE (2)
⅝" × 6¾" × 10"

¼" DEEP × ⅝"
GROOVE FOR
FACING

BACK
⅛" × 10" × 10¾"

10"

10¾"

⅛" × ¼" DEEP
DADO FOR
BACK

HALF
ROUND
EDGE

6¾"

½" BEFORE
SHAPING EDGE

10¾"

BOTTOM
⅝" × 7½" × 12¼"

3/16"

⅛" WIDE × ¼"
DADO FOR
BACK

¼" × ¼" DADO
FOR SIDE

5½"

7½"

12¼"

EDGE PROFILE

lumber will not be readily available in this thickness so it will be necessary either to plane or resaw heavier stock to the appropriate thickness.

The half-round cutouts in the three inside drawers were shaped with a 1½-in. Forstner bit, but they could be cut with a band or saber saw. Do not assemble the drawers at this time.

Cut the doors and bevel three edges to make the raised panels. The edges where the doors meet are not beveled, but cut at a 2-degree angle to provide swinging clearance. Also cut the raised panel for the top drawer front. Profile the edges of the top, bottom and the fronts of the sides.

Assemble the sides, bottom, back and front facing with glue and clamps. The top is set in place but not glued. After the glue has set, assemble the drawers and check for fit. The top drawer is not as deep as the three inner drawers to allow for the music movement, which is fitted in place after the top drawer assembly is complete. A wood bumper is added to the back of the drawer to shut off the music when the drawer is closed. When the musical movement operates properly, the top can be glued to the cabinet.

Cut the pediment, profile the edges and mount it to the rear edge of the top with glue and three flathead wood screws. Make the base as shown. The front and sides have a splined miter joint. The back fits in dadoes in the side pieces. Assemble with glue and clamps; when dry, attach to the cabinet with glue and wood screws in counterbored holes.

Mount the doors with the hardware you have selected and attach magnetic catches.

Finish the cabinet and drawers. After the finish has dried, place a lining material such as velvet in the drawers with the dividers removed. The dividers sit on top of the lining material and help hold it in place, or it can be glued in with white glue.

Half-round cutout finger pulls are made with Forstner bit in drill press. Band saw or saber saw could be used.

To make raised panels, 1/16 in. deep kerf first is made 3/8 in. from edge. Then 30 degree cut is made even with kerf.

Cabinet and drawers are assembled with top off. Note mounting of music movement. It should operate properly before gluing on top.

Cassette Tape Storage Projects

With more and more products that use cassette tapes on the market, storage of the tapes can become a problem. Here are two projects you can build as an alternative to commercial units.

Standard cassettes measure ¾ × 2¾ × 4¼ in. long. The wall-mounted storage unit holds 60 tapes on end and they protrude about a half inch for easy grasping. Storage capacity is easily increased by changing the length of the dividers, top and bottom, or by adding additional shelves. For example, if you want twenty tapes per shelf instead of fifteen as shown in the drawing on the next page, add one inch for each additional tape. The dividers would be 20¾ in. long and the top and bottom would be 21¾ in. long. Each additional shelf would add 4¾ in. to the length of the sides, and the size of the back would increase accordingly.

For cabinet storage, the tapes are stored on end in drawers. The cabinet shown in one photo was built for a library to hold computer cassette tapes and takes up less than five square feet of table space. If you are planning to build a stereo cabinet, you might want to include a cassette storage drawer (drawing on page 248).

Since there are so many dadoes to cut in this project, a jig is used to space the dadoes uniformly and to speed up cutting them. The jig is a piece of straight hardwood ¾ × 3 × 20 in. long with two dadoes in the bottom and a thin strip of wood fastened in one of the slots.

Cut the two dadoes in the bottom edge of the board so that they are exactly ¼ in. apart. The distance between the dadoes determines the distance between the dadoes in the workpiece. After the first dado is cut, the workpiece is placed so that dado fits over the thin strip in the jig. Then the next dado is cut. The process is repeated until all the dadoes are cut in each piece.

Since the storage rack requires so little lumber, it won't cost much to use a good-quality hardwood. Cut the ¾-in. stock for the dividers, sides, top and bottom to the proper width, but leave an inch or two of extra stock at the ends to form the joints. Cut the rabbets for the back on the top, bottom and sides before you cut the dadoes. This will help prevent chipping off the corners of the partitions between the slots.

Then use the jig to cut the dadoes in the top, bottom and dividers. Be sure to leave enough stock at each end to make the joints. Also be sure the dadoes on both sides of the dividers line up.

Cut the dadoes in the sides to receive the ends of the dividers. These can be measured and marked on the workpiece and passed through the saw with the miter gauge. If you plan to make several storage units, you might want to make another jig to space these dadoes uniformly.

Cut the miters at both ends of the top, bottom and sides as shown in the drawing. Then cut the dividers to proper length, leaving ½ in. of solid stock at each end. Before assembly, sand off any fuzz left from cutting the dadoes and joints.

Cut the plywood back and test fit it in the "dry assembly." Assemble the unit with glue and small finishing nails. Use a web clamp to hold the assembly together while nailing. The unit mounts to the wall with round head screws positioned so the heads don't line up with the tape slots.

The three-drawer cabinet utilizes the same setup to cut the dadoes in the dividers and drawer sides as the wall-mounted unit. In the drawer unit, the dividers are spaced 2½ in. apart instead of 4 in.

Since there are more than 50 dadoes to cut in the front and back for the dividers, it would save time to make another jig to cut the dadoes for the dividers. Make the drawers first, and then build the cabinet to fit the drawers. The measurements given in the drawing allow for full-extension drawer slides which require ¾-in. clearance on each side and ¼-in. clearance at the rear of the drawer. Some drawer slides require only ½-in. clearance on each side, so allow for this when building the cabinet. Buy the slides first.

The drawer sides are the same as the dividers, except they are dadoed on one side only. Cut the rabbets in the sides, front and back first. Then cut the dadoes.

The drawer fronts overlap the drawer opening ⅜ in. on all sides. Use small brads through the bottom to hold the front and dividers together during assembly. The back can be bradded directly to the dividers.

Assemble the cabinet as shown in the drawing, but attach the drawer-slide supports with screws only. They may have to be adjusted

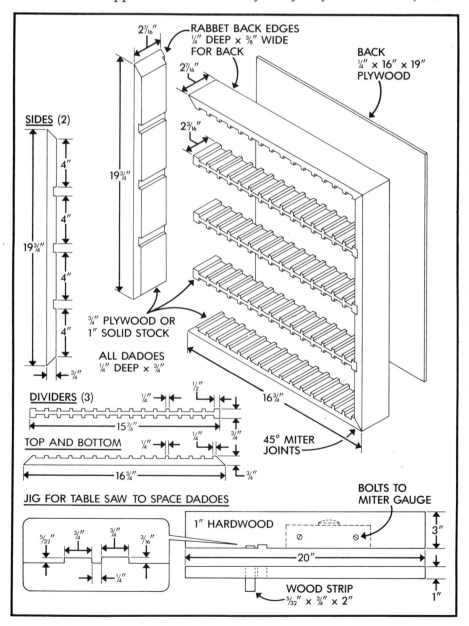

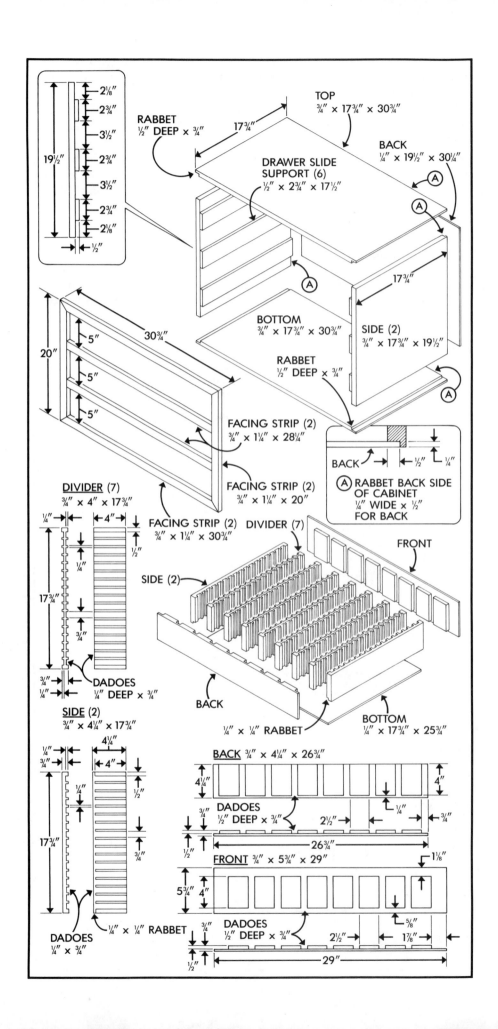

RABBET
½″ DEEP × ¾″

2⅛″
2¾″
3½″
2¾″
3½″
2¾″
2⅛″

19½″

½″

TOP
¾″ × 17¾″ × 30¾″

17¾″

BACK
¼″ × 19½″ × 30¼″

DRAWER SLIDE
SUPPORT (6)
½″ × 2¾″ × 17½″

Ⓐ

Ⓐ

17¾″

Ⓐ

BOTTOM
¾″ × 17¾″ × 30¾″

SIDE (2)
¾″ × 17¾″ × 19½″

RABBET
½″ DEEP × ¾″

Ⓐ

30¾″

20″

5″

5″

5″

FACING STRIP (2)
¾″ × 1¼″ × 28¼″

FACING STRIP (2)
¾″ × 1¼″ × 20″

BACK

½″ ¼″

Ⓐ RABBET BACK SIDE
OF CABINET
¼″ WIDE × ½″
FOR BACK

DIVIDER (7)
¾″ × 4″ × 17¾″

¼″ 4″ ½″

¼″

17¾″

¾″

¾″
¼″

DADOES
¼″ DEEP × ¾″

FACING STRIP (2)
¾″ × 1¼″ × 30¾″

DIVIDER (7)

SIDE (2)

FRONT

BACK

BOTTOM
¼″ × 17¾″ × 25¾″

¼″ × ¼″ RABBET

SIDE (2)
¾″ × 4¼″ × 17¾″

¼″
¾″

4¼″

4″

¼″

½″

17¾″

¾″

DADOES
¼″ × ¾″

¼″ × ¼″ RABBET

BACK ¾″ × 4¼″ × 26¾″

4¼″   4″

DADOES
½″ DEEP × ¾″   2½″   ¾″

¾″   ¼″

½″   26¾″

FRONT ¾″ × 5¾″ × 29″

1⅛″

5¾″   4″

DADOES
½″ DEEP × ¾″   2½″   1⅞″

5/8″

¾″

½″   29″

later to get the drawers to slide smoothly. Use glue and finishing nails to join the top, bottom and sides as well as the facing. Leave off the back until you've finished fitting the drawers.

Install the drawer-slide hardware to the drawers and the slide supports. Then insert a drawer in its opening and close it so the lip fits snugly against the facing on all sides. Use padded bar clamps to hold the drawer in place while adjusting the drawer-slide supports. It may be necessary to shim them out a little or to make them thinner to get the drawers to slide in and out properly. When the adjustment is right, fasten the slide supports to the sides of the cabinet. Then install the back. Finish to suit.

Laminated Nativity Picture

Various parts of the figures are cut from balsa wood 1/16 in. thick. Use sharp knife or thin blade in scroll saw.

Window scene is assembled from pieces of 1/16 in. balsa. Upper edges of "hills" are stained light brown color.

Cut-out pieces of nativity scene are first arranged on cardboard, then glued to plywood backing in their proper order.

This freestanding three-dimensional picture gives the illusion of viewing the nativity scene through the open stable door, with Bethlehem's hills in sight through the window in the back wall.

Rough-cut cedar, which is rough only on the top surface, comes ⅞ in. thick and is resawed ⅛ in. thick to make the planks in the back wall, the ceiling and the angled support beam. The full thickness is used for the base and the three pieces that form the door frame.

The figures and the scene in the window are laminated from pieces of balsa ¹⁄₁₆ in. thick, while the stones for the floor are ⅛-in. balsa. After you cut out the stones, round their edges and space them slightly apart.

Cut out the various pieces as detailed, noting that two or more layers are used to create a three-dimensional appearance. Place the various pieces on a piece of cardboard somewhat larger than the backing board that is a rectangle of ¼-in. plywood. Cut the backing board to

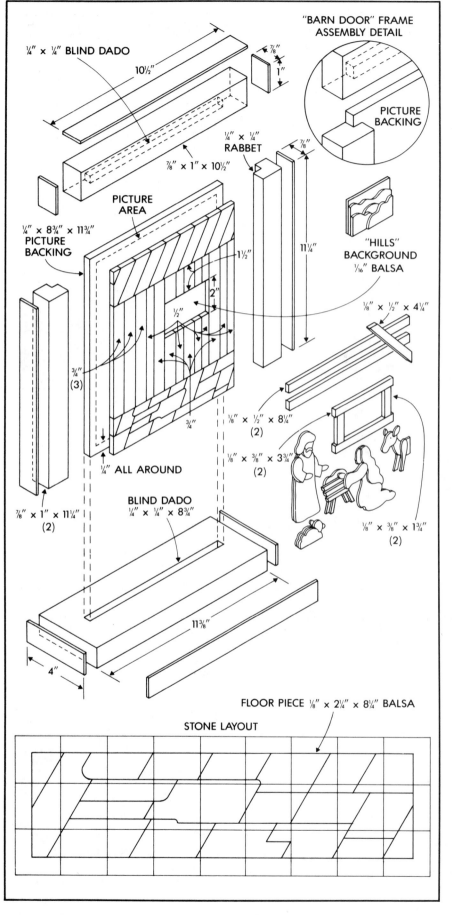

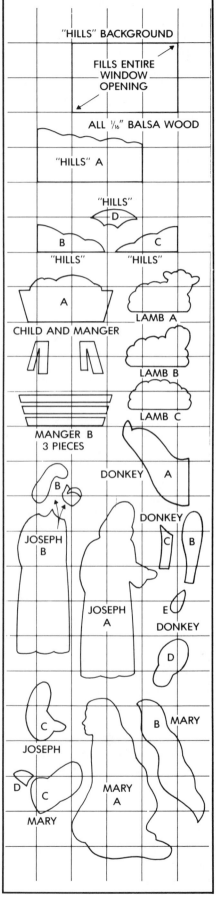

8¾ × 11¾ in., then draw a line ¼ in. from each edge to delineate the picture area. Keep all parts of the picture inside these lines.

Pick up the various pieces from the cardboard and transfer them to the plywood, gluing them in place.

When the picture is complete, put it aside until the glue sets completely. In the meantime, cut the base piece and make a blind dado in it as detailed. Cut the two side pieces of the "door frame" and the top piece to the dimensions shown, then make rabbets in the side pieces. The top piece has a stopped dado in it.

The completed picture is glued into the dado in the base piece, then the two side frames are glued to the picture edges and to the base. The top piece of the door frame now is glued to the top edge of the picture and the tops of the side door frame pieces.

Spray the finished project with a clear acrylic that deepens the color of the cedar and adds to the contrast between the cedar and the light-colored balsa wood.

Other types of wood can be used for the nativity picture, but rough-cut cedar is authentic in appearance. A 4-ft. length of cedar 1 × 12 provides all the stock needed.

Cube-shaped Caddy

When the lid is on this caddy, it is an attractive cube with circle motifs on the sides, ends and top. When you lift the lid, two decks of playing cards are revealed. Walnut was used for the caddy shown but any hardwood would be suitable, and small pieces from the scrap box can be utilized. The caddy not only makes a nice gift, it could be a good seller in a gift shop.

Cut all pieces to size from dimensions given in the Materials List on the next page. Cut rabbets on the edges and bottoms of the sides of the box. Also cut dadoes on the edges and ends of the sides of the lid. Make templates for the pattern layouts, mark the sides and lid of the box and drill the holes. Clamp the various pieces to a scrap board so when you drill through the pieces the wood does not split and splinter on the underside.

No nails or screws are used for the assembly. Clamp and glue box framework, fit in the bottom. Lid is assembled in same manner.

Sand the pieces, then glue the box sides together around the bottom. Do the same with the lid and top. Cut the half-round notches in the two opposing sides of the box liner; they allow gripping the decks of cards to remove them.

Fit the liner pieces into the box, gluing the mitered corners as well as the faces of the liners to the inside surfaces of the box. The liner pieces should fit snugly so the miters are tight. Finally, position the divider so it is in the center of the box, mark its location, then remove it and apply glue. Replace it and clamp if necessary until the glue sets.

When you are sure the glue is set completely, do your final sanding. Make sure the lid fits properly, then stain and finish the caddy. Clear satin polyurethane was applied to the caddy shown.

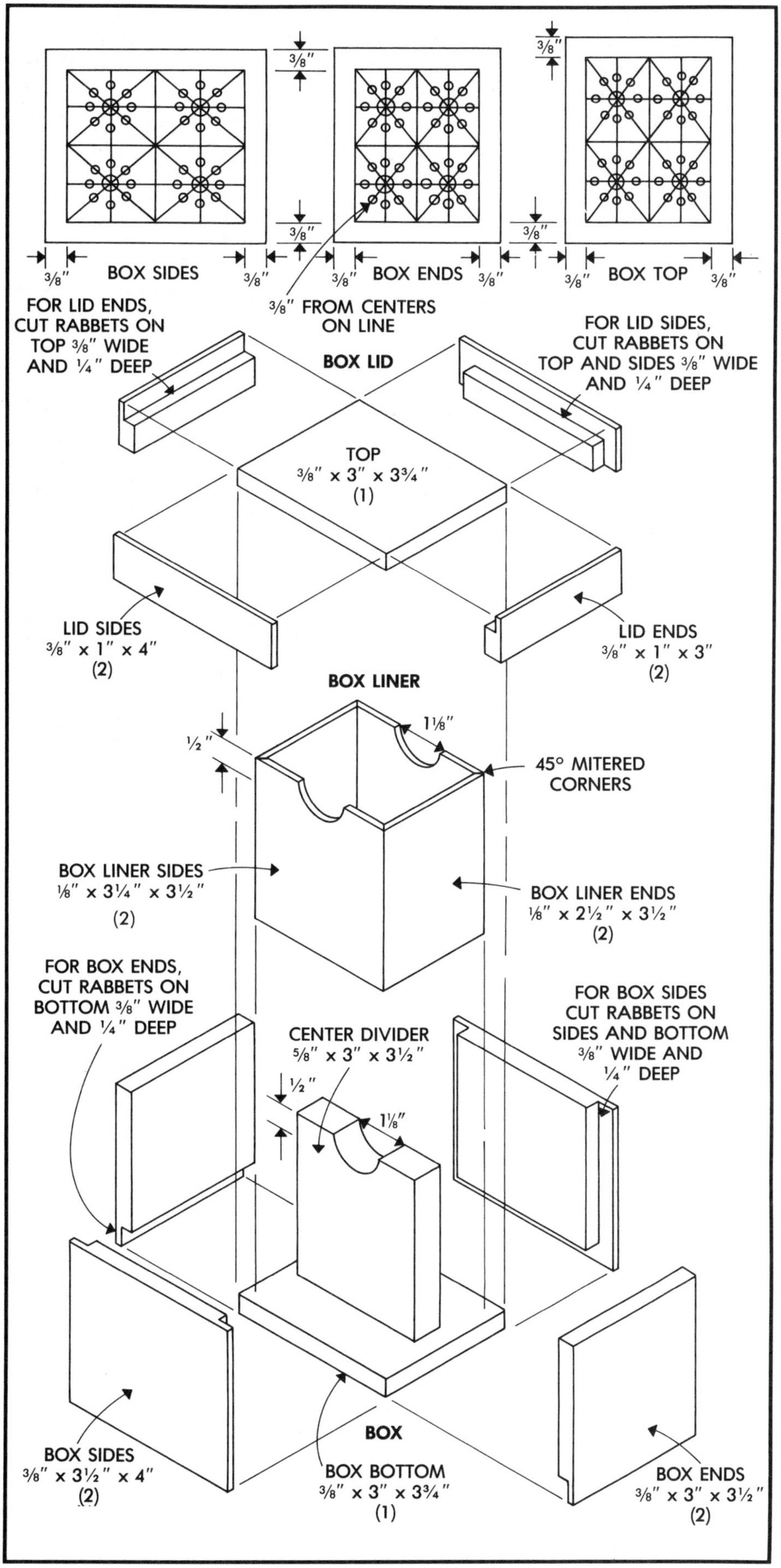
3/8"
3/8"
3/8"
3/8"
3/8"
BOX SIDES
3/8"
3/8"
BOX ENDS
3/8"
3/8"
BOX TOP
3/8"
3/8" FROM CENTERS ON LINE
FOR LID ENDS, CUT RABBETS ON TOP 3/8" WIDE AND 1/4" DEEP
BOX LID
FOR LID SIDES, CUT RABBETS ON TOP AND SIDES 3/8" WIDE AND 1/4" DEEP
TOP 3/8" x 3" x 3¾" (1)
LID SIDES 3/8" x 1" x 4" (2)
LID ENDS 3/8" x 1" x 3" (2)
BOX LINER
1/2"
1⅛"
45° MITERED CORNERS
BOX LINER SIDES 1/8" x 3¼" x 3½" (2)
BOX LINER ENDS 1/8" x 2½" x 3½" (2)
FOR BOX ENDS, CUT RABBETS ON BOTTOM 3/8" WIDE AND 1/4" DEEP
CENTER DIVIDER 5/8" x 3" x 3½"
1/2"
1⅛"
FOR BOX SIDES CUT RABBETS ON SIDES AND BOTTOM 3/8" WIDE AND 1/4" DEEP
BOX
BOX SIDES 3/8" x 3½" x 4" (2)
BOX BOTTOM 3/8" x 3" x 3¾" (1)
BOX ENDS 3/8" x 3" x 3½" (2)

MATERIALS LIST

Box:

Side, 3/8" × 3½" × 4" (2)
End, 3/8" × 3" × 3½" (2)
Bottom, 3/8" × 3" × 3¾" (1)

Lid:

Side, 3/8" × 1" × 4" (2)
End, 3/8" × 1" × 3" (2)
Top, 3/8" × 3" × 3¾" (1)

Box Liner:

Side, 1/8" × 3¼" × 3½" (2)
End, 1/8" × 2½" × 3½" (2)
Divider, 5/8" × 3" × 3½" (1)

INDEX